The Fall of Apartheid
The Inside Story from Smuts to Mbeki

Robert Harvey

First published in hardcover 2001

First published in paperback 2003 by
PALGRAVE MACMILLAN
Houndmills, Basingstoke, Hampshire RG21 6XS and
175 Fifth Avenue, New York, N. Y. 10010
Companies and representatives throughout the world

PALGRAVE MACMILLAN is the global academic imprint of the Palgrave Macmillan division of St. Martin's Press, LLC and of Palgrave Macmillan Ltd. Macmillan® is a registered trademark in the United States, United Kingdom and other countries. Palgrave is a registered trademark in the European Union and other countries.

This book is printed on paper suitable for recycling and made from fully managed and sustained forest sources.

A catalogue record for this book is available from the British Library.

Library of Congress Cataloging-in-Publication Data
Harvey, Robert, 1953–
     The fall of apartheid : the inside story from Smuts to Mbeki / Robert Harvey
        p. cm.
     Includes bibliographical references and index.
     ISBN 1–4039–1574–1 (pbk.) ISBN-13 978-1-4039-1574-0 (pbk.)
        1. Apartheid—South Africa. 2. South Africa—Politics and government—
     –1989–1994. 3. South Africa—Politics and government—1994– 4. South
     Africa—Social conditions—1961–1994. 5. South Africa—Social
     conditions—1994– I. Title.

DT1757.H37 2003
320.968'09'045—dc21

                                                    2003048229

10   9   8   7   6   5   4   3   2   1
12   11   10   09   08   07   06   05   04   03

Transferred to Digital Printing 2008

The Fall of Apartheid

For Betty and Alan Young

Contents

Preface

By Anthony Sampson

The story of South Africa's peaceful revolution has already become a twentieth-century epic: an exciting tale full of unexpected heroes, but also a crucial study in political science, with important lessons in the art of negotiation and persuasion. It is a story with several plots and contrasted settings: the growing rebellion of blacks inside South Africa, threatening to take it into an irreversible civil war; Nelson Mandela, isolated in jail, secretly discussing with an intelligence team the possibility of talks between the government and the African National Congress; Oliver Tambo and his fellow exiles of the ANC in Lusaka, with their own ideas about dialogue and sanctions, increasingly anxious that Mandela might be selling out; the British government, dominated by Margaret Thatcher, attempting to bring pressure on the South African government under P. W. Botha while refusing to recognize the ANC. Behind the main scenes many independent-minded and courageous individuals were seeking to make contacts to avert the terrifying prospect of a race war. The eventual resolution was the result of many pressures, direct and indirect. But certainly among the most useful and illuminating meeting-places were the confidential gatherings in Britain where Afrikaner intellectuals and businessmen were able to meet ANC leaders in exile, where the two sides could communicate with each other away from the public eye, with a growing common understanding which provided a precious basis of trust for the formal negotiations which followed.

It is this part of the story which this book reveals for the first time in vivid detail, with a remarkable empathy for both sides. Robert Harvey's account is the more interesting because it avoids the stereotypes of intransigent Boer reactionaries or dogmatic black revolutionaries. He takes care to represent the Afrikaners' dilemma in the perspective of their unhappy and heroic history, and to portray ANC leaders as sympathetic individuals who faced their own hardships and internal problems. The historical flashbacks show without moralizing or caricaturing how the confrontations between Africans and Afrikaners became increasingly dangerous and inevitable; while his accounts of the secret meetings bring the characters to life, talking in their secluded and compact settings, with the intimacy of a play. The outstanding personalities, including the Afrikaner academic

Willie Esterhuyse and the ANC negotiator Thabo Mbeki, are shown interacting as credible human beings, as they share the common dread of escalating conflict, and understand each other's fears and aspirations.

The sponsorship of the secret talks in Britain was achieved in an unexpected way, worthy of a political thriller. Consolidated Gold Fields was an improbable benefactor; the company once dominated by Cecil Rhodes was seen as one of the most conservative in South Africa, and their centenary had just been commemorated by a company history by the right-wing polemicist Paul Johnson which was contemptuous of the ANC. And Gold Fields was soon to have its own problems in trying to fend off takeover bids, eventually becoming part of the Hanson Group. It was all the more remarkable that its chairman, Rudolph Agnew, should have been persuaded by his political adviser Michael Young to finance the meetings between Afrikaners and the ANC at the company's own country house, Mells; and that Lord Hanson would continue the commitment (with some other supporters, including British Airways, who provided the air tickets). But the meetings which resulted from Agnew's decision were the more realistic for having conservative sponsorship; and it was ironic that Afrikaner businessmen found they could do business with the African politicians at a time when Margaret Thatcher still regarded them as outlaws. The achievement of Michael Young, who had initiated the process through his contacts with the ANC President, Oliver Tambo, is a reminder of how adventurous individuals can break logjams when conventional diplomacy has failed, and how realistic business contacts can be more fruitful than negotiations between governments trapped in their ideologies.

But this story also has some lessons which go beyond political science, and help to illuminate not just the South African problems, but more general problems of establishing candid communications and trust. We see how goodwill develops as each becomes more open in discussing their problems with their own people; how they achieve a camaraderie both through common setbacks and through breakthroughs; and how talks acquire their own atmosphere, assumptions and momentum as they exchange confidences. Thus the ANC group were encouraged by the Afrikaners' reports that their civil and military leadership were at odds; while the Afrikaners were impressed by Mbeki's candid explanation of the ANC's difficulties in restraining their guerrillas from bombing 'soft targets'. The formal speech-making and defensive attitudes gave way to disarming exchanges about each other's difficulties, and the acceptance of common sense instead of dogma. As Mof Terreblanche put it: 'Commonsense is the most wonderful thing to reach understanding.'

Today the account of the secret meetings has a special interest for the light it throws on the character of Thabo Mbeki, now President of South Africa, who is still regarded by many observers as an enigmatic figure with a secretive history as an exiled leader. In this book we see how Mbeki led his delegation with extraordinary confidence, with a mixture of flexibility and fixed purpose, gaining the trust of Afrikaners while never forfeiting his position with his own colleagues, and apparently confident of his own position. He did not appear to see Mandela as the future leader of the ANC after he left prison, let alone an eventual President of his country: Mbeki stressed to the Afrikaners that Tambo and Sisulu were both Mandela's seniors. Reading this book, it is hard to see Mbeki as a natural deputy by nature, subservient to his president, Oliver Tambo, as some critics have depicted him. Certainly he took care to keep in touch with Tambo and his colleagues; but Mbeki during the talks appears as an obvious leader with his own clear plans for navigating the routes to power.

How far these secret talks contributed to the peaceful transition in South Africa is a question that must eventually be left to future historians. But undoubtedly they played a part in establishing trust before the settlement was eventually thrashed out. They were a kind of dress rehearsal, as one Afrikaner participant described it; or as Thabo Mbeki said afterwards, 'a negotiation within a negotiation'. It was in the nature of their informal basis that they could not be binding or decisive; but the informality was the key to their success in communicating at a time when communication was thought by most politicians to be either impossible or undersirable.

Acknowledgements

In writing this book I owe thanks first and foremost to Michael Young, who gave me full access to his unique record of the Mells Park Talks that initiated the dialogue between the ANC and the Afrikaner community, as well as truly unlimited generosity with his time, and for reading the manuscript with such care. I also owe a great debt to Anthony Sampson, with his huge experience of South Africa, for his support and time, for reading the manuscript correcting many errors (the ones remaining are my responsibility alone), as well as for his generous Preface.

I also owe many others in or concerned with South Africa for the time they gave me as I embarked on this piece of contemporary historical detective work in 1995, but only completed last year. They include, in no particular order, the late Oliver Tambo and (now President) Thabo Mbeki, whom I met and questioned as a member of the House of Commons Foreign Affairs Committee; Cyril Ramaphosa; Aziz Pahad; The Rt Hon Lord Howe of Aberavon; Dr Willem Pretorius; Sir Robin Renwick; Rudolph Agnew; Prof. Sampie Terreblanche; Mof Terreblanche; Attie du Plessis; Ebbe Domisse; Dr Vyvyan Bickford-Smith; and John Peake (who also first kindled my interest in South Africa). Michael Hart, of Exeter College, Oxford, with his colossal knowledge of South Africa, provided many helpful insights, and Dr David Atterton and David Potter of Guinness Mahon many useful introductions. My warm thanks also to Robert Johnson. To those who wish to deepen their understanding of the mindset behind apartheid, Ivor Wilkins and Hans Strydom's *The Super Afrikaners* (1978) is a goldmine; I am enormously grateful for their researches.

Gillon Aitken, as always, has been a fund of wisdom and advice, and has never ceased to believe in the book. My warmest thanks to Tim Farmiloe, the legendary Macmillan editor who commissioned this book (his third from me) and to my other thorough editors at Palgrave. I am grateful indeed to my assistant, Jenny Thomas, who must by now know the book by heart, and her historian husband Geoffrey. I am particularly grateful to Nicola Harrison for her skill and hard work in coordinating many aspects of the research. I owe a huge debt to my mother and sister and family, always closely supportive; to my friends in Meifod and London; and to my beloved Jane and Oliver who have travelled with me on another journey of political and historical discovery.

Introduction

Always interested in South Africa, I first became actively involved in its affairs as a member of the House of Commons Foreign Affairs Committee, when it staged its pioneering inquiry into the subject under the chairmanship of Sir Anthony Kershaw. The other members were Denis Canavan MP, the Rt. Hon. David Howell MP, Sir Ivan Lawrence MP, Sir Jim Lester MP, Ian Mikardo MP, Nigel Spearing MP, The Rt. Hon. Norman St John-Stevas MP, The Rt. Hon. Peter Thomas QC MP, Sir Bowen Wells MP and Michael Welsh MP.

Sir Anthony, a former British Foreign Office minister of great shrewdness, with a refreshingly open mind, took the bold decision of inviting the ANC's principal leaders in exile to testify, including Oliver Tambo, Thabo Mbeki (now South Africa's President), and Aziz Pahad, and the Foreign Secretary, Sir Geoffrey Howe, and his senior officials, as well as senior representatives of all shades of the political spectrum both in South Africa and in Britain. The first public hearing with ANC leaders was in October 1985, the second in June 1986. The subsequent report advocated direct British dialogue with the ANC, clearly the principal representative of black opinion in South Africa, and thus proved to be a milestone in international recognition of the organization, which had previously been viewed by the British government as a 'terrorist' body, on a level with the IRA.

I was entirely unaware at the time, as was almost everybody else, that on Tambo and Mbeki's second visit they had set up contact with the public affairs director of Consolidated Gold Fields, Michael Young, who initiated the first direct talks between the ANC high command, led by Tambo and Mbeki, and senior representatives of the Afrikaner community, reporting directly to their government. The historic importance of these talks in dispelling suspicion on both sides and in permitting nuts-and-bolts discussions of how to proceed peacefully towards majority rule cannot, in my opinion, be overstated. Young subsequently gave me access to the written record of these conversations, which took place at different venues in Britain, mostly at the Consolidated Gold Fields country house at Mells Park. These meetings remained, astonishingly, a closely guarded secret almost to the end, until exposed in the *Sunday Times*.

On subsequent visits to South Africa, I became fascinated by the whole extraordinary story of how apartheid, one of the most unique and remarkable political perversions of the twentieth century (an epoch characterized by such aberrations), came into being, secured its ascendancy over the richest and most developed society in sub-Saharan Africa, a former British colony, and then, even more astonishingly, as that society appeared to race towards mutual self-destruction, collapsed. This 'miracle' was not achieved out of the blue, although it appeared so at the time, but through the heroic and drawn-out struggle of South Africa's blacks, aided by a few liberal whites, the patience and intelligence of the more enlightened members of the Afrikaner community, and the prolonged dialogue between blacks and whites that began at Mells Park and ended with the constitutional agreement between Cyril Ramaphosa and Roelf Meyer in 1993.

The blacks, although heroic, did not win in battle; the whites, although hard-pressed, did not surrender unconditionally. The white tribe of Africa, the Afrikaners, who had invented the bizarre creed of apartheid, as suddenly abandoned it and decided to reconcile with their fellow South Africans, overwhelmingly in the majority, some 10–15 years in advance of the point when military pressure would have become overwhelming – according to both the senior black and white leaders I spoke to when preparing this book. In so doing, even after they had performed such terrible cruelties, they at last earned the right to be recognized as true South Africans themselves, not inter-lopers; and in accepting them, black South Africans showed an awesome and humbling magnanimity. That reconciliation is a beacon now shining from a country that is now the economically developed leader of a continent that all too often, over the past few decades, has seemed bereft of hope.

Prelude

On 16 June 1999, a trim, reserved, impeccably dressed man with a grey beard was sworn in as South Africa's new president, succeeding a giant of the century, a modern icon whose awesome strength and magnanimity after decades in prison had made possible reconciliation between the races after more than 70 years of institutionalized racial repression. In that crystal clear, blue-skied winter's day, surrounded by foreign dignitaries such as the Ruritanian-attired Colonel Qaddafi of Libya and an almost exclusively black audience of politicians, bureaucrats and senior military figures, including the gold brocaded figure of the country's would-be Evita, Winnie Mandela, Thabo Mbeki seemed far too small to be stepping into Nelson Mandela's shoes. Yet this man had played almost as crucial a role in the sudden unravelling of apartheid as his famous predecessor, one which is almost entirely unknown and began just under 12 years before in the utterly implausible setting of the Compleat Angler Hotel in Marlow – the first of a series of historic meetings at secret locations in Britain at which white South Afrikanerdom first confronted its nemesis.

* * *

Black and white. That has been the definition of the struggle in South Africa. Black and white, not grey or technicolour. As long as South Africa was in the grip of one of the most evil systems the twentieth century has evolved – institutional racism, on a par with Nazism and Leninism – the struggle had to be seen in such terms. In war there is friend and foe, good and bad.

Now that the conflict is won, subtler shades are permissible. As in any fight, there were good men and bad on both sides; the complex conditions that incubated such evil can be analysed; the oppressors can be seen in almost as tragic a light as the oppressed; the panoramic complexity of human nature behind the front lines on either side can be examined. The tribal, political, social and intellectual divisions that fissure all peoples re-emerge once the smoke of battle has cleared. War is the great simplifier; in peace the complexity of human nature reasserts itself.

So it was with the end of the war against apartheid in 1994. The

1

heroes of this book are the men on both sides who stared down the bitter hatreds induced by an inhumane system and murderous conflict and dared to talk peace in South Africa's darkest hour. Even to acknowledge this achievement requires a shedding of stereotypes. There were 'good' Afrikaners; there were anti-apartheid fighters – indeed their very leaders – prepared to negotiate with the hated enemy. These men on both sides saw that it was possible to end a conflagration before it swept out of control and reduced a whole country to ashes.

There can be no question that the black majority won South Africa's bitterly fought racial war. Equally, there can be no doubt that the white surrender was conditional and took place well before military considerations alone would have dictated. For so much bloodshed to have been averted required a staggering degree of foresight, leadership and statesmanship on both sides. There was no white Mandela, no Lincoln, prepared to lead and reconcile. But there were a number of whites – in the end a majority – who understood the inhumanity of apartheid and the inevitability of change if South Africa was to avert its Armageddon.

This book is partly about them and their equally far-sighted inter-locutors in the ANC. South Africa is a tragic land, with many heroic martyrs who have paid in blood, suffering and imprisonment. Less well known are its peace-makers, seven of whom, in addition to Nelson Mandela, F. W. de Klerk, and Thabo Mbeki, form the subject of this book. Their names are Aziz Pahad; Jacob Zuma; Neil Barnard; Willie Esterhuyse; Wimpie de Klerk; Sampie Terreblanche; and Michael Young. They were the interlocutors in a four-year secret nego-tiation that kept a flicker of hope alive during South Africa's dog days of 1986–90, sitting in parallel to the extraordinary prison-cell negoti-ations between Mandela and the government which ultimately paved the way for the full-blown talks that led to peace in South Africa two years later.

Part I
The Elect

1
A Stranger in Stellenbosch

In February 1986 of a despairing year, a man in his early forties steered a hired car on to the freeway that leads out of Cape Town into the vast South African interior. It was one of those clear Cape days, with only a few clouds in the sky and a sun that would have been oppressive but for the winds from two oceans that periodically flushed away the city's smog and continued to give it a perpetually fresh, exuberant atmosphere.

Leaving the flathead crag of Table Mountain to his right and the old port, now being converted to a modern shopping and leisure centre, to his left, Michael Young's car coasted along the freeway for nearly 20 minutes before turning onto a wide paved road that led directly to the nearest cluster of mountains to the Cape. The country was gloriously open and fertile: this was wine country, where great vineyards extended to yield the subtle, smoky tastes that, such was the country's international isolation, had been unknown for generations in the world outside.

Young could smell the rancid grapes as he drove past extensive one-storey Dutch ranches with turreted doors and old slave quarters. Ahead were the imposing, rugged ranges of Stellenbosch, the Jonkershoer Nature Reserve, Simonsberg and Bottelaryberg jutting ruggedly and precipitately out of the flat plain. Young's destination was an arcadian town beneath the mountains, a finely designed grid of buildings enfrocked by long, delightful avenues of single-storey, spacious villas with huge, manicured gardens, swimming pools and tennis courts.

For Young, as for any first timer, this seemed like some provincial paradise transplanted from the lower German Alps. Tanned, long-limbed white girls with immaculate blond hair streaming in the breeze behind them bicycled along boulevards adorned with trees and flowers. Young men in open-necked shirts made their way across streets clutching tennis rackets or satchels of books.

It was in fact not a provincial rest and recreation centre – although it was also that, a departure point for tourists to visit the 'winelands', and hike in the mountains. It was a university town, as the slightly more staid and utilitarian buildings in the centre attested. Not just any university town: unlike Cape University, a turbulent centre of protest which was traditionally the enclave of the English-speaking community, or Witwatersrand, the academically highly regarded melting pot near Johannesburg, this was Stellenbosch, the elect university of Afrikanerdom, where the best, richest and brightest of the white tribe that had dominated South Africa for four decades went to study, the academic hothouse of the inward-looking and secretive Afrikaner community.

Stellenbosch was not a place that even English-descended white South Africans were comfortable in. This pleasant country town that did not look like a university at all was the intellectual heartland of Afrikanerdom, the place where the academic foundations for apartheid, one of the three most hated creeds in the modern world (the others being fascism/Nazism and communism), had been laid. Hendrik Verwoerd, architect of apartheid, had himself long been a professor there, while his successor, Johannes Vorster, had become its chancellor.

* * *

Now Young, not just English-speaking but a Briton, the traditional historical enemy of the Afrikaners, had arrived on an extraordinary mission, as ambitious as it was daunting: to make contact with and persuade dissidents within the Afrikaner intellectual establishment to place their careers and even lives on the line talking directly with the organization responsible for the terror and guerrilla warfare gnawing at the edges of the fabric of South African society – the African Nationalist Congress. It was rather as if some foreign neutral had arrived in the heart of Berlin in 1944 to suggest that leading Nazi intellectuals should talk directly to senior members of the British government.

The ANC, to all white South Africans, was the enemy, and the terrorist enemy at that, increasingly targeting civilians in its attacks. To the academics at Stellenbosch, the ANC was the very antithesis of their creed. Young was white and was political adviser to the London parent company of one of South Africa's most famous companies, Gold Fields. That was almost all there was going for him.

He cut a solitary figure as he arrived at the sprawling, comfortable, ranch-like home of one of his only two contacts in this Afrikaner heartland. Senior academics at Stellenbosch lived well: it was, after all, the university that had incubated the high priest of apartheid, Hendrik Verwoerd.

Young's sense of unreality was further heightened when, in place of the square, firm-jawed, thick-featured countenance of most of the Afrikaners he knew, he was confronted by a bear-like man with owlish eyes that inspected him even as he talked, and a mop of unruly white hair. His expression was at once quizzical, apologetic, and alert. He was the personification of the absent-minded professor, speaking in a great unstoppable rush of words. He was homely, courteous, never pausing to draw breath – save that his talk was lucid, fascinating, displaying an impressive intellect and a recollection of dates and events that went back decades, as though photographed in his mind. Young could imagine how popular he must have been among his students.

This was Professor Sampie Terreblanche, one of the most formidable minds in South Africa, an economist of world repute, and one of the finest intellects in Afrikanerdom. Terreblanche had shocked the Afrikaner community and his own colleagues at Stellenbosch by emerging as a clear dissident towards apartheid not just within the masonic cloisters of Afrikanerdom, which was just acceptable, but broadcasting this to the world outside, which was not. He was regarded as having betrayed the white tribe of Africa.

Young was soon to discover that this very virtue was to prove Terreblanche's greatest drawback – at least for the purpose Young had in mind. The price of Terreblanche's courage was that he had acquired a pariah status among Afrikaners, and could open few gates into that community. Meanwhile Young was bemused by the cordiality and brilliance of his host.

Terreblanche had grown up a member of one of the best-known Afrikaner establishment families; in youth he had been an enthusiastic supporter of Jan Smuts. Intellectually precocious, Terreblanche was soon an adviser to government, and in the early 1970s became actively involved in politics. Steeped in his Afrikaner background, he remained committed to the apartheid system, although adhering to its liberal wing.

His Rubicon came on 16 June, 1976, two days after the Soweto riots begin in which hundreds were killed. A parliamentary committee was set up under the redoubtable Erika Theron to improve the conditions of the coloured community; Terreblanche was a member. It visited several coloured townships – which were themselves comparatively prosperous by comparison with the black ones. For a young man cosseted by life in the bosom of Afrikaner prosperity, the experience came as an appalling shock: the absence of facilities, lighting, electricity, running water, sewerage, appalled him.

The commission proposed substantial, if not revolutionary, reform, including the repeal of the mixed marriages act and the section of the immorality act which prohibited sexual liaisons across the colour bar. The then prime minister, Johannes Vorster, ignored, indeed denounced the report. Terreblanche was now confirmed as a passionate advocate on the radical wing of the National Party.

In 1978, to his delight, the reformist candidate for the succession to Vorster, P. W. Botha, from the Cape, became leader of the National Party. 'We sought bloodless reform. We were doing our best,' insists Terreblanche. For five years of expectation followed by disappointment, he continued to hope that the Botha regime was capable of initiating real reform.

In 1982 Andries Treurnicht had led a right-wing breakaway to found the Conservative Party, and Terreblanche and his followers believed that at long last Botha had a free hand to fulfil his promise. But little happened. Over the next two years, Terreblanche finally became disillusioned about the National Party's capacity for renewal.

* * *

On 16 December 1984 he broke ranks with senior Afrikaner academics by urging that apartheid should be abandoned – a huge intellectual leap for a pillar of the Afrikaner academic establishment, if for no one else. He had been appalled by Botha's attempt to institute apartheid in a tricameral legislature in which the blacks would still not be represented. The climax was reached at just about the time that Terreblanche met Young for the first time. On 20 February 1987, the Stellenbosch professor, along with 28 other senior members of the liberal Afrikaner establishment, sought a meeting with Botha where they confronted the president with proposals for fundamental reform. In Terreblanche's words, 'there was an explosion. Botha started shouting at me for several minutes, and I shouted back at him.'

Terreblanche resigned from the National Party the following day. Terreblanche and other reformist Stellenbosch intellectuals then further angered Afrikaner opinion by openly setting out their criticisms of the government. In a statement issued on 7 March 1987, they publicly voiced their opposition for the first time:

We, the signatories, are members of a discussion group of teachers and researchers at the University of Stellenbosch that have met on a regular basis since October 1985. The group was founded as a result of our concern about the deteriorating security situation in the country during 1985, as well as about the tempo and direction of reform in South Africa. The stagnation of the reform process since May, 1986, increased our concern. Initially the group refrained from issuing public statements and preferred to express our concern and to encourage the acceleration of reform and negotiations between credible, representative leaders of all communities by means of correspondence, submissions and meetings with prominent government leaders – including the state president himself. According to our judgment, this modus operandi proved unsuccessful. We cannot, therefore, refrain from issuing a public statement any longer ...

We are not only concerned about the tempo of the reform process in South Africa, but also about its character and direction. We are convinced that the process of negotiation about the accommodation of all (particularly black) South Africans in the decision-making process is seriously retarded by the government's hesitance to issue signs of hope for those concerned. We understand that a new dispensation cannot become a reality overnight, and that stability has to be maintained during the transitional period. However, the government has an inalienable responsibility to create hope for the future for all South African citizens.

In our opinion, this hope can only be created if the government is willing to issue a clear and unambiguous declaration of intent on two issues: ... Its intention to abolish all residuals of apartheid (the Group Areas Act; the statutory definition of groups on the basis of race; the three-chamber parliament; and the Separate Amenities Act); ... The government should secondly declare its unambiguous intention to share power effectively with blacks. All South African citizens must be represented in the central parliament of the country and on all other levels of decision-making in such a way that they have an effective say, which is acceptable for a majority, in the decision-making process. This implies that we recognize that a situation will eventually be reached in South Africa in which the whites, as this group is currently defined by statute, will relinquish their exclusive and decisive ability to enforce decisions which have consequences for all South Africa's people. The broadening of democracy in South Africa requires, at the same time, the constitutional entrenchment of democratic institutions such as a representative parliament, an independent judiciary, free elections, freedom of speech etc, in order to protect individuals and groups against the abuse of power by the authorities.

* * *

Young was received with great warmth by Terreblanche, but found himself frustrated when he sought the latter's help to set up contacts with other Afrikaners. The Englishman did not know the full extent of the professor's brush with apartheid. He was now a leper, an outcast to his tribe, a man who had broken with the close-knit Afrikaner community. Terreblanche feared that any introduction from him would be tainted; he would perhaps have limited value in furthering Young on his mission. He was enthusiastic himself about the idea of meeting senior ANC representatives (he had already done so on an informal basis), and eager to participate in the discussions. But Terreblanche was damaged goods: he had been too brave too soon.

If Young's second introduction were to prove as frustrating as his first, his mission would have been over before it began. It was to Professor Willie Esterhuyse, another Stellenbosch academic with a less formidable international reputation than Terreblanche, but a considerable one among Afrikaners as an adviser to governments who, although highly critical of the Botha government, retained his connections and had not burnt his boats by publicly denouncing it. Descended remotely from a princely Hungarian family, the Esterhazys, the professor too came from Afrikaner founding-father aristocracy.

When the Englishman met Esterhuyse at the university's spartan Schumann economic faculty building, he was surprised to find himself greeted by as great a contrast with Terreblanche as could possibly be imagined. Esterhuyse was tall, well-built, good-looking, with a creased, rugged face that belonged more to a Boer country landowner than an academic. Only the slightly long and unkempt mop of greying hair, in a country where crew cuts are considered dangerously radical and hirsute, betrayed his academic origins. Possessed of a booming, gravel voice, he moved slowly and with a deliberation completely at odds with the speed of his mind.

Unlike Terreblanche, who wore his cleverness on his sleeve, Esterhuyse's was concealed beneath a veneer of extrovert *bonhomie*; but the eyes were watchful, appraising, shrewd. More than that – and again in contrast to Terreblanche – he was more a politician than an academic, and maybe more a member of the intelligence community than a politician. His conversation was illuminating rather for what he did not say than for the slightly bland surface of what he did. His most disconcerting habit when faced by a question he did not want to answer, was to retreat into vagueness, professing implausible ignorance – where a more skilled politician returns the ball on the other side of the court, answering in a direction unintended by the questioner, but of use to both.

For all the calculator in him, he was a warm, likeable man, accustomed to long hikes in the mountains with family and friends, and a courageous intellectual opponent of apartheid. As early as 1979 he had written a book in Afrikaans, *Apartheid Must Go*, which had broken new ground within the Afrikaner community. He had the shrewdness – unlike the impulsive Terreblanche – to realize that he would be more effective at despatching the system by staying within the Afrikaner family than from outside. It was from him that Young, to his relief, got his first leads. They talked at length, and Esterhuyse furnished Young with four more names to approach from the Afrikaner establishment, while confirming that he too was willing to participate in the talks. Young had made the first breakthrough.

* * *

What the two Afrikaners thought of Young as he departed for Cape Town is a matter for conjecture – although all three became firm friends afterwards. His own career could hardly have been less conventional – or less likely to fit him for the position he now occupied, political adviser to one of the most conservative companies in the world, Consolidated Gold Fields, parent of the South African mining giant.

Young hailed from Newcastle, from a farming family, with interests in the coal mining industry. His father was an accountant who worked first for the Co-op and moved to Milford Haven and then Wellington in Shropshire, where he worked as company secretary for a variety of industries. His family was politically interested and he became active as a Young Conservative in Wellington. After studying at York, he became vice-chairman of the Federation of Conservative Students and chairman of the York University Conservative Association, before being recruited into the Conservative Research Department to look after its international desk.

He had passed into the front rank of British Conservatism at the age of 25 as a foreign affairs adviser to Sir Alec Douglas-Home, then foreign secretary, and later to Edward Heath, the former British prime minister, in opposition. He rubbed shoulders in the job with all the principals of Conservative politics.

When Heath, to whom Young is personally and politically close, was defeated by a more robust exponent of free-market conservatism, Margaret Thatcher, he continued to act as her principal foreign affairs adviser as well as that of Lord Carrington, her shadow foreign secretary. He had met Thatcher when she was education minister and disliked her 'radical libertarian belief in absolute truth'. He considered her 'intellectually difficult and politically fearful'. He backed her deputy, William Whitelaw, as a moderating force. But he became disillusioned with Whitelaw, 'who had the opportunity to rein her in but didn't do so'. Young joined the left-of-centre Lollards group within the Conservative Party, led by William Van Straubenzee; but wearying of the 'pusillanimous liberal wing of the Conservative Party', he went to his old mentor, Heath, and discussed his intention of joining the Liberals. He informed both Whitelaw, who was 'polite but privately vituperative', and Van Straubenzee, who stopped speaking to him.

He played a key role, along with the party's African expert in parliament, Lynda Chalker, in advising Carrington at all costs not to throw Britain's lot in with the party led by Bishop Abel Muzorewa, which had won the country's first half-free elections, from which Zimbabwe's two main parties were excluded. Young proved to be right: when fully free elections were held, Robert Mugabe's Zanu-Patriotic Front swept the board, consigning Muzorewa to oblivion.

Young's disillusion with the free-market doctrines of the Thatcher government after 1979 soon became complete. While retaining close links with Heath's private office, he resigned from the party, joining the Liberal Democrats under David Steel. The break was not easy for him personally. His mother was a prominent Conservative branch secretary in the Penrith and Borders seat of deputy prime minister Whitelaw, who was a friend of his parents, and he felt that she 'suffered' from his decision. Yet she loyally resigned her post and gave him her unstinting support, sitting outside the polling station taking numbers for her son. He felt he owed her a great debt for this. He was selected to fight Whitelaw's safe seat on the English-Scottish frontier in 1983.

The result was remarkable, in an election in which the Liberal–Social Democratic alliance probably reached its high-water mark. Young increased the Liberal vote sharply, coming a respectable second to the astonished Whitelaw, now a household name. Within a year Whitelaw had been elevated to the House of Lords and Young had a second, unexpected chance at the seat. He ran the Conservative, David Maclean, to within 500 votes, as much through the sheer moderation of his personality as through any electoral dislike of his opponent.

At the next general election in 1987 the Liberal vote returned to its more normal level of just under 15,000 against Conservative support of just under 34,000. Young had one more try at that election, standing for the Isle of Wight before returning to his business career. It had been a political career of courage, brilliance and, by conventional standards, extreme foolishness.

* * *

If Young had not stood on principle so hard, in the natural order of things he could have expected comfortably to sail into a safe Conservative seat for his past service to the party. But his refusal to cooperate with Thatcherism lost him his political investment. That his boldness was not proof of a fatal lack of political judgement was, however, to become apparent with his initiative in South Africa. By now, though, Young had had enough of politics and looked to his business career, joining Gold Fields as its public affairs director.

His very unconventionality was apparent from the first in his job at Consolidated Gold Fields. In an act that would have horrified the starchy, tough-minded local management of Gold Fields South Africa, he made contact, through an effort to raise money for black education and enterprise, with a matriarchal figure in the Soweto township, Sebolela Mohiani. Large and colourfully dressed, she was one of many who sought to channel the efforts of black youths deprived of fathers – many of whom were overseas or fighting with the ANC – as well as education – a result of black boycotts – to social and productive purposes.

She took him to visit a shabeen (unlicensed bar) on the edge of Soweto. In the yard outside, Young sipped African beer and was nauseated to witness a cow being ritually slaughtered: 'quite a remarkable experience for someone coming from twentieth-century London'.

On another occasion he was driven into Soweto proper, past roadblocks, sheltering in the bottom of the car to avoid being stopped by the police – it was as illegal as it was dangerous for a white man to enter a black township at night – to a shabeen, across a muddy yard, which consisted of a simple shack with a corrugated iron roof and dust floor. Dakar was being smoked.

His hosts were young, educated blacks who astonished him with their attitude of tolerance and forgiveness towards their white oppressors. Young argued that after all the blacks had suffered he would not be surprised if they were angry, murderous, vengeful. They replied that the whites were 'here to stay, we'll get nowhere fighting them'.

Sadly, Sebolela Mohiani was soon to be killed in a car crash in possibly suspect circumstances; she had been a well-known activist. Young, meanwhile, was reinforced in his conviction that a negotiated settlement was possible; he had been to the grass roots and sipped beer with unwashed militants, as no conventional mediator had.

2
A Seed of Hope

The germination of a peace initiative, like any evolutionary process, starts from small, chance beginnings. Such was a meeting held in the comfortable London home of possibly Britain's best-known liberal journalist, Anthony Sampson, on the afternoon of 24 October 1986, as South Africa appeared to be racing headlong towards final damnation. The meeting was one of the first on a week-long visit arranged for the leader of the African Nationalist Congress in exile, Oliver Tambo, and his party. It was held in Sampson's ground floor drawing room just off London's prestigious Holland Park Avenue, tucked behind the wealth and traffic chaos of prosperous Kensington.

Tambo had been invited to London by Sampson's longtime friend David Astor, former proprietor and editor of the *Observer* and a famous and long-standing opponent of apartheid. It might have seemed a perennial gathering of liberals of the more woolly-minded and earnest sort, but for the fact that some of Britain's top businessmen, at last convinced not just that white South Africa was morally indefensible but doomed, had chosen to attend.

Apart from Young, they included Sir Christopher Hogg, the abrasive chairman of Courtaulds, who insisted that his workers in South Africa be as well paid as those in Britain; Sir Alistair Frame, the ebullient chairman of Rio Tinto Zinc; Gordon Adam, the director for Africa of Barclays Bank, which was thinking of disengaging from South Africa; Sir James Spooner, a friend of Sampson's and a senior director of a number of companies who was personally opposed to apartheid; David Sainsbury, the supermarket tycoon, vigorously anti-apartheid and a financial contributor to the Social Democratic Party; Patrick Gillam, managing director of BP South Africa, a longtime critic of apartheid; Ray Allen, a director of ICI, which had been heavily involved in the country in the past; Neil Forster, chairman of the United Kingdom–South Africa Trading Association, a pro-apartheid front (he insisted his members should not know of his attendance); and Young.

Sampson recalls the discussions as being 'quite tense'. While most were sympathetic in their questioning, Forster was openly hostile. Young found Tambo refreshingly flexible on economic issues. On the same trip, Tambo also had lunch with the Editor of *The Economist*, Andrew Knight, along with the Barclays Bank Chairman, Sir Martin Jacomb, and the immensely wealthy and urbane *Economist* chairman and merchant banker, Evelyn de Rothschild.

After unveiling a statue in honour of Nelson Mandela on 28 October, Tambo went on to a private meeting of Conservative MPs led with foresight and courage by the former foreign office minister Sir Anthony Kershaw, who was also chairman of the highly influential House of Commons Foreign Affairs Select Committee. The following day, after attending a meeting at the Royal Institute of International Affairs at Chatham House, the ANC arrived at a public session of the Foreign Affairs Committee.

As a member of the latter, I attended this, and was impressed by the remarkable moderation displayed by the ANC team, while I retained a degree of scepticism as to its depth. Tambo was sincere and soft-spoken. Thabo Mbeki, his deputy, was well-groomed and highly articulate. After further meetings with editors and businessmen, Tambo and his party left on 31 October. It had been a highly significant trip: he and his colleagues had begun to cross the line (even in the minds of Conservative politicians and businessmen) that divides a terrorist revolutionary movement from a legitimate and politically sensitive resistance organization against an oppressor government. The anti-apartheid movement had always been well-supported in Britain on all sides of the political spectrum. Now it became possible to be a supporter of the ANC (as opposed to the revered martyr figure of Nelson Mandela) as well.

* * *

It would be hard to imagine two persons less like each other on the surface than Michael Young and his chairman, Rudolph Agnew. The latter was the grandson of a New Zealander, J. A. Agnew, who had risen to become chairman of Consolidated Gold Fields in 1933. This scion of a Gold Fields prince was born a year later, educated at

Downside, one of Britain's top Catholic public schools, and had served as an officer in the 8th King's Royal Hussars between 1953 and 1957. He joined Consolidated Gold Fields in 1957, entering a fast track to becoming deputy chairman in 1978. His club was the Cavalry and Guards. His recreation was shooting. In 1983 he became chairman.

One of his detractors describes him as 'the most appalling old reactionary'. On the surface affable, blimpish and establishment through and through, he is a big man with a large head, a frank expression and shrewd eyes that size you up as he makes self-deprecatory jokes. He is straightforward, to the point, and has a disconcerting habit of making some quite serious point and then breaking out into a broad laugh and utterly disarming grin.

Those who worked for him make clear that he was no mere figurehead for the company, but an intelligent, steely and decisive man whose highly strung nervousness is in fact concealed behind a veneer of old-boy bluffness – as is often the style with the British business establishment. (The disadvantage of this approach is that it sometimes conceals genuine obtuseness, and it is not always easy to tell the difference.) Young, for one, who held opposed political views to Agnew – an ardent admirer of Mrs Thatcher – was intensely loyal, and saw a different side to him: 'He was a Rupert of the Rhine figure: patrician, tall, good-looking, with style. He exuded leadership and commanded loyalty, but didn't always think through the consequences of his actions as precisely as he should. He indulged me but made jokes at my expense, calling me a wimp and wet and loyal to a lost leader – Ted Heath; I would reply that he was to the right of Genghis Khan.'

In fact, Agnew was a merchant buccaneer and adventurer. He explained his philosophy to the writer Paul Johnson:

> I am going for growth in assets and earnings. These will largely depend on successful earnings and good acquisitions. Because we are placing so much emphasis on exploration, we will go increasingly to the great mineral provinces of the world – to the Americas, to South Africa, to the South Pacific, to Australasia …
>
> There are sirens seeking to distract us, the short-term considerations that companies are increasingly subjected to – earnings per share, league tables, analysts' reviews and so on. I lump them together under the general heading of vanities: Chief Executives hate to see their companies described as 'dull'.

But my starting point is the romantic nineteenth-century attitude. The mining industry is a great adventure. Sure, it should be highly profitable. But it is not a game susceptible to stockbrokers' charts because of its very nature. You have to cope with great political pressures. You need good nerves, a long-term view.

It is an industry which is very involved with people – including the sheer physical safety of people. Our founders, Cecil Rhodes and Charles Rudd, epitomize the typical dichotomy of mining. On the one hand you have the ruthless merchant-adventurer type, on the other the conservative professional needed to support the lead given by the adventurous ... To me, Gold Fields is a great story of success and failure – and success again. It reflects the genius of the British race, which is a genius for merchant adventuring in obscure parts of the world. The question, if you agree with my romantic vision, is whether Gold Fields lives up to its tradition of adventure, or whether we're faceless men working solely for our pensions.

This contempt for analysts' reviews was to rebound on him as successive takeover bids were to be mounted for Gold Fields; but he was not a man to live any other way. His deputy, Anthony Hichens, put it even more bluntly:

We have always had a buccaneering outlook. We have a go. We take risks. We look for new things to do. Our top people are encouraged to take risks and not mortally punished if the risks do not come off. This attitude is sharply different from more orderly and logical companies. It may even lead to a certain amount of confusion.

When I first joined the company I found it hard to find out what they were doing, because the willingness to take risks is hard to grasp as a company strategy, and it certainly can't be put down in a formal strategy paper. But you learn by example. We're enormously proud of the West Wits Line – but the risks we took were breathtaking. But this happened because the company is used to having a go, and executives knew their careers would not be blighted if there was a failure.

A flavour of the romance involved in mining is captured by Adriaan Louw, a former chairman of Consolidated Gold Fields South Africa:

Mines can be rich, painted, modern tools and toys. But they can also be happy when they're poor because people care for them. It is usually done by one person, a good manager, who creates the spirit of the mine. Colonel S. R. Fleischer put his spirit into Sub Nigel, which he once managed. That was a happy mine. The spirit of West Driefontein was implanted by Stan Gibbs, a protégé of Fleischer. That was and is a happy mine too. The two years I spent as manager of West Drie was the best time of my life – to stay there I almost turned down promotion to a head office job.

Agnew little expected that he would fall prey – having successfully fended off the predatory Anglo-American bid to gain control of Consolidated Gold Fields – to that most modern of buccaneers, the financial holding company, in the guise of Hanson Trust. In fact it may have been precisely Agnew's inattention to the share league tables, analysts' reviews and other 'vanities' of 'faceless men' that was to render his company liable to takeover. But that is beyond the scope of this book.

* * *

Young knew that his boss, like other business leaders with South African interests, was looking for an insurance policy in case the apartheid regime should collapse. He was believed to favour Chief Mangosuthu Buthelezi, who had committed himself to a Western-style free enterprise system and – ironically, in view of later events – a non-violent approach to power sharing with the whites, although he was also committed to the principle of majority rule, like the ANC, to which he had once belonged.

Agnew, moreover, was a major contributor to Conservative Party funds and on first-name terms with the Prime Minister, Margaret Thatcher, who would invite him to dinner at 10 Downing Street. In addition, Gold Fields had lost much of its central control over Gold Fields South Africa, which was run by Robin Plumridge, whom Young viewed as 'volatile, prejudiced, narrow and puritanical with very little foresight'. Gold Fields South Africa supported the most conservative wing of the National Party and took care, whenever Agnew and Young visited, carefully to chaperone them throughout the visit. Only when Young was in a private capacity could he slip away to meet his unconventional contacts.

* * *

For Young to approach Agnew – conservative, establishment, deeply hemmed in by pro-apartheid subordinates – and suggest the company start a dialogue with the ANC must have seemed like a schoolboy asking his headmaster permission to visit the town brothel. What induced Agnew to say yes, apart from his buccaneering spirit? He takes up the story:

> I was intrigued by Michael's suggestion. It could do some good. Apartheid was a form of government which couldn't last. It wasn't a matter of right or wrong. Whatever the idealists believed, it was like socialism: it didn't work. The ANC were an important movement. It wouldn't do any harm to start a dialogue. I considered Inkatha a factional movement. If anyone wants to talk, that is a good thing.
>
> There was no deep wisdom involved in my decision. It was a gut reaction. I had confidence in Michael Young. Michael must get the credit for persuading me that the ANC was the logical alternative. But of course it was quite dangerous. If word had got out it would have been damaging. I consulted very few people – just the finance director and maybe the deputy chairman. Michael was very concerned about security being essential to the talks. One advantage of Mells Park is that it was the last place to look for such talks.

For Agnew the talks were to be 'of much greater significance than I originally thought. They were one of the tributaries that fed the main river of a peaceful settlement in South Africa.' They continued only until 'the main river took over'. In fact Agnew was to authorize a total expenditure of between £500,000 and £1 million on the talks – an astonishing figure at the time even for a company of Gold Fields's size. This took place without the authorization of the shareholders or the knowledge of any but two of his directors, and over the head of his South African subsidiary. It was indeed quite dangerous and expensive, for a decision based only on 'gut instinct'.

Surely, but surely, given his first-name relationship with Margaret Thatcher and P. W. Botha, he picked up the telephone to ask whether this would be a helpful initiative? Agnew vehemently denies this. 'I wouldn't have dared tell anyone,' he chortles.

Be that as it may, the Mells Park dialogue was to prove of immense use to President Botha and his office, who knew about it soon enough, as well as to the ANC. Unwittingly, Young was setting up a crucial channel of communication desperately sought by both sides. Without even knowing it, he was to be the last section in a bridge already three-quarters constructed at both ends – or, to change the metaphor, the courier between two sides that had only corresponded hitherto through distant, and easily misread, smoke signals.

* * *

Sampson and Astor's slow, patient attempt to introduce the ANC to the business community and to conservatives who had so long viewed it as a terrorist organization continued. Of the 10 present at the meeting at Sampson's house, 7 asked to keep in touch. The larger-than-life Sir John Harvey-Jones, chairman of ICI, also now expressed cautious interest.

On 15 December, Sampson had a lengthy meeting with the ANC leader at Gatwick airport. The ANC leader told the veteran journalist that the contacts with journalists and businessmen 'have changed a lot', having a major impact on opinion within South Africa, which Tambo ironically described as 'still really a British colony'. He reported grimly that there was no real evidence that Botha was willing to negotiate.

Tambo insisted that his main objective now was real negotiations between the ANC and the government. He also reported that the South African army was growing more powerful and moderate and had favoured the Nkomati Accord with President Machel of Mozambique. With respect to the Commonwealth 'eminent persons group' about to visit South Africa, Tambo counselled against them meeting Mandela alone – although he acknowledged that the latter would also consult with his colleagues before making any statement – a first sign of the edginess between the external ANC leader and its internal living martyr.

Tambo may have favoured Sampson's business contacts because they bypassed the British Communist Party, which tended to try and keep ANC visitors to London to themselves. Tambo expressed the desire to influence West German opinion, but acknowledged it was a difficult nut to crack.

The pace of Tambo's courting of Western governments continued relentlessly. Just over a month later, Sampson met Tambo again on his way back from the United States. He had seen Henry Kissinger, as a result of an introduction from his good friend Andrew Knight, and had been pleasantly surprised. 'I won't say anything which will stop you saying what you want,' the former US Secretary of State told

Tambo in a typically convoluted seal of approval. Kissinger had not appreciated before that the ANC was not closely associated with the Communists – his old obsession.

Sampson snorted at Kissinger's patronizing tone towards Tambo: the Americans had for so long been dealing with regimes that had supported apartheid. Tambo pointed out that he had told Kissinger he had come to America in 1960, 1961 and again in 1962, and received no support; while in Moscow Tambo had been given more money than expected.

He informed Kissinger, 'our people will decide and they're not very interested in a socialist state: the Communists will know that they will only be one group among many: they will be pressing for communism but not really expecting it'. Tambo had already shortly before seen Mikhail Gorbachev, the new leader of the Soviet Communist Party. Gorbachev had been well informed and interesting, quite unlike Brezhnev; the new Soviet leader was a man who had impressed Tambo as enjoying a good argument, like Kissinger himself. However, for the first time the Soviet Communist Party had applied real pressure on Tambo on a matter of policy – to suggest that the ANC revise its economic policy in order to place less emphasis on nationalization! This was the first of a number of crucial meetings in which the Soviet leader increasingly inclined towards the freer-market approach of Tambo's deputy, Thabo Mbeki

On his American trip the ANC leader lunched at General Motors and met John Reed of Citibank, who listened with a sympathetic ear. Tambo also confirmed that he got on well with Lynda Chalker, whom he met at Samora Machel's funeral. Surprisingly, he also found himself at ease with the British foreign secretary, Sir Geoffrey Howe, considering him 'very honest'. When they disagreed, he had told Tambo, 'we're both lawyers, so we must disagree'. Both ministers were flouting Thatcher's edict that there should be no ministerial contact with the ANC.

Tambo's sense of growing international acceptance had buoyed him up; he expected the West Germans to start talking to the ANC soon. 'Botha can't keep people in the laager for very long; he's much more isolated now,' Tambo told Sampson. The latter now arranged for Tambo to address a larger audience of senior businessmen on 24 June. This was to be a full-blown affair, held under David Astor's auspices at the plush Connaught Rooms, including no fewer than 23 senior men.

The guest list read like a Who's Who of British tycoons. They included former Chancellor of the Exchequer Lord Barber, Chairman of Standard Chartered Bank; Sir Timothy Bevan, Chairman of Barclays Bank; Sir Alistair Frame of Rio Tinto Zinc; Lord Greenhill of SG Warburg, a former head of the foreign office; Sir Martin Jacomb of Barclays de Zoete Wedd; Evelyn de Rothschild; George Soros of the Soros Fund of New York which was later to become globally renowned; and Sir James Spooner of Morgan Crucible – as well as one of the youngest present, Michael Young, representing Consolidated Gold Fields.

The ANC delegation was also full-blown this time: apart from Tambo and Mbeki, there were Mac Maharaj, Aziz Pahad and Jacob Zuma. Tambo spoke eloquently, emphasizing that the ANC's minimum requirement was for a one-man-one-vote state. Some of the businessmen expressed concern that the blacks were not ready for this. Tambo showed no sign of impatience: he was thoughtful and reflective in his replies.

Young, observing him for the second time, saw him as 'a small, elegant, precise man'. Deeply impressed, Young went up to Tambo afterwards and asked him what a company with large interests in South Africa could do to make a difference.

Tambo thought for a while, holding my hand for what seemed an eternity, and then asked if I could help him build a bridge between the ANC and those Afrikaners close to the government. He told me that no means of communication existed and, without this, progress was impossible. I told him I would think about what he had asked and be in touch again.

Thabo Mbeki was present throughout this exchange. He asked if I could help arrange a meeting between the ANC leader and the foreign office minister responsible for Africa, Lynda Chalker. Margaret Thatcher had directed that officials could talk to the ANC but ministers might not. I was aware of this edict, as of course were the ANC, but they were anxious to begin a dialogue with British government ministers, since officials had been unable to take discussions further than noting the ANC position and reiterating the policy of Her Majesty's government towards South Africa.

As it happened, Lynda Chalker and I are long-standing friends and on that basis I telephoned her at the Foreign Office from a pay phone in the Connaught Rooms and asked if she would receive Oliver Tambo the following afternoon. To her great credit, and notwithstanding the Prime Minister's edict, she agreed to meet the ANC leader. This meeting constituted the first contact between the

ANC and a British minister. [In fact the informal encounter at Machel's funeral had paved the way; but this latest meeting was at an official level.]

Lynda felt the chill wind of Thatcher's displeasure and was carpeted subsequently for this breach of instruction and for being the first Conservative government minister publicly to advocate one-man-one-vote in South Africa during a Commons debate on June 17th. What Chalker had done was to place the ANC–British government relationship on an entirely different and more proactive footing. The box into which Margaret Thatcher had placed the relationship had been broken.

Following this meeting, this senior executive of the company that had made its name in the smoke and dust of the Johannesburg gold rush approached his boss, Rudolph Agnew, in the stately surroundings of St James's Square, London's clubland. What Young had unwittingly taken on was not just Thatcher but the legacy of nearly half a millennium of a people's history. Decades of anti-apartheid struggle have served to simplify history beyond recognition. Afrikaners believed they were a superior but native African tribe whose territories had been encroached upon by warlike and primitive black tribes from the north. To the blacks and their outside sympathizers, the Afrikaners were no more than particularly barbarous colonial plunderers who enslaved and repressed their peoples. The truth was altogether more complicated.

The Afrikaner soul, which Young had stumbled upon at an awesome turning point in its history, had been shaped by an extraordinary kaleidoscope of human virtue and vice. It ranged from pioneering adventurism, extreme hardship, fortitude, courage, family-based trust in the Lord, devotion to simple Christian values, the assertion of national freedom and independence, bravery in conflict, suffering under extreme adversity of terrain, disease and slaughter, anti-colonialism, cultural assertion and pride; through to plunder, the murder of innocents, the stealing of others' lands, narrow-mindedness, obscurantism, bigotry, racial introversion and an overwhelming sense of social inferiority towards fellow whites which resulted in a compensating assertion of racial superiority against the indigenous population, wholesale slaughter and, finally, the imposition of the most elaborate pseudo-scientific theory of social engineering outside the Communist scriptures, based on race, rather than class (Nazi ranters and scribblers do not deserve to be characterized as theorists at all).

It is misleading, and ultimately ignorant, simply to lump together Afrikaner racialism with cruder nationalistic, ethnic and sectarian manifestations elsewhere in the world – nationalistic, ethnic and sectarian though apartheid undoubtedly was at the grass roots. It was more than that. It represented the yearnings of a strange, wandering people sandwiched between colonial oppression and a huge, threatening black underclass – an almost unique phenomenon in history; and it represented the intellectualization, the elevation of a crude human emotion – ethnic self-assertion – into an elaborate social, political, cultural and even scientific construct by a sophisticated elite.

Arguably, all political theory is a variety of this: Marxism-Leninism, for example, can be described as the intellectual justification for the base human emotion of envy; capitalist free-market theories gave intellectual respectability to the exploitation of man by man; and so on. Nazism, and to a lesser extent fascism, were crude momentary responses to particular historical conditions – the destruction of an old order without the emergence of a new social consensus, economic depression, an eruption of raw popular nationalism – that can hardly be distinguished with the label of ideology.

Apartheid in South Africa was something more: it was the ideology of race, carefully elaborated in intellectual terms, not by a handful of men to satisfy their own lust for power, but by a developed and sophisticated community – its political, social, academic and business leaders – over a period of some 70 years, as long as the Russian revolution was to last. The Afrikaners were not to assert, as the Germans did of Nazism, that this was an aberration, a minority view thrust upon them. Most Afrikaners identified with apartheid – although its most extreme form was indeed imposed by the hard-line minority among them. Even liberal Afrikaners were to turn against apartheid as a creed that could not work, rather than on moral grounds.

As a political creed it was unique and, its detractors would say, uniquely evil. It was nothing less than an ideology that justified not just colonization as such – the conquest and rule of the territories of peoples in a weaker state of political and military development by the stronger – but the wholesale replacement of an indigenous people by a settler people. As such it might even be applied to the experience of North America, Australia and New Zealand – with the key difference that in these cases there were fewer indigenous peoples, and the settlers found it easier to exterminate or marginalize them without even requiring the justification of a twentieth-century ideology. These attitudes were only beginning to recede by the time Young first encountered, like some latter-day Bartolomeu Dias, the elaborate creed of a tribe of 2 million people.

Apartheid was nothing less than the philosophy of a white tribe 'gone native', which in many respects had taken on the assertiveness of the more warlike of the very people it despised for their backwardness. Apartheid became the expression of the Afrikaner state, born of the 400-year history of a remarkable, sometimes heroic, sometimes contemptible people. This history explains both the unique phenomenon of apartheid, and the reasons why it was to disintegrate more suddenly than anyone would have thought possible – as fast as Communism, or the Berlin Wall.

Young was to be one of the very first to venture into the intellectual heart of Afrikanerdom, Stellenbosch University, and its nerve centre, the Broederbond, and discover to his astonishment that this seemingly impregnable fortress of defiance, ideology and brute force had already crumbled away. Nothing remained but the façade, which required just a gentle push from within – as in Russia – to topple over into dust.

3
Defeat in War, Victory in Peace

The history of modern South Africa might be said to have begun in May 1902, when a host of bedraggled Boer leaders converged on Vereeniging. The Boers, according to a witness, were, 'starving, ragged men, clad in skins or sacking, their bodies covered with sores, from lack of salt and food ... their appearance was a great shock to us, who came from the better-conditioned forces in the Cape.'

It was Jan Smuts, the young state attorney of Transvaal Free State, whose eloquence won the day.

> We represent not only ourselves, but also the thousands who are dead and have made the last sacrifice for their people, the prisoners of war scattered all over the world, and the women and children who are dying out by thousands in the concentration camps of the enemy; we represent the blood and the tears of an entire nation. They call upon us, from the prisoner-of-war camps, from the concentration camps, from the grave, from the field and from the womb of the future, to decide wisely and to avoid all measures which may lead to the decline and then extermination of the Afrikaner people, and thus frustrate the objects for which they made all their sacrifices ...
>
> As soon as we are convinced that, humanly speaking, there is no reasonable chance to retain our independence as republics, it clearly becomes our duty to stop the struggle in order that we may not perhaps sacrifice our people and our future for a mere idea which cannot be realized ... Perhaps it is [God's] will to lead the people of South Africa through defeat and humiliation, yea, even through the valley of the shadow of death, to a better future and brighter day.

General Christiaan De Wet, the Boers' greatest war leader, at last gave way, and peace was signed on relatively generous terms from the British. But the Boers gave up their independence.

One satisfaction the Boers could derive was that they had killed some 7,000 British soldiers and wounded 20,000, compared with around 4,000 Boer deaths in battle. Yet it had been a futile war, one which in retrospect the Boers could not possibly have won. They were soon to adopt much more intelligent tactics.

The war was to underline, once again, the terrible history of struggle that seemed forever the Boer lot. Their forces demoralized, their lands laid waste, thousands killed or wounded, so many perishing in concentration camps, repression, defeat – all contributed to the Boer sense of being history's victims, of trekking from one setback to another, of a journey without end. The original conquerors of South Africa (although they distanced themselves from the Dutch), they had been dispossessed by the British. They had sought to flee from the British yoke, and the British had come after them and taken over their lands. They freed themselves briefly, but once again the British had been triumphant after a merciless war.

Martyrdom, even masochism, had become part of the Afrikaner psyche. Struggle was their lot. Every advance seemed to be followed by a setback. While Britain had a major responsibility for the Boer War – it could be portrayed as just an imperialist grab for the gold fields – it must have percolated through even the thick skins of Boer self-righteousness that they were not entirely blameless.

The Boers' corrupt and obscurantist government had sought to disenfranchise not just the blacks but the British on their territory, daring the colonial authorities to do nothing about it. It had been the Boers who launched the war just as compromise seemed in sight. Even the most vituperative critics of the British empire can hardly have expected the British to do nothing as tens of thousands of their own people were stripped of their political rights and as millions of pounds flowed into the development of the Reef without securing any corresponding political influence. The Boers had, to a great extent, brought the war upon themselves. Wallowing in self-pity after their defeat did not become them. They were soon to discover that the British authorities, while skilled at winning wars, were also remarkably adept at losing the peace.

* * *

The post-war strategy of the British Governor-General, Lord Milners, was three-pronged: to encourage enough English settlers into the Orange Free State and the Transvaal to reverse Afrikaner domination; to force English upon the Afrikaner-speaking Boers; and to rule the two Boer provinces directly from Cape Town. All three were to prove disastrous failures. Only 1,200 English settlers were persuaded to emigrate to the two Republics.

'Anglicization' proved not only a failure, but counter-productive, heightening the Boer sense of cultural persecution and resistance. Children were permitted to speak Dutch only three hours a week at school, or forced to carry a placard saying, 'I am a donkey, I spoke Dutch'. Milner argued that 'next to the composition of the population, the thing which matters most is education ... Dutch should only be used to teach English, and English to teach everything else.' One historian of the period, Dan O'Meara, writes:

Within the imperialist colonial state, a clear cultural oppression operated against Afrikaans speakers. Long before the war ended the independence of the Republics, so generating a fierce cultural response, the language of the Cape had inspired a strong cultural nationalism. More importantly, in an essentially peripheral economy dominated by the ideology of imperialist interest, for those Afrikaners unprepared to accept cultural assimilation, and who possessed a modicum of training, rendering them unsuitable for manual labour, employment opportunities were limited. English was the language of the economy.

The Afrikaners chafed bitterly under this repression, and formulated their own ideology for promoting their language should they ever attain power over the English. The British bore the blame for this white-on-white cultural apartheid, and for planting the seeds of retaliatory hatred among the Afrikaners.

* * *

The economic objectives of the British, meanwhile, had been frustrated: if it proved almost incredibly difficult to force blacks down the gold mines – which had ground to a halt during the Boer war – it proved even harder to entice Afrikaners, however destitute.

In despair, the British were forced to do what they had done the previous century in order to bring in cheap labour to work the sugar plantations of Natal: look to the Far East. Between 1860 and 1911 some 150,000 Indians were shipped to Natal as 'indentured' labour – contracted for three to five years – and made to live in 'coolie lines' (primitive barracks) and work ceaselessly, under pain of being flogged. The Natal *Witness* summed up the prevailing attitude to the Indians:

> The ordinary Coolie ... and his family cannot be admitted into close fellowship and union with us and our families. He is introduced for the same reason as mules might be introduced from Montevideo, oxen from Madagascar, or sugar machinery from Glasgow. The object for which he is brought is to supply labour and that alone. He is not one of us, he is in every respect an alien; he only comes to perform a certain amount of work, and return to India ...

So appalling were the conditions in which the Indians worked that in 1871 the British Raj, hardly a beacon of liberalism, sought to ban the trade. 'We cannot permit emigration [to Natal] to be resumed until we are satisfied that the colonial authorities are aware of their duties towards Indian emigrants and that effectual measures have been taken to ensure that class of Her Majesty's subjects of all protection in Natal ...'

The conditions of the next great labour migration – Chinese workers for the gold mines – were little better. Between 1904 and 1906, some 64,000 arrived, again on three-year contracts, housed in compounds under strict pass-law conditions and prevented from doing skilled jobs. As the mines began to operate to full capacity again, at last the Africans returned to work them. There were soon some 94,000 blacks, 51,000 Chinese and 18,000 whites, contributing to producing around a third of all world gold production. The Chinese were all repatriated by 1910, leaving as their legacy the renewal of the gold mines and a rule that non-whites were permitted to carry out only unskilled labour.

* * *

Milner's third great failure was not long in coming. The Boers had an extraordinary stroke of good luck – that in the immediate aftermath of the war they were not led by stubborn civilian farmers as before, but by progressive military leaders, of whom Louis Botha and Jan Smuts were to be effective and skilful beyond any in their community. In

1906, a Liberal government had come to power in Britain, believing that the Boer War had been expensive and immoral. Smuts, taking advantage, went to London and pressed the new administration that the time had come to end direct rule from the Cape and restore a measure of self-government to the two Boer provinces. Boer parties proceeded to win elections to their parliaments by substantial majorities over Cape parties.

Milner himself was hardly enlightened on racial matters. 'A political equality of white and black is impossible,' he asserted. The white man must rule, 'because he is elevated by many, many steps above the black man; steps which it will take the latter centuries to climb; and which it is quite possible that the vast bulk of the black population will never be able to climb at all.'

* * *

Smuts and Botha now proceeded to press for a constitutional convention to set up a new basis for South Africa – something which was welcome to the British, who had always wanted a union. The Afrikaners believed they could dominate the new union and set it up on their terms – and they turned out to be right. The convention decided on a unitary constitution. When Cape leaders sought to entrench black voting rights in the new constitution, they accepted a compromise proposal by Smuts that would allow each province to retain its own method.

Smuts thus secured a vital concession for the Afrikaners: a weighted voting system that would give around a third as many more seats to sparsely populated country areas than to urban areas. This was to entrench Afrikaner domination of white South African politics. Astonishingly, the British colonial authorities went along with this. The Liberal government in Britain lacked interest in South Africa, and certainly held no brief for black voters. Thus British Liberals were responsible for the fateful decision that first awarded power over South Africa to the Afrikaners and gave away the rights not just of English-speakers but of blacks.

The colonial authorities, it seems, had not done their sums. Given the electoral bias towards the countryside, and with blacks disenfranchised in their provinces, the Afrikaners now secured a majority of seats in the white-dominated parliament. In May 1910 the constitution was promulgated and Botha became the first prime minister of a united South Africa.

Eight years after the Boer defeat, their principal military commander was in charge not just of the voortrekker republics, but the whole country. It was a reversal of fortunes without precedent in history, and proof, if such were needed, that the British Empire was nothing if not magnanimous. The Campbell-Bannerman and Asquith governments in Britain had been negligent of the interests of the majority in South Africa to the point of criminality. In order to bolster a 'liberal' view of colonial self-government they had installed in power the Boer minority which preached racial oppression of the overwhelming majority in the country – the blacks. Worse, it was proposed to grant the Boers an undemocratic majority in parliament at the expense of the English-speaking community.

The Afrikaners took power and did not relinquish it for 84 years. South African politics was now to be decided by internal feuding within the Afrikaner tribe, not by reasoned argument between the country's main communities.

What followed was a series of tribal bloodlettings within the Afrikaner community which resulted in the centre of gravity, already dangerously skewed towards the racist right, moving even more sharply towards the extremists in 1924, veering briefly back to moderation, Afrikaner-style, in 1934, and then returning to extreme right-wing rule under a conspiratorial, tribal-based volkstaat in 1948. This permitted a glimmer of reform only in 1966, and a little more in 1978, before disintegrating in 1990.

In spite of securing power, the Afrikaners continued to suffer from a persecution complex. Yet black Africans had better cause to complain about British feebleness in resisting Boer demands. Within a decade of the loss of the Orange Free State and the Transvaal, the Afrikaners were in power in all of South Africa, with the British their junior partners – and soon not even that.

Britain was guilty not of repressing the Boers after the war, but of spinelessness towards them; it had won the Boer War, only to give away the peace.

* * *

A more serious charge still can be laid against the British – and indeed was, by, of all people, the Afrikaners: that the former, not the Afrikaners, were the originators of the whole system of white supremacy that was eventually to congeal into the cold desert of apartheid.

It is certainly possible to substantiate this at the beginning of the century. Milner and the British authorities believed firmly in keeping the black man in his place. They still saw the blacks as a potential reservoir of labour for the new industrial South Africa, and their social policies were shaped by their economic priorities. The majority of British-descended whites shared the Boer prejudices against the blacks. For the great bulk of the English-speaking community, the established order – a white overclass and a black and 'coloured' underclass – was natural and preferable to any change.

Yet the elevation of white supremacy to quasi-religious status – based on the supposed threat that the blacks posed to the whites (*oie swatgevaar*, the 'black threat', was a peculiarly Afrikaner obsession, founded on the grim view of the previous century that the blacks were primitive, 'heathen', uncivilized and occupied a position somewhere between the white man and animals). Moreover, at a time when around the world the franchise was being quietly extended to a wider community – to women, to all adults – the Afrikaners were to make it their mission to withdraw what few political rights the blacks had succeeded in acquiring under the British.

Because, by the end of the Second World War, it had become unacceptable to base a state on racial discrimination, the Afrikaners were then obliged to go down the tortuous route of finding a legalistic justification for their gut prejudices. Apartheid and the doctrine of separate development provided this, with increasingly perverse and unnatural results, as the ideology, which was originally a convenient figleaf for a state based on white domination and black labour, became the bizarre driving force of South African society.

The tenets and direction of English-based law in the Cape inevitably tended towards the granting of black rights and extension of the franchise (as in Britain itself). That was the bias of the law and the Cape liberals that upheld it, whatever the basic prejudices of many English speakers and the inherently racialist economic engineering of men like Rhodes and Milner. The Afrikaners instead created a legal and governmental framework that enshrined racism, a constitutional Frankenstein that was soon to get the better of them and continue powering ahead when even Afrikaners realized it was unworkable and grotesque.

The legacy of British colonial rule was racism and economic oppression; but not institutional, legal and ideological oppression, the hallmarks, indeed the uniqueness, of apartheid. The foundations of a state based no longer merely on whites driving the blacks off their best land, but using them as an underclass in a white-run economy, were laid, sure enough, when South Africa was still British ruled and with the support of most of the country's English speakers. But it was the Afrikaners who were in the driving seat after 1910, the Afrikaners to whom race was a matter of obsession, not of mere convenience, and the Afrikaners who set the racial agenda.

The British guilt thereafter was that of association and inertia. Milner's own attitude was that he believed in 'a self-governing white community supported by a well-treated and justly governed black labour [force] from Cape Town to the Zambezi.' In 1903 Milner set up the South African Native Affairs Congress (SANAC), headed by Sir Godfrey Lagden, a former native commissioner for the Transvaal.

The first thing that the commission concluded was that the basis for 'natural selection' already existed, in the form of the 'traditional homelands' of the blacks – the Zulus in Natal, the Xhosa in the eastern Cape and the Sotho in Basutoland, for example – a policy of 'reserves' similar to the one that had been applied in North America, with the considerable difference that the whites were a small minority in a country overwhelmingly black-dominated. In order to get blacks to work in white industries, it would be necessary to limit the amount of land available to them. The principle was that male blacks must go and live in white areas, under stringent supervision, and return to their families from time to time in the homelands.

In chillingly inhuman language, Lagden argued that 'a man cannot go with his wife and children and his goods ... on to the labour market. He must have a dumping ground. Every rabbit must have a warren where he can live and burrow and breed, and every native must have a warren too.' The commission recommended that education for the blacks would be beneficial for South Africa in the long term. But in the short run the African was not yet ready, and it would be too expensive.

As to political rights, the commission did not recommend any change in the growing black vote in the Cape, where they might eventually become the majority, but deemed it impossible to apply the same rights to the franchise to the other three provinces. Traditional black structures should be strengthened so that they had a right to make representation to the white government 'without conferring on them political power in any aggressive sense, or weakening in any way the unchallenged mastery, supremacy and power of the ruling race'.

The principal elements of South African society as it was to endure for most of the century were laid down in this report – but it did not specifically affect the black franchise or the spread of black education. Nor was Lagden's commission in fact binding, although it did represent the views of the more tough-minded representatives of the English-descended community.

4
The Broeders – Stormtroopers of Apartheid

The real foundations for apartheid were put in place shortly after Botha took power, and the architect was none other than the supposed 'liberal' of the Afrikaner community, Jan Smuts. His views, in fact, were hardly that. As he said in London in 1917,

> With us there are certain axioms now in regard to the relations of black and white; and the principal one is no intermixture of blood between the two colours. It has now become an accepted axiom in our dealings with the natives that it is dishonourable to mix white and black blood ... We have felt more and more that if we are to solve our native question it is useless to try to govern black and white in the same system, to subject them to the same institutions of government and legislation. They are different not only in colour but in minds and political capacity, and their political institutions should be different while always proceeding on the basis of self-government.
>
> Instead of mixing up black and white in the old haphazard way, which instead of lifting up the black degraded the white, we are now trying to lay down a policy of keeping them apart as much as possible in our institutions. Thus in South Africa you will have in the long run large areas cultivated by blacks and governed by blacks, where they will look after themselves in all their forms of living and development, while in the rest of the country you will have your white communities which will govern themselves separately according to the accepted European principles. The natives will, of course, be free to go and to work in the white areas, but as far as possible the administration of white and black will be separated, and such that each will be satisfied and developed according to its own proper lives.

This expressed the essence of apartheid more than 30 years before the first 'extremist' apartheid government took power. In swift succession, Smuts rammed through the 1911 Mines and Works Act, which 'reserved' skilled jobs as being beyond the 'competency' of blacks; and the 1913 Natives Land Act, which ear-marked the reservations for the sole use of black workers mainly in Zululand, Ciskei and Transkei, just 7 per cent of the land area of South Africa. Elsewhere blacks were forbidden to own land, but they could be tenants.

The act caused massive suffering. As evidence to the Beaumont Commission on the subject expressed it, the act

> puts them back in their rearing of their stock and ruins what they term their bank. It causes our people to be derelicts and helpless. We beg the commission to approach the government and make our grievance clear and find a haven of refuge for our oppressed. There is winter in the Native's Land Act. In winter the trees are stripped and leafless.
>
> ... Owing to our vagrant condition year after year and the absence of any security of tenure, we are unable to erect substantial dwellings capable of sheltering us and our little ones from rain, wind and cold. The occupation of the tumble-down dwellings to which we are condemned has had a marked effect on our health. Also it has never been practicable to make provision for education. Requests to landlords for permission to erect schools are met with refusal, notwithstanding that in some cases we lease land and in others sow on half shares. On top of this, when a landlord wishes to get rid of a tenant he has to go, however unwilling, and leave behind him, without compensation, any improvements he may have effected in the way of dwellings ...

The 1920 Natives Affairs Act appointed district councils, based on tribal divisions, to give blacks a separate administration from the whites. The 1923 Natives (Urban Areas) Act sought to regulate the flood of blacks to the cities. In Cape Town, for example, huge squatter settlements had sprung up, arousing violent feelings even in that bastion of white liberalism. The city's chief medical officer commented that the conditions of Africans were 'very undesirable, both from the point of view of sanitation and socially, by bringing uncleanly, half-civilized units into intimate contact with the more cleanly and civilized portion of the community.'

The act forced local authorities to provide adequate living for

Africans in shanties, but it also strictly regulated them, pushing them out of city centres and requiring them to use passes. Surplus labour was deported. This legislation was the result of a report by a Transvaal local government commission headed by Frederick Stallard, which stated baldly that 'it should be an organized principle that natives – men, women and children – should only be permitted within municipal areas in so far and for as long as their presence is demanded by the wants of the white population ... The masterless native in urban areas is a source of danger and is a cause of degradation for both black and white ... If the native is to be regarded as a permanent element in municipal areas ... there can be no justification for basing his exclusion from the franchise on the simple ground of colour.'

The architect of apartheid was in fact Jan Smuts, not Alfred Milner 10 years earlier, and not Hendrik Verwoerd more than 40 years later.

* * *

Botha's policy of reconciliation between the Afrikaner and English communities, which had allowed the Afrikaners to win power in 1910, was soon outflanked by Barry Hertzog, a thin-lipped, walrus-moustached bigot for whom black issues were central to his assertion of Afrikanerdom. In 1912 he declared he would rather live in a dunghill than stay in the British Empire, and he was sacked by Botha the following year, forming the National Party in opposition to the ruling South Africa Party.

Hertzog's right-hand man in Cape Province was Daniel Malan, who favoured outright Afrikaner domination over the English. Meanwhile, Gustav Prezler had launched a magazine called *The Sentinel,* championing 'Afrikaner' – a mixture of Dutch, English, Xhosa, and Malay words which had previously been the language of the poor whites and 'coloureds'. In 1925 it was to replace Dutch as the official language of the non-English-speaking whites.

Botha remained firmly in charge, however, and he made the decision in 1914 to enter the First World War alongside Britain, making preparations to invade German South West Africa. The Boer war heroes Koos de la Rey and Christiaan de Wet strongly disagreed, and decided to stage a coup. By chance de la Rey was shot dead at a police road block, and the plot fizzled out in a futile rebellion; de Wet was eventually captured. But Botha had lost a great deal of Afrikaner support, and in the following year's election he won 95,000 votes to Hertzog's 77,000, forcing him into coalition with the English-speaking Unionists – a deal regarded as treachery by many Boers. The country was deeply divided over the war, with frequent clashes between pro-war factions and anti-war Afrikaner factions. Botha died in 1919, upset by the antagonism of his own people, and was succeeded by Smuts. He, however, faced the brunt of the Depression, which hit the country's poor whites, and was in turn swept from power by Hertzog.

The latter's greatest obsession was the removal of the Cape franchise from the blacks – the last vestige of South Africa's liberal origins under the British and their last hope of participation in the country's politics. In 1925 he urged its abandonment and the following year tabled four bills to do away with it. In 1927, however, his bills were defeated in parliament. Only in 1935, when he formed the 'fusion' government, did he receive the necessary two-thirds backing, using Smuts' support to get the measure through with an overwhelming 168 votes to 11, after the National party's leader had conjured up the image of an 'intermingling of blood' and domination by the Africans. Their land reserves were doubled in compensation.

Hertzog presided over a modest economic recovery from the postwar slump. But the 1920s also saw the spread of whites, squeezed off the land by larger farms and enterprises, and joining the ranks of the poor and hard-working blacks in Africa's major industries. This was exacerbated by the onset of the Great Depression after 1929, forcing Hertzog to ally with Smuts in coalition.

* * *

The combination of three things – the growth of Afrikaner nationalism, the increasing insecurity and poverty of a large part of the white community, and, eventually, the joining together of two of South Africa's two main Boer parties – incubated a new and more radical Afrikaner nationalism. In the difficult conditions of industrialized South Africa in the mid-twentieth century, this was to draw its inspiration from the voortrekker pioneers of a century before and the Elysian simplicity of a pure white pastoral lifestyle that had existed only briefly then, if at all.

The new ideology was pioneered by an organization that started from ludicrously small beginnings and which, with all the implausibility of a Conan Doyle story woven around some masonic mid-Western conspiracy, united the underground of anti-British movements in the Transvaal into an extraordinarily powerful and pervasive network. The Afrikaner clique seized power in 1948 and rode through the high noon of apartheid until its fall nearly half a century later. It was the first documented example of a secret society taking over a government.

On the night of 17 April 1918, Malan, the hardline leader of the National party in the Cape, was addressing a meeting in Johannesburg. A pro-war mob broke into the meeting and beat up many of those attending. Three teenagers present, led by a bespectacled, intense, sharp-faced youth, Henning Klopper, met the next day to declare that they would form an organization to defend the Afrikaner. Two months later they held a meeting to form Jong Suidafrika. This was soon renamed Die Afrikaner Broederbond – the Afrikaner Brotherhood.

Although it was initially seen as 'nothing more than a semi-religious organization', one veteran recalls that 'we formed the Broederbond as a kind of counterpart of societies and clubs which, in those days, were exclusively English-speaking. Those were hard days for the Afrikaner. Everything was English and Afrikaans-speaking people found it hard to make out. We decided the Broederbond would be for Afrikaners only – any Afrikaner – and that it would be a sort of cultural society. We started raising funds to build up a library and we invited prominent Afrikaners to give lectures. There was nothing sinister about the Bond in those days.'

But by 1921 the organization had become secret, and members were forbidden to tell even their wives about their membership. Its initiation ceremony involved new recruits stabbing a dummy, in a red winding sheet bearing the word 'traitor', with a dagger. The 'chaplain' conducting the ceremony would intone, 'he who betrays the Bond will be destroyed by the Bond. The Bond never forgets. Its vengeance is swift and sure. Never yet has a traitor escaped its just punishment.' This might seem harmless schoolboy nonsense – except for the fact that the Bond soon became quite astonishingly powerful.

By 1935 the power of the secret society within Afrikanerdom – itself the dominant force within the country – was such that Hertzog, the right-wing prime minister, devoted a major speech to attacking it. Malan had walked out of Hertzog's party in disgust at the formation of the 'fusion' alliance with Smuts, to found his own 'Purified National Party' (HNP).

Hertzog declared sweepingly,

We see now in what close relationship the Afrikaner Broederbond stands to the Purified National Party. The leaders and moving spirits of the one are the leaders and moving spirits of the other. There can be no doubt, therefore, that the secret Broederbond is nothing less than the Purified National Party busy working secretly underground, and that the Purified National Party is nothing but the secret Afrikaner Broederbond which conducts its activities on the surface. Between the two, the unification of Afrikanerdom is being bartered for a republican-cum-Calvinistic bond.

By departing from the sphere of national culture and mixing in politics, the Afrikaner Broederbond has shed its youthful innocence and has suddenly become a grave menace to the rest and peace of our social community as well as to the irreproachable purity of our public life and civil administration, even where it operates in the economic-cultural sphere.

To realize the nature and extent of the danger with which we are now being threatened by the secret machinations and activities of the Broederbond, it is necessary for me to impart to you certain information from secret documents of the Bond regarding its organization, members and several other particulars. The strictness with which the Bond's activities are kept a secret appears from the fact that only very few persons outside its organization know of its existence, although it has existed for 17 years and although there are few towns and villages in the Free State where it is not in operation, or where it has no organization.

The members of the Bond are not many – at the outside 2,000. But the power of the Bond does not lie in its membership, but in its secret organization, which, for instance, is spread over the whole Free State like a network for the purpose of active propaganda.

Hertzog went on to accuse it of 'blind race animosity, which secretly seeks racial domination and bossism'. It should be remembered that the prime minister himself represented the hard-line wing of Afrikanerdom, which had broken with the 'liberal' Smuts, himself the initiator of most of the country's founding apartheid legislation.

The Bond's three main concerns were language, the pursuit of Afrikaner education, and the concept of Broeder helping Broeder in business. Its secret agenda was political – the installation of Malan in power, and the capturing of influential positions throughout the country for Broeders at the expense of non-Broeder Afrikaners and the English community.

* * *

In 1938 there occurred an event as significant for the Afrikaners as Mussolini's march on Rome in 1922 or the burning of the Reichstag in Germany in 1933. Klopper organized the great ox-wagon trek to commemorate the centenary of the great trek. It struck a huge chord among that proud, rootless people. It was perhaps the greatest single display of Afrikaner consciousness in their history. When in August two stinkwood ox wagons, the Piet Retief and the Andries Pretorius, set out for the journey from Cape Town to Pretoria's Voortrekker Monument, Klopper and his fellow Broeders in the first, some 100,000 people turned out to see them off. All along the way they were greeted by crowds, and other wagons joined them, the men wearing voortrekker costume and the women frocks and bonnets.

At the monument a huge torchlit rally was held and a giant bonfire ignited. Daniel Malan thundered to 60,000 people that 'as the muzzle load had clashed with the assegai in the past', it was the Afrikaners' duty 'to make South Africa a white man's land'. As T. C. Robertson of the *Rand Daily Mail* reported,

> The great Voortrekker camp on Monument Koppie stirred with life tonight. Ten thousand visitors from all over South Africa had trekked in, and the smoke from their campfires drifted low over the long rows of white tents. It was a scene with those hard contrasts of light and shade, of silence and noise, which provided the stark qualities of a film set.
>
> Powerful floodlights played on the tents and accentuated the red glare of the campfires against the white canvas. In the valley, a mile below the hill where the foundations of the Voortrekker Monument were silhouetted against the evening sky, a choir of 1,000 children were singing Afrikaner songs. The chorus of the melodies vibrated among the tents, and men and women round the campfires stopped to listen.
>
> But the heroes of the camp are the burghers of the commando. They sit loosely in their saddles and yet manage to ride with the swagger and bravado of Roman cavalry in a triumphal procession. Looking at these commandos one can understand why they have been described as the greatest and most mobile fighting unit in the world ... Scenes of enthusiasm and crowds of a size never before seen in Pretoria marked the arrival of the wagons, and their progress through the flag-bedecked streets was the signal for the pealing of church bells, the firing of guns and the ceaseless cheering of thousands of people ...

The two torches, brought by relays of Voortrekkers from Cape Town and Dingaan's Kraal, arrived in the valley below the Monument tonight. Three thousand boys and girls, carrying torches, met them on the hill above the aerodrome. They marched down towards the camp like a winding river of fire more than a mile long. There a crowd of 60,000 stood waiting in silent amazement.

Then, as the chain of light wound past them, they started cheering – more lustily and enthusiastically than I have ever heard a South African crowd cheer. Women rushed forward and burned the corners of their handkerchiefs and kappies in the flame of the two torches, to keep as momentoes of the great event ... A score of women knelt in silent prayer in the darkness round the bare foundations of the Voortrekker Monument tonight.

I saw the outlines of their kappies silhouetted against the brilliant lights of Pretoria – the Voortrekker City – in the valley below. The action of these 20 women was characteristic of the reverent spirit that is prevailing at the Monument. Although a soft rain was falling, they climbed the steep slopes of Monument Koppie through the thick growth of protea bushes and long grass. From the camp the echo of the massed choirs singing hymns could be heard. In the south the lights of the city of gold, where the modern Voortrekkers are fighting their battle, could be seen twinkling over the hills.

Malan went on to fight the 1938 election on an unashamedly segregationist platform – but he was defeated by a landslide after some six years of economic recovery fuelled by a sharp rise in the gold price.

* * *

A year later, however, Hertzog recommended to his cabinet that South Africa stay out of the war that had just broken out in Europe. Smuts opposed this along with 6 of the other 11 ministers present. After a fierce debate in parliament, Smuts won by 80 votes to 67, and Hertzog resigned as prime minister.

Within days Hertzog had left the United Party and, together with Malan, recreated the National Party. The latter intoned, 'in spirit I see the figures of Piet Retief, Andries Pretorius, Sarel Cilliers, Hendrik Potgieter and ... it is as though I hear them saying: "Even when you were divided we loved you, but now that you are one, our love for you is doubled".' However, Hertzog's old enemies in the Broederbond were to exact a bitter revenge. Insistent that Afrikaans become the main language taught in schools – he favoured neutrality between Afrikaans and English – they drove him out of the party and to a bitter and lonely death in 1942.

Smuts, now in power, shied away from a confrontation with the Broederbond during the war – although the Ossewabrandwag, formed at the time of the trek centenary, became a Nazi front, boasting around 400,000 members, including Klopper and the brother of future prime minister Johannes Vorster (who himself was interned for three years during the war for pro-German sympathies). However, Smuts' director of military intelligence kept a close eye on the Bond. As he reported:

> Racial separation, which had been part of South Africa's way of life for generations, received a new impetus from Nazism and German-oriented Afrikaners. This attitude spilled on to English–Afrikaner relationships as well as between white and non-white. As indicated before, a number of leading Afrikaners had become impressed by Hitler's success in propagating the doctrines of national socialism in Germany. The Nationalists, particularly, found themselves in sympathy with his ideas of building up a pure Nordic race which would rule Europe after getting rid of Jews and capitalists. Hitler's regimentation of the German youth and particularly his use of symbol slogans and national rallies to create a feeling of national consciousness were soon copied in building up an exclusive Afrikaner nationalism. Behind it all was the thoughtful planning and pervasive organization of the Broederbond ...

Smuts at last acted against the Bond in 1944, ordering civil servants and teachers to resign from it or be dismissed. He launched a furious tirade, describing it as a 'dangerous, cunning, political, Fascist organization of which no civil servant, if he was to retain his loyalty to the state and the administration, could be allowed to be a member.'

Some 1,000 civil servants resigned, while others lay low. In a subsequent parliamentary debate, Smuts performed unimpressively. However, it didn't matter: he was South Africa's most powerful and internationally respected prime minister this century, leading the South African delegation to the opening of the United Nations at San Francisco, and there drafting the preamble to the UN Charter.

That South Africa should be so respected was, just four short years later, remarkable. In part this had been secured by Smuts' statesman-like decision to join the anti-Nazi coalition; in part by his decisions to relax the pass laws and improve the training and working conditions of blacks as a means of harnessing them to the war effort; but also as a result of a remarkable report compiled by the secretary for native affairs, Douglas Smit, drawing attention to the 'tremendous price of the laws – including the loss of labour owing to the regular mass detention of blacks'. In language remarkable for its time, Smit added, 'the harassing and constant interference with the freedom of movement of Natives gives rise to a burning sense of grievance and injustice which has an unsettling effect on the Native population as a whole. The application of these laws also has the undesirable feature of introducing large numbers of Natives to the machinery of criminal law and makes many become familiar at an early age with prison.'

For the first time since the end of English-speaking rule in South Africa in 1908, it seemed in 1945 that there was hope of a slightly more enlightened view on race from an Afrikaner government. As Smuts' biographer, Bernard Friedman, writes, 'Smuts could afford to ignore his opponents. His star was definitely in the ascendant. After the general election of 1943 he was at the height of his power. After VE day – victory in Europe – he was at the height of his prestige. He had brought his country through years of bitter adversity to ultimate triumph. At home his authority as Prime Minister was complete and unchallengeable; he was in full control of the destiny of his country. Abroad his prestige was immense – no other Commonwealth states-man outside of Britain had ever attained such heights.'

This was the more remarkable in that he had been more responsible than any in having laid the foundations of apartheid legislation, and his betrayal had permitted the abolition of the Cape franchise. This statesman abroad had been an inveterate racist at home, if not so visceral and mean-spirited a one as Hertzog or Malan. Yet Smuts' obsession with global concerns was viewed as a disadvantage in South Africa.

In particular, during the war, black obeisance to segregationist laws had begun to break down. As thousands of impoverished blacks flooded to the cities, the government appointed a commission under Henry Fagan to look at the reality of native laws. Complete segrega-tion, it concluded, was 'totally impracticable; the flow of Africans to the cities cannot be reversed; indeed it would be good for industry if they stayed.'

These sensible but revolutionary conclusions were bitterly resisted by the opposition HNP, led by Malan, who raised the spectre of *oorstroming* – becoming inundated or overcome. Its own report, drawn up by segregationist Paul Sauer, urged that 'detribalization' be stopped, and that Africans should only be allowed in as temporary workers, returning to the homelands afterwards. The Sauer report for the first time introduced the explicit concept of apartheid – although, as we have seen, its origins were far older.

Malan took up the refrain with vigour. Africans would have to 'develop along their own lines in their true fatherland, the Reserves'. The HNP 'realizes the danger of the flood of Africans moving to the cities and undertakes to protect the white character of our cities and to provide a forceful and effective way for the safety of individuals and property and the peaceful life of the inhabitants.' Undoubtedly this populist racist struck a chord among South Africans wondering whether even Smuts was beginning to weaken in his anti-black resolve.

The HNP also benefited from a return to post-war politics as usual. Before the Depression, the National Party under Hertzog had been the majority white party. During the Depression and war, Afrikaners had gone along with coalition. Now they returned to their traditional allegiances, particularly as disillusionment with wartime privations, rationing and economic difficulties continued, while the HNP openly and passionately played the race card.

To widespread astonishment, Smuts was toppled in the general election on 26 May 1948, just as Churchill had been defeated three years earlier in Britain. Malan's HNP jumped from 48 seats to 70, while Smuts' United Party slumped from 89 to 65. The rump of Hertzog's movement, the Afrikaner Party, allied to the HNP, won 9 seats, and the Labour Party 6.

In fact the UP, the Labour Party and other more moderate splinter parties had won far more votes – 624,000 compared with 444,000 – than the HNP and the AP; but the bias in favour of rural voting gave the extremists the edge. Smuts himself was narrowly defeated by Witzel du Plessis, a former civil servant who had resigned rather than leave the Broederbond. Smuts lamented, 'to think that I have been beaten by the Broederbond'. He at least was clear about what had happened.

5
The Volkstaat

Even the blacks were unaware of the full extent of the horror about to
be unleashed. As Albert Luthuli, head of the ANC, commented lacon-
ically, 'the Nationalist win did not either surprise nor extremely
interest us, although we did realize that there would probably be an
intensification of the hardships and indignities which had always
come our way. Nevertheless, I think it is true that very few, if any, of
us understood how swift the deterioration was to be.'

The United Party hoped the setback was only temporary; they, no
more than the blacks, foresaw the grim determination with which the
party of the Broederbond would now install itself as the new ruling
class, equipped with an ideology of race unparallelled anywhere else
in the world. As Ivor Wilkins and Hans Strydom, historians of the
Broederbond, recount,

> It was indeed the Broederbond's hour of greatest triumph. A small
> band of brothers in 1918, they were now the group with political
> control of the whole country. Never would they let power slip from
> the hands of the Super-Afrikaners. They would reform the country
> politically and socially on racial lines, with a zeal never witnessed
> before in the world. The campaign they had planned so painstak-
> ingly over the years to build up their secret structure had finally
> given them the biggest prize of all – absolute control. Not a day, not
> an hour, could be lost in putting their stamp on everything.
>
> The world would look on in wonderment at a secret society that
> gained political control and transformed a sophisticated country
> almost beyond recognition. It must surely rank as one of the most
> fascinating political stories of our time.

Malan was the first Broeder to become prime minister. Arguably, he was the organization's presiding genius, and Klopper had been no more than his fanatical, sinister lieutenant. Only 2 of the 12 members of the new cabinet were not Broeders, and all were Afrikaners, making a nonsense of the idea that South Africa's government should seek to represent both white communities.

Broeders were promoted to senior civil service jobs. Major-General Evered Poole, an English speaker who was deputy chief of staff at only 46 and expected to move to the top job, was shunted off to become head of the military mission in West Germany. The military intelligence chief, a dedicated anti-Broederbonder, was fired and his files on the organization seized. The head of the railways and the chairman of the state trading company were also replaced by Broeders.

The entire senior management of the South Africa Broadcasting Corporation was taken over by Broeders. The new chairman, Dr Piet Meyer, a future chairman of the Broederbond, who was to dominate the enterprise for 20 years, made his contempt for South Africa's English speakers plain. The Boederbond's objective, he said, could be

nothing less than the complete political nationalizing and eventual cultural Afrikanerization of our English-speaking citizens – if it can still be done. We will not be able to stop the process of complete cultural integration of Afrikaans- and English-speaking if we have only limited control of this process. Therefore we can envisage only the deliberate Afrikanerizing of the English-speakers, or tacit acceptance of the unintentional but certain Anglicizing of the Afrikaner. The objective of nationalizing the English-speakers politically will be of permanent value, ensuring the continued existence of the Afrikaner, only if it is coupled with the Afrikanerizing of the economy.

The Afrikanerizing of the English-speakers is an educational task – it must start in the schools. The Afrikanerizing of the English-speaker entails the English-speaker accepting the Afrikaner outlook and philosophy as his own; integrating his ideals and lifestyle with that of the Afrikaner; recognizing the Afrikaner's history as his history; and recognizing Afrikaans as his national language next to English as the international language of the two white groups ... We will then talk of Afrikaans-speaking and English-speaking Afrikaners.

Another of Meyer's objectives was the need for South Africa finally to break the hated imperial link and become a republic. As he later put it,

In the second phase of our organization's existence, from about 1934, it deliberately worked for the establishment of the Republic of South Africa, separate from the Commonwealth. It saw this as the most important condition and method through which English-speaking citizens could be persuaded to become loyal South Africans and, with the dedicated Afrikaner, safeguard the future of southern Africa as a permanent home for the separate white and non-white groups.

On race, the Broederbond had set out its views plainly as early as 1933:

Total segregation should not only be the ideal, but the immediate practical policy of the state. The purchase and separation of suitable and adequate areas for habitation by natives' families, and tribes living on farms and smaller reserves, should take place at any cost ... A native who has reached a stipulated age will be allowed, with the permission of his tribal chief and the commissioner, to go temporarily to white areas to work on farms and in towns and cities. But he will not be allowed to take his family.

The detribalized native must as far as possible be encouraged to move to these native areas. Those who cannot do so must be housed in separate locations where they will enjoy no political rights and own no property because they must be viewed as temporary occupants who live in the white area of their own choice and for gain. Unemployed natives should be forced to leave these locations and move to the native areas after having been allowed a reasonable time to obtain work.

The blacks were to be treated as foreigners in their own country. One prominent Broeder academic, G. Cronje, went as far as to equate the Boers and the Bantu.

The Boer people have themselves gone through the crucible of imperialist and capitalist domination and exploitation. They still show the wounds and the bruises of it all. Their national life and culture have been disrupted. As a nation they almost perished because they serve the interests of other people. They know what it means to see their own destroyed, but they also know what it means to promote through their own efforts a national revival and restoration ... The Boer national can therefore fully understand the sufferings of the bantu. It is that same imperialism and capitalism, having them believe that the foreigner is better than what is their own, which seeks to destroy their tribal life.

Cronje believed in 'the nationalist Afrikaners meeting in the Broederbond and elsewhere, talking into the small hours and cogitating on the new vision of a policy which would finally put an end to the inchoate state of the country. A massive black proletariat was building up in the ghettos of the cities, posing a threat to the survival of the white race and especially of the Afrikaner nation, as lately conceived and described.'

* * *

A single-minded, dedicated zealot, also a Broeder, came to office in 1950 as minister of native affairs. He had a profound effect on the history of his country. Thickset, visionary, outspoken, possessed of an almost obsessive certitude belied by a genial, even friendly, appearance, Hendrik Verwoerd had been born in Amsterdam, the son of a shopkeeper who emigrated first to Rhodesia, then to South Africa. By birth not an Afrikaner at all, Verwoerd studied at Stellenbosch, then in Germany, and returned to become professor of sociology at Stellenbosch.

During the depression he became sympathetic to the plight of poor whites and in 1937 became prominent in Transvaal politics, as well as editor of *Die Transvaaler*, which was convicted as being a vehicle of German propaganda during the war. Verwoed spelt out his views in his first major speech in the senate: 'I want to state here unequivocally now the attitude of this side of the House, that South Africa is white man's country and that he must remain the master here. In the reserves we are prepared to allow the Natives to be the masters, we are not masters there. But within the European areas, we, the white people in South Africa, are and shall remain the masters.'

His ally, Meyer, spelt out the messianic, quasi-religious concept of the battle between good and evil espoused by the Broederbond:

In our efforts to find a morally defensible Christian way of coexistence between white and non-white in our country and on our borders, the Broederbond came in direct contact with the two biggest and most dangerous present-day forces of the dark bedevilling relations, namely communism and liberalism. These are forces which enter the spirit of the people and cannot be stopped by solely political and military defence methods – forces which must be fought on religious, cultural and political grounds.

It was therefore the Afrikaans churches and the Afrikaner Broederbond which worked for the closure of the British embassy in Pretoria, started the battle against communism through the formation of well-disposed organizations in the trade union field, especially in the clothing and mining industries, and which alerted the nation and the country to the danger through the church congress on communism and later the Volkscongres on communism.

Indeed, one of the keys to the Broederbond concept of Afrikanerdom was religion. Afrikanerdom and the whole concept of apartheid – apartness – is bound up with the mystical exclusiveness of Calvinist Protestantism. As a Broederbond document puts it, 'The history of the Afrikaner nation cannot be written without the history of the Afrikaans churches ... Consider the Church's missionary policy and action on the basis of separate ecclesiastical organizations for various national, language and cultural communities. Consider also the meaning that the Church's deliberations about our race relations in the light of scripture had for our political, social and constitutional arrangements. The fact that the Afrikaans churches clearly declared themselves against integration and blood-mixing between white and non-white gave the Afrikaner nation incalculable moral support.'

Calvinism itself preached apartness between the Elect, who were predetermined to eternal life, and their damned brethren. Apartheid was a logical extension. As the Dutch Reformed Church commission put it,

> Every nation and race will be able to perform the greatest service to God and the world if it keeps its own national attributes, received from God's own hand, pure with honour and gratitude ... God divided men into races, languages and nations. Differences are not only willed by God but perpetuated by Him. Equality between Natives, Coloured and Europeans includes a misappreciation of the fact that God, in His providence, made people into different races and nations ... far from the word of God encouraging equality, it is an established spiritual principle that in every community ordina-

tion, there is a fixed relationship between authorities ... Those who are culturally and spiritually advanced have a mission to leadership and protection of the less advanced ... The Natives must be led and formed towards independence so that eventually they will be equal to the Europeans, but each on his own territory and each serving God in his own fatherland.

Piet Meyer, chairman of the Broederbond at the apex of its power, expressed the religious undercurrent at a huge meeting at Tweefontein on the Eastern Rand in 1963: 'The struggle against South Africa is aimed at rooting out the last vestiges of white Christendom. We have accepted it thus: we want to be a Christian nation. In that spirit we stand here. Christ is the highest, the most powerful weapon against Communism. As a nation, we want to be an instrument in the hands of God to take on the struggle against Communism.'

In 1934, the then Broederbond chairman had set out its ultimate goal: 'The primary consideration is whether Afrikanerdom will reach its ultimate destiny of domination in South Africa. Brothers, the key to South Africa's problems is not whether one party or another shall obtain the whiphand, but whether the Afrikaner Broederbond shall govern South Africa.'

* * *

What followed, under Malan and Verwoerd, after 1948, was the scientific application of these tenets. A close observer of Verwoerd says he was a man 'with a closed mathematical mind who applied his ideas with precision regardless of the human consequences'. Thus the whole concept of South African racialism had evolved over the years from straightforward contempt for a 'heathen, subhuman' people in their own country in the eighteenth century, through to the economic exploitation of the blacks as a pool of mass labour in the nineteenth century, through to Smuts' cynical attempts to continue this while trying to keep the races as separate as possible.

When urban migration threatened to break down separation in the 1940s, there was a white backlash, and segregation was enforced by social engineering of a ferocity and application seen rarely outside the Communist bloc. The primitive Broederbond creators of apartheid became the prisoners of ideology. It is impossible to justify notions of racial superiority intellectually, although the Afrikaners passionately believed in them, so the theory of 'separate but equal' development –

which in practice was entirely unequal – had to be vigorously proclaimed. While the old English establishment had not been too concerned at racial mixing, provided cheap black labour was available, the apostles of apartheid believed in the latter accompanied by the most rigorous racial screening taken to almost incredible legal lengths and expense.

It was an ethic of racial privilege imposed by the minority within Afrikanerdom. To protect them from being overwhelmed, they must be protected and placed above all of South Africa's peoples – even their fellow English-speaking whites. Thus their supremacy was born of a deep-rooted historical sense of inferiority and a feeling of being under threat.

The scientific application of apartheid was as remorseless as an advancing ox wagon. In 1949 the Prohibition of Mixed Marriages Act was the first major piece of legislative apartheid (there were only about 100 such marriages a year). The following year, sex between the races was banned under a provision of the Immorality Act.

The same year the Population Representation Act, in terms reminiscent of Nazi legislation to establish how Jewish particular Germans were, drew up definitions of race based on appearance as well as descent. The 'pencil in the hair' test was established as one rule of thumb. If the pencil stayed, the hair was fuzzy and the person classified as black or coloured. If it fell out, the person had straight hair, and was white. Families were split up as a result of these arbitrary classifications.

The Group Areas Act gave the government powers to laboriously separate the races in the urban suburbs. The Reservation of Separate Amenities Act of 1953 provided for separate public facilities in buses, trains, post offices, public conveniences and so on. The young P. W. Botha justified this baldly by saying 'to gain a clear view regarding fair treatment and the rights of non-Europeans, we should first answer another question and that is: do we stand for the domination and supremacy of the European or not? For if you stand for the domination and supremacy of the European, then everything you do must be in the first place calculated to ensure that domination.'

Verwoerd introduced the Native Laws Amendment Act in 1952. This extended greater controls on African movement to all towns and cities; made it compulsory for women to carry passes; and gave the authorities power to remove 'idle or undesirable' natives. All Africans had to carry a reference book, 96 pages long, containing details of their lives. Africans were stripped of their right to appeal against removal orders, which could be enforced to maintain 'peace and order', and the police were given the right to raid their homes without warrants. The Prevention of Illegal Squatting Act of 1951 lived up to its name.

* * *

The second plank of Verwoerd's policy was the establishment of the homelands and the creation of a tier of tribal authorities with limited powers. This, the 'acceptable' face of apartheid, which at least had the virtue of consistency, ran into two immense obstacles. It was directly counter to the natural evolution of a modern society – from country to town – and there was far too little land made available to the blacks.

As South Africa's industrial society grew ever more complex, the unscrambling of its peoples and the return of the majority to tribal homelands they had abandoned was a step back in time, a turning back of the clock to an idealized voortrekker past. To make it work, either the terrible separation of black urban workers from their families in the homelands would have to continue or the whites would increasingly have to take over unskilled jobs – which they were unwilling to do. The whites could not continue to live off cheap black labour and yet be separated from the blacks.

The Tomlinson Commission, set up by the government, also estimated that there was barely enough tribal land to meet the basic requirements of the black population of South Africa. By the end of the century there would only be enough to meet the requirements of two-thirds of the population. Verwoerd angrily rejected the report. However, as the 1950s progressed, it became apparent that a colossal enforced movement of people was necessary to make the homelands policy work. The more criticism South Africa attracted from abroad, the more it sought to justify its actions on the basis of the homelands policy for self-government and full political rights there for blacks, and the more social engineering was necessary to put history into reverse – to return Africans to the countryside they had come from.

The chairman of the Bantu Affairs Committee in 1968, for example, argued with sweet reasonableness that the Bantu were not 'one single people' but

> divided by language, culture and traditions into several peoples or nations ... Fortunately for each of these people or nations, history left to them within the borders of the present Republic large tracts

of land which serve as their homelands. The government's policy is, therefore, not a racial policy based on the colour of the skin of the inhabitants of the Republic, but a policy based on the reality and the fact that within the borders of the Republic there are found the White nation and several Bantu nations. The government's policy, therefore, is not a policy of discrimination on the ground of race or colour, but a policy of differentiation on the ground of nationhood of different nations, granting to each self-determination within the borders of their homelands – hence this policy of separate development.

6
The Mathematician

This colossal public relations exercise turned ideological trap involved the relocation of a staggering 3.5 million people altogether – the kind of forcible migration only achieved in places like Stalinist Russia and Nazi-occupied Europe, or after major wars. In the 1960s alone, some 1.8 million Africans were removed from the white areas, and some 600,000 Indians, coloured and Chinese relocated (only around 40,000 whites lived in 'black' areas). Huge numbers were settled in dormitories just outside the homelands, so that they should be easily available to come and work in white areas. Forcible removals could not be appealed against, and were often carried out by the army as well as the police.

Chilling and heart-breaking scenes were repeated up and down the country. When Sophiatown, the primarily black but bohemian area of Johannesburg, was segregated, one woman described how five white men arrived. 'Before we had even opened the front door, I just heard the hammer on the pillar of the verandah ... a big sound that made me wonder if I was dying. That sound went right into my heart and I shall never forget it ... We had to take everything and throw it outside, just as it is, a chair just as it is – that's how [they] removed [us] ... I felt such pity for my husband ... because he had built that house with his ... bare hands. That house was our one and only little kingdom. We had freedom there in Sophiatown and that day I felt we were losing our rights ... my friends in the yard and that old spirit of the people I lived with.'

Afterwards, according to a local journalist, Sophiatown looked 'like a bombed city ... the few citizens who remain are hounded out of their houses for not possessing permits ... hundreds sleep on verandahs, live with friends and live in the ruins ... and the rains are coming.' District Six, Cape Town's inner-city black neighbourhood, suffered the same fate. So did the squatter camps. As the *Sunday Tribune* wrote in 1977, they became 'an eye-smarting hell of teargas and snarling dogs, of laughing officials and policemen, of homeless families crouched pitifully with their meagre possessions beside the road.'

At Crossroads a year later, according to the *Rand Daily Mail*, 'squatters were dragged by their clothing and beaten with batons and sticks during the second raid in less than six hours. Passes were grabbed by the police and other officials and thrown to the ground or temporarily confiscated. Ten policemen were injured when they were stoned in an earlier raid ... a squatter had been shot dead and soon a baby was to die on his mother's back as they were trampled by panic-stricken squatters attempting to escape yet another teargas attack.'

Such scenes were repeated all over the country. The Minister of Cooperation and Development, Piet Koornhof, justified this human anguish in coldly reasonable terms:

> In resettling a community every endeavour is made to ensure that work opportunities in the resettlement area are comparable with those in the area from which resettlement is undertaken ... Resettlement is made as attractive as possible in order to obtain the co-operation of the people concerned, and to achieve this, the Department ... undertakes the development of residential areas prior to resettlement. This entails the supply of treated water by pipelines to central points throughout the area where water is obtainable from taps; the provision of temporary prefabricated houses for each family and in addition tents are available if required to enable people to complete their own dwellings in their own time; the provision of sanitary facilities, schools, a clinic and the provision of roads in the area.

A group of Stellenbosch theology students later wrote, 'God forgive us, because we know not what we have done', in the Afrikaner newspaper *Die Burger*.

By 1981 four homelands – Transkei, Bophuthatswana, Venda and Ciskei – had been given their independence, and six others awarded self-government. They enjoyed a real measure of autonomy. But the homelands were geographical nonsenses and – with the exception of Transkei – a patchwork of territories dotted all over white South Africa, encompassing just a fraction of its land area.

The coloureds were treated marginally better. As a Broederbond document spelt out, 'The coloured preference points will eventually develop into coloured conurbations where the glories of first-class citizenship unfold for them ... work opportunities will develop for them in their own municipalities, transport undertakings, industries, large and small businesses, construction and property firms and in other directions characteristic of large conurbations. While a number of coloured cities are being established according to a set plan, all existing coloured areas can be retained. The conurbations need provide only for the 2.7 million additional coloured people to be accommodated by the turn of the century...'

The Indians were not so lucky, as the racial engineers went about their grotesque work. Another Broederbond paper declared, 'the Indians are presently accepted as an indigenous national group, as citizens of South Africa who must make a living in the white area. At the same time, the policy is clear that this must happen in a separate area. In the period exceeding the 100 years they have been in the country, the Indians have become less acceptable, rather than more, to other national groups in respect of possible assimilation. For everybody except the Indians, repatriation or resettlement in another country remains the most acceptable solution. If that is not possible, then an alternative plan is for a separate geographic home where the present process of physical and political separation can be completed.'

* * *

The other side of the coin of this human suffering on a grand scale and the establishment of the homelands was the stripping of blacks and coloureds of what few political rights they enjoyed in the white areas. In 1950 the Suppression of Communism Act banned the party, and the sole Communist member of the House of Assembly was forced out two years later. The Criminal Law Amendment Act of 1953 made it an offence to protest against any law, while the Riotous Assemblies Act made it an offence to picket during strikes.

In April 1952, the main opposition movements, the ANC and the South African Indian Congress, held a rally of 50,000 people outside Johannesburg to protest these measures; in June an even larger event was staged. The government responded with arrests and seizures of records, detaining a total of 8,400 people by December. Effectively, South Africa was now crossing the chasm that divides an oligarchic, authoritarian-based state still retaining the panoply of law, from that of a totalitarian police state, in which all citizens lack elemental political freedoms and the black majority any rights at all. Rioting broke out in October in Port Elizabeth, Johannesburg, Kimberley and, with particular savagery, in East London. The Criminal Law Amendment Act and the Public Safety Act effectively outlawed protest. James Moroka, the ANC leader, and other prominent blacks were arrested. Moroka was replaced as ANC leader by Albert Luthuli. Black peaceful resistance went underground until 1955, when the ANC held its 'Congress of the People' in an open field near Soweto to draft the Freedom Charter, the ANC's political testament for the next 35 years. The whole assembly was surrounded and the names of participants taken. In 1956, 56 leading black activists were arrested and the Treason Trial opened the following year, becoming a carnival for the accused until the eventual acquittal of the last 30 in 1961. Boycotts of segregated busing became frequent, and finally ended in violence.

The Nationalists' last targets were the 48,000 coloured voters still on the Cape electoral roll; the blacks had been removed in 1936. Nationalist minister Ben Schoeman said bluntly, 'we will take the Hottentots off the white-man's voters' roll'. In 1951 the Separate Representation of Voters Bill, giving the coloureds a separate voters' roll and the right to elect four white MPs, one senator and two members of the provincial council, was passed by simple majority in parliament – even though constitutional changes were supposed to be approved by two-thirds majority.

The appellate division of the supreme court declared the act unconstitutional. Malan promptly submitted a bill making parliament the highest court in the land. This in turn was declared unconstitutional. Malan now sought a two-thirds majority from the electorate in the 1953 election. He won comfortably – 94 seats to 61 – but did not secure the necessary two-thirds majority. A further attempt to amend the law failed in 1954.

Malan, the dour, tough-minded old Broederbond bigot, was now 80. It was time to step down after six years as prime minister, only this last piece of business in snuffing out South Africa's elemental liberties left incomplete. He favoured Eben Donges as his successor, but the job went instead to an old rival, J. G. Strijdom, who was himself elderly and ill. Strijdom had two further Broederbond goals: to scrap the coloured roll once and for all and to have South Africa throw over the final traces of British imperial domination by becoming a republic. Thus the Afrikaners' remaining old enemies – the coloureds and the British – were to be punched simultaneously in the eyes.

Within a year Strijdom had packed the appellate bench with 6 placemen, enlarging it from 5 members to 11. He then arbitrarily doubled the number of senators from 48 to 89, ensuring that almost all were National Party members chosen by a simple majority of parliamentary members in each province. This enlarged the vote from 29 Nationalists and 19 opposition members in the senate to 77 Nationalists and 12 opposition members. In 1956 the two houses sat together, and this time the government had engineered the necessary two-thirds majority to pass a constitutional measure. The new court went along with this.

The last vestige of representation for non-whites was stripped away through such blatantly undemocratic measures. South Africa was now a full-fledged racial autocracy, steam-rollered through by means that were undemocratic, even in respect of the white constitution, by the controlling wing of Afrikanerdom.

Strijdom had less success achieving his dream of a republic. This task was to be left to his successor, Hendrik Verwoerd, who succeeded after the former's death in 1958. As a Broederbond party official explained,

> During the Prime Ministership of Advocate J. G. Strijdom, we co-operated with the National Party to develop South Africa as quickly as possible towards a Republic. At a special annual meeting, where Advocate Strijdom took part, the basis and form of the coming Republic was thoroughly thrashed out. It was, however, Dr H. F. Verwoerd, who was for a long time a member of our executive council, who called in the active co-operation of our organization when he, as Prime Minister, decided to call a referendum for or against our becoming a Republic. We not only used our funds to elicit public support for the Republic, but also used the power of our own members, and of outside supporters, to this end.

In 1960 Verwoerd took the immense gamble of holding a referendum of white voters in the republic with no guarantee of success. In the event it was a fairly close run: the republicans won by 851,458 to 775,878 for the crown. South Africa promptly withdrew from the Commonwealth, in accordance with Broederbond policy that 'departure from the Commonwealth as soon as possible remains a cardinal aspect of our republican aim'.

Dr Piet Meyer, the Broederbond chairman, was later to comment that the organization and the National Party after 1948 had 'placed South Africa clearly, firmly and inexorably on the road to an independent republic – they and Afrikanerdom had had enough of the road of "honour" which always ended with participation in British wars. The republican road was not a road of abstract constitutional freedom, but of embracing spiritual freedom in which the Afrikaner could always be himself ...' The descendants of the trekboers, the voortrekkers and the Boers had set their country squarely and proudly against the rest of the world. They had at last created their isolated, racist nirvana based on Afrikaner supremacy and the segregation of even the white community in South Africa.

* * *

1960 was also to be a watershed of another sort in South Africa. Two years before, a group of extremists had split from the weakened ANC, in disgust with its multiracial approach, urging 'Africa for Africans' – an exclusive black struggle. Its leader was Robert Sobukwe, a charismatic 35-year-old lecturer at the University of Witwatersrand; the new movement called itself the Pan-Africanist Congress. Sobukwe decided to stage an anti-pass-law campaign by leading a crowd of blacks who had left their passes at home and defying the police to arrest them. Two major demonstrations in Evaton and Boipatong were disrupted by police intimidation and low-flying jets.

In Sharpeville, however, around 4,000 jeered and waved at the jets. The crowd was peaceful and good-humoured. At 1.15, after a scuffle at the front of the crowd, inexperienced policemen, without orders or warning shots, suddenly opened fire. One witness described the scene:

> We heard the chatter of a machine gun, then another, then another. There were hundreds of women, some of them laughing. They must have thought the police were firing blanks. One woman was hit about ten yards from our car. Her companion, a young man, went back when she fell. He thought she had stumbled. Then he turned her over and saw that her chest had been shot away. He looked at the blood on his hand and said: 'My God, she's gone!'
>
> Hundreds of kids were running too. One little boy had on an old blanket coat, which he held up behind his head thinking, perhaps, that it might save him from the bullets. Some of the children, hardly as tall as the grass, were leaping like rabbits. Some were shot, too. Still the shooting went on. One of the policemen was standing on top of a Saracen, and it looked as though he was firing his sten gun into the crowd. He was swinging it around in a wide arc from

his hip as though he were panning a movie camera. Two other officers were with him and it looked as if they were firing pistols ... When the shooting started it did not stop until there was no living thing in the huge compound in front of the police station.

When the shooting stopped 69 lay dead and 180 wounded. It was as though South Africa had reverted to the savagery of the bloodletting of a century before. The massacre attracted world-wide revulsion and condemnation, as well as triggering off a spate of marches and protests, most ruthlessly suppressed.

The ANC and PAC were banned just over a fortnight later. Oliver Tambo, one of the ANC's leaders, was chosen to flee into Bechuanaland to set up an ANC movement in exile. The organization decided to set up a military wing, Umkhonto we Sizwe, Spear of the Nation.

Sharpeville meanwhile had triggered financial panic. The stock exchange fell sharply, as did the rand. Currency reserves fell from $315 million to $142 million. The government introduced import and foreign exchange controls restricting the repatriation of profits and capital as an emergency measure. They had the desired effect: the economy recovered by the end of 1961.

By April 1960, the state of emergency had been lifted, although protests continued in Pondoland. In May 1961, Nelson Mandela of the ANC and others called for a three-day general strike. After a huge police crackdown and the arrest of some 10,000 people, the strike fizzled out. Two fateful portents for South Africa's future followed. Mandela received ANC approval to go over to armed violence as the only means of fighting the regime effectively; and for the first time international action began to be taken against South Africa.

The British and Canadian governments, as well as Australia, supported a resolution at the United Nations calling for unspecified action against apartheid. The ANC president, Albert Luthuli, was awarded the Nobel Peace Prize. The two weapons that brought apartheid to its knees 30 years later had made their first appearance.

The armed struggle, to begin with, was not impressive. In December 1961 a series of bombings, supposedly concentrated on economic and political targets without endangering lives, were staged. Altogether around 200 were carried out between 1962 and 1963. Meanwhile the PAC launched a series of much more vicious, ill-coordinated attacks, including an attempt at an armed uprising by 250 men in November 1962, and the murder of 5 whites in 1963. Hundreds of PAC members were arrested over the next few months; with Sobukwe already in jail,

Potlako Leballo, its second-in-command, soon joined him. The organization was effectively crippled.

Mandela, on his return from a 6-month training course in Algeria, was arrested on 5 August, 1962. The black decision to move over to armed struggle, at Mandela's urging, was a godsend to the whites. While the blacks' attacks were largely ineffective, the state apparatus now had ample justification for an unprecedented crackdown. Was Mandela thus responsible for the greatest error in the black liberation struggle for South Africa? Certainly a strong case can be made for this view. For the armed struggle was to prove a sputtering failure over the next 30 years. The regime was to be brought down by courageous, spontaneous mass flare-ups like the Soweto riots, internal mass mobilization and strike action, the growing isolation of the country from its neighbours, the impact of international sanctions, and above all the evolution of South African society itself. The armed struggle was a poor relation in this context, but it did provide the government with the pretext it needed for the institutionalized savagery of the next quarter century. Non-violence and passive resistance might have been more effective, in the view of many.

Two men had been placed in charge of security in South Africa, and were responsible for the fearsome machinery of repression. John Vorster, the minister of justice, introduced the Sabotage Act of June 1962, which allowed him to place anyone the government defined as an 'agitator' under house arrest, made it possible to ban and fine newspapers, and defined a series of activities such as trespass and the illegal possession of weapons as dangers to public order, carrying stiff sentences. The General Law Amendment Act allowed police to hold suspects without warrants or access to a lawyer for 90 days.

Vorster's ally was Hendrik van den Bergh, the new head of the state security police, granted huge powers to pursue the opposition. He was the creator of the crassly acronymed Bureau of State Security (BOSS), which became a byword for terror. In July, 1963, shatteringly, virtually the whole leadership of Umkhonto was arrested at its headquarters farm in Lilliesleaf, Rivonia, along with piles of documents detailing their plans for insurrection and civil war. Govan Mbeki, Walter Sisulu, Raymond Mhlaba and Ahmed Kathrada were among them.

They, along with Mandela, were put on trial in October. In June 1964, Mandela and 8 of the others were sentenced to life imprisonment and flown to Robben Island to begin their sentences. A bomb planted at Johannesburg station the following month, which killed one person and injured more than 20, appeared to be the last indiscriminate fling of a pathetic and extinguished resistance movement.

7
Afrikaner Darkness

The next 14 years were, as it were, the crowning glory of the Afrikaner Republic, marred only by the murder of Verwoerd, the architect of apartheid, by an apparently deranged knifeman in parliament in 1966. Vorster, much less ideological than his predecessor and with a lower public profile abroad, but the hub of the huge repressive apparatus, took control. South Africa was now both a totalitarian country and a police state. The great majority of the population was subject to massive controls, social engineering and arbitrary arrest. The black opposition had been incarcerated or cowed; the press was muzzled by threats. Only the continuing debates between rival white communities gave the country the appearance of pluralism, but the electoral roll was effectively rigged in favour of the National Party.

It was also the first, and probably only, avowedly racial autocracy (as opposed to colonial regime) in world history. During the 1960s and early 1970s there seemed little reason to believe it could not survive for decades. The economy was booming as never before. Growth throughout the 1960s averaged 6 per cent a year, with foreign investment rising from $3 billion in 1963 to $7 billion in 1972. Nearly half of South Africa's imports were in the shape of capital goods for the new industries.

The country's old dependence on Britain, which accounted for nearly 29 per cent of imports and nearly a third of exports in 1962, fell to 21 per cent and 27 per cent respectively over the next decade. In 1974 West Germany became the biggest exporter to South Africa, while West German investment rose from just 70 million rand in 1965 to R1.5 million in 1972, second only to Britain and before that of the United States.

The French, meanwhile, filled the gap opened up by Britain's decision in 1964 to end arms sales to South Africa. South African defence spending jumped from $60 million in 1960 to $475 million in 1964, some $700 million in 1973 and fully $1 billion in 1975. The French supplied South Africa with 120 helicopters, 60 Mirage fighter bombers and three submarines, as well as a licence to manufacture Mirages, and a nuclear capacity both for energy and weapons.

South Africa was booming, its trade was diversifying. The new prosperity was ushering in the Broederbond's Afrikaner dream: a middle-class society dominated by them. There seemed little reason not to believe in a 1,000-year Volkstaat. Repression had apparently worked well. The Broederbond's 12,000 members, divided into 500 cells, now packed town and city councils, school boards, agricultural unions, radio and television, industry and commerce, banks and building societies, the departments of education, planning, roads and public works, hospital services, universities, state corporations, the civil service and, of course, politics, where they controlled the office of prime minister, most of the cabinet, much of the National Party caucus, the senior defence establishment (the defence minister, P. W. Botha, and Van den Bergh were members), the giant Afrikaner combine Sanlam, and the five main Afrikaner universities (Vorster, when he resigned as prime minister, was to become chancellor of Stellenbosch University).

In three areas, in particular, the Broederbond made gigantic strides against its mortal English-speaking enemies: in penetrating the business community, hitherto dominated by English speakers; in the increasing use of Afrikaans in education; and in countering English immigration into South Africa.

Piet Meyer, chairman of the Broederbond in 1966, argued that the English-speaking community must be absorbed into Afrikanerdom, or the reverse would happen; in his paranoid rendition, the two could not co-exist.

The aim can be nothing but the complete nationalizing and eventual cultural Afrikanerizing of our English-speaking co-citizens – if it can still be done. We will not be able to stop the process of complete cultural integration of Afrikaans- and English-speaking if we have only limited control of this process. Therefore we can only envisage either the deliberate Afrikanerizing of the English-speakers, or the silent acceptance of the unintentional but certain Anglicizing of the Afrikaner. The drive to nationalize the English-speakers politically will not be of permanent value, ensuring the continued existence of the Afrikaner, unless it is coupled with the Afrikanerizing of the economy.

The Afrikanerizing of the English-speakers is an educational task: it must start in the schools. It entails the English-speaker accepting the Afrikaner outlook and philosophy as his own, integrating his ideals and life-style with that of the Afrikaner, embracing the Afrikaner's history as his own, and regarding Afrikaans as his national language next to English as the international language of the two groups, while both remain official languages. We will then talk of Afrikaans-speaking and English-speaking Afrikaners.

This was a neat reversion to Milner's failed policy at the beginning of the twentieth century. Another Broederbond chairman put this in the context of economic power:

If there is one thing vital to keeping the Broederbond alive in the ranks of the Afrikaner nation, now and in the future, it is the conviction that fulfilment cannot be attained by the Afrikaner without maximum economic control. Especially now that we put so much emphasis on unavoidable co-operation between the Afrikaans- and English-speaking, we must ensure – even if it must be done discreetly – that the Afrikaner is the senior partner. Without that there will be something missing from our status and independence. Therefore the Broederbond should give urgent attention to it now.

The most articulate spokesman of the right, Andries Treurnicht, in a secret Broederbond document, set this out explicitly: 'Are the English-speakers really a nation in South Africa equal in nature and status to the Afrikaner nation? The answer cannot be "Yes" so the question arises of whether we can speak of "two language groups" or "the two national groups" as if an Afrikaner nation and an English-speaking nation were equal in status to the Afrikaner nation. There are not two white nations in South Africa. There is only one. That nation is the Afrikaner nation ... In view of this, it is time to invite the English-speakers to become absorbed into the [Afrikaner] nation. Groups like Jews and Greeks are of course excluded here: "English-speakers" means those of British descent.'

Rarely is the Afrikaner obsession with nationhood, race and descent better illustrated. The Afrikaners were as, if not more, obsessed with the British threat as the black threat. The only terms on which

English-descended South Africans could be dealt with involved their absorption into the Afrikaner nation. The Afrikaners were not just white supremacists, but Afrikaner supremacists. Even nearly half the whites had inferior status, in their eyes, to the Boer tribe.

In economic terms, Sanlam had become the second largest complex in the country, second only to Anglo-American, with assets worth two-thirds of the value of all foreign investment in the country. The Volkskas banking group and the tobacco and liquor conglomerate giant, the Rembrandt group, were also among the biggest major companies in South Africa.

On immigration, the Afrikaners exerted a strict control to ensure their narrow majority was maintained – 1.8 million Afrikaners to 1.15 million English speakers (and the Afrikaner birthrate was higher). 'We are not prepared to sacrifice our traditional way of life, language and culture but are prepared to accept large-scale immigration as one of the most important aids in our struggle. Yet recruitment overseas has raised doubts in the minds of the folk because the majority of immigrants are English-speaking ... and many belong to the Roman Catholic Church. Just as in the past, the Afrikaner feels threatened by foreign elements,' argued a Broederbond document in 1964.

* * *

Yet it was education that proved the most controversial battleground and provided the spark for trouble ahead – indeed, that ignited black consciousness unquenchably. Dr Andries Treurnicht, the eloquent, smooth, and extremely tough-minded deputy education minister, spelt out the Afrikaners' bitterness in a speech in 1968:

> For too long ... the Afrikaner had to suffer the insult of an alien cultural stamp being forced on to the education of his children in the persistent Anglicisation process. It became the logical and compelling demand of his own nationalism that his education should be in his own language and should form young lives for the Afrikaner community. And because the nation's origins and growth were so closely connected with the work, doctrines and activities of the church, it was obvious that the national life should be Christian in its education.

In 1948, the National Party congress had embraced an education policy that preached that 'creation took place in six calendar days and fossils must be explained presumably as examples of degeneration since the flood ... God had given to each people a country and a task. It was the Afrikaner's task to rule South Africa, and nobody had the right to question what was divinely ordained. Teachers who refused to subscribe to these doctrines would simply not be appointed.' As Wilkins and Strydom were later to comment:

> The Afrikaner Cultural Organization (FAK) helped to promote the ideology in an educational frenzy: it stressed all things Afrikaner: language, music, song, literature, dress, customs, experiences. For example, the concentration camps established by the English in the Boer War are constantly recalled to bolster nationalistic feelings. The FAK has even purchased one of these camps to serve as physical evidence of Afrikaner grievances.
>
> The Voortrekkers, who represented die-hard resistance to British suzerainty, are brandished before die volk like a cloth before a bull. Van Riebeeck has been all but deified. His statue at Cape Town greets the visitor to South Africa and reminds the Briton that the Dutch were there first.

It was the Boer War all over again, with the Boers winning this time. Fatally, the Afrikaners now tried not just to Afrikanerize the English-speaking whites, but to impose Afrikaans as a second white language on the blacks, who of course, already spoke their own languages in addition to English. A Broederbond memo complained bitterly that 'Afrikaans as spoken word is neglected in Bantu education. Broeders in responsible circles (Cabinet) have confirmed that much has already been done to give Afrikaans its rightful pace, but that there were many problems. It is recommended that the Executive refer this issue to Broeders in the department with "the request that serious attention should be paid continuously to the use of Afrikaans in Bantu education".'

In 1974 a circular was sent out by the all-powerful department of Bantu education saying that arithmetic, mathematics and social sciences must be taught in Afrikaans while science, woodwork and arts and crafts should be taught in English. Fourteen years after Sharpeville and the crushing of black resistance, this ignited a whole new wave of young black protest that ultimately toppled the regime. The headmaster of Soweto's biggest school, Wilkie Xambule, as the Afrikanerization drive intensified, commented simply that, 'The main reason ... that young blacks these days tend to be radical is that they see Afrikaans as part of the people in authority.' Another teacher commented, 'They come home after school saying how much they hate Afrikaans, but it is only because they are forced to study it'.

* * *

Yet the first ominous rumble of thunder in the skies of the peaceful and prosperous white totalitarian state of South Africa came from outside the country's borders. On 25 April 1974, there was curious upheaval in a small, run-down European country thousands of miles away. Marcelo Caetano, Portugal's dictator, was deposed in a military coup by a group of young captains and majors disillusioned by the cost in lives and money of maintaining the country's sprawling overseas dominions, the last European empire. Portugal's new rulers immediately set independence dates for Mozambique, to South Africa's east, in June 1975 and Angola, to the west, in November 1975.

Within months, the South African representative at the UN, Pik Botha, had delegates rubbing their eyes in disbelief when he said, 'we do have discriminatory laws. But it is not because the whites in South Africa have any herrenvolk [superior race] complex. We are not better than the black people, we are not cleverer than they are ... we shall do everything in our power to move away from discrimination based on race or colour.'

Pik Botha himself in fact reflected a minority current of opinion within the Afrikaner community that the white volkstaat was not in the long run sustainable; but for him to say so publicly was astonishing. The awful truth for the Afrikaners was that they had been living in a fool's paradise of protective security. They were losing their cordon of surrounding states. Black rule was now extending to the country's very borders.

Already, with a wave of strikes after 1972, the pullout by the British Royal Navy from the Simonstown base, the effects of the oil shock in 1974, and a falling gold price and decline in foreign investment, the good times were beginning to falter. With the fall of Mozambique, the prospect of ANC bases along the border was so appalling that the South Africans stepped forward to declare their friendship towards the country's Marxist president, Samora Machel, and a willingness to fund the Cabora Bassa hydroelectric power scheme to pay for the use of the port at Laurenco Marques (Maputo). Machel promised in return not to help the ANC. 'We do not pretend to be saviours or reformers of South Africa. That belongs to the people of South Africa.'

Matters were not so simple in Angola, where the Marxist Popular Movement for the Liberation of Angola (MPLA) had seized power in Luanda while rival movements – the National Front for the Liberation of Angola (FNLA) and the United Front for the Total Liberation of Angola (Unita), led by the charismatic Jonas Savimbi in the south, raised the standard of rebellion, supported by a variety of anti-Marxist forces including the French, Zambia's President Kenneth Kaunda, Tanzanian President Julius Nyerere, the Chinese, and the Americans. In 1975 a ferocious battle between the liberation movements in the north left 20,000 dead. With Russian backing, a first contingent of 20,000 Cuban troops was brought in to help the MPLA.

South Africa had at first been unwilling to get involved: Angola, after all, did not have a common border and did not directly threaten South Africa. But both the French and the Americans pressed them to counter the Soviet–Cuban influence, providing arms to South Africa as an inducement. In October the Republic, as much to curry favour among such influential friends as from any other motive, at last agreed to a full-scale attack. South African forces blazed their way in less than three weeks to within 12 kilometres of the capital. Then they came up against Cubans equipped with mortars, armoured cars, tanks and Mig-21 fighter aircraft.

The South Africans would probably have won a pitched battle; but the price would have been high, and the stakes hardly seemed worth it in a war the country had been lukewarm to enter. If the South Africans had captured Luanda, what would they then have done – defended the capital indefinitely? The Democrat-controlled United States senate, meanwhile, snubbed President Ford and his Secretary of State, Henry Kissinger, by cutting off military aid to anti-MPLA forces.

South Africa was now on its own. In January 1976 it withdrew back into Namibia. It had earned international condemnation for 'aggression', while the Americans had been quick to disavow it and the French had cut off arms supplies. Increasingly, South Africa was forced to fall back on a curious group of international friends for arms supplies and other strategic goods – Israel, Kenya, Iran, Paraguay, Uruguay, and China. More ominous still, with Rhodesia's borders now porous to guerrillas on two sides, from Angola and Mozambique, that country's time under white rule was running out. As civil war broke out there, South Africa was faced by the possibility of another hostile black state on its borders.

* * *

These developments were cause for concern, but not alarm, to Vorster and the South African government. The first real indication of the internal struggle to come took place in June 1976. The government had plenty of warning, as the obscurantist education minister, M. C. Botha, and his hardline deputy, Treurnicht, relentlessly pushed ahead with forcing Afrikaans upon the seething black schools.

A series of schools boycotted the move from February of that year onwards; they were shut down. Incidents of sporadic violence erupted. By 11 June a Soweto residents' committee was declaring, 'we reject Afrikaans as a medium of instruction because it is the language of the oppressor'. The principal of Soweto's main school, Orlando, declared, 'Schoolchildren are doing exactly what the parents and everybody feels about Afrikaans – only they have the courage to stand up against it.'

On 14 June a local councillor perceptively warned that, with tensions escalating, another Sharpeville was on the cards. The children 'won't take anything we say because they think we have neglected them. We have failed to help them in their struggle for change in schools. They are now angry and prepared to fight and we are afraid the situation may become chaotic at any time.'

In fact, these young students, growing up in a South Africa where black resistance had been extinct for almost two decades, had become receptive to the radical Black Consciousness views of Steve Biko, head of the South African Students' Organization. Biko argued that to look to white liberals for reform was a delusion. The blacks had to fight alone for their own rights.

> The integration they talk about … is artificial … a one-way course, with the whites doing all the talking and the blacks the listening … One sees a perfect example of what oppression has done to the blacks. They have been made to feel inferior for so long that for them it is comforting to drink tea, wine or beer with whites who seem to treat them as equals. This serves to boost up their own ego to the extent of making them feel slightly superior to those blacks who do not get similar treatment from whites. These are the sort of blacks who are a danger to the community.

On 16 June 1976, the starting point for the events that were to result in a handover to black rule 18 years later and the real turning point in South Africa's post-1948 history, teenage blacks organized a march for 7 a.m. in Soweto, to be followed by a mass rally in Orlando Stadium.

The march began peacefully enough, with thousands joining it, although scuffles soon broke out with police.

At just past 9.00 around 50 police arrived, and stone-throwing and sporadic shooting broke out during which a 13-year-old boy, Hector Peterson, was shot and carried out mortally wounded by a student; a photograph of this appalled the world. The police retreated, and the crowd marched on the offices of the West Rand Administration building, lynching two employees. Over the following days of unrest, police reinforcements poured in. Hundreds of teenagers were shot and more than 140 vehicles and 139 buildings destroyed.

Undeterred, Treurnicht reaffirmed that, 'In the white areas of South Africa [Soweto was in a 'white area'], where the government erects the buildings, grants subsidies and pays the teachers, it is our right to decide on language policy. The same applies to schools in areas where there is no compulsory education. Why are pupils sent to schools if language policy does not suit them?'

On 18 June Vorster got tough. 'The government will not be intimidated. Orders have been given to maintain order at all costs.' The Riotous Assemblies Act was introduced, banning all outdoor political meetings save for sports. The government approach was that repression had worked after Sharpeville, and would do so again.

Yet this was no one-off event like Sharpeville. Violence flared up all over the country. Some 80 separate outbreaks took place over the following few weeks. In Soweto, for a year and a half, running battles with the police were a regular occurrence, as were school boycotts and mass arrests. In Cape Town in August alone 30 people died in township protests; around the university and training schools of the Western Cape there were violent clashes that resulted in 30 more deaths. The generation who were teenagers at the time of Soweto were to provide the up-and-coming political class of the 1990s. Many slipped out of the country to fight for the ANC and the PAC.

* * *

In August 1977 the protesters acquired their most prominent martyr to date: Steve Biko had been detained, but not charged, for 26 days. He was held naked, 'to prevent him hanging himself with his clothes', in leg irons, and interrogated by five gaolers. He was hit by a severe blow or blows – according to police, inflicted when he banged his head against a wall – and seriously injured, placed naked in the back of a landrover for the 1,000-mile journey from Port Elizabeth to

Pretoria, where he died, according to his counsel, 'a miserable and lonely death on a mat on a stone floor of a prison cell'. Almost certainly, he was deliberately murdered by the authorities in revenge for Soweto.

The riots reverberated around the world: gold shares fell 75 cents and diamond shares 15 cents; business confidence was badly shaken. Harry Oppenheimer of Anglo-American joined forces with Afrikaner Anton Rupert to set up the Urban Foundation, a deliberate attempt to encourage the growth of a black middle class as an ally against youthful black radicalism. Training, adult education and housing and urban policies were its priorities. It provided funds for these and recommended scrapping discrimination in land ownership and the occupation of squatters' camps – whose population by 1990 was 5.7 million, an ineradicable social problem that flouted tidy apartheid planning and showed the doctrine's unworkability.

Black resistance, although subdued by 1978, did not fizzle out as in 1962. It sputtered on in the growing number of ill-planned sabotage attacks staged by the ANC and PAC. In 1980 a refinery in Sasolburg in the Orange Free State was spectacularly set alight for several days, and the Koeburg nuclear power station was attacked as well. Tokyo Sexwale, one of the ANC supporters seized for high treason in 1978, memorably summed up the attitude of his generation:

It was during my primary school years that the bare facts concerning the realities of South African society and its discrepancies began to unfold before me. I remember a period in the early 1960s, when there was a great deal of political tension, and we often used to encounter armed police in Soweto ... I remember the humiliation to which my parents were subjected by whites in shops and in other places where we encountered them, and the poverty.

All these things had their influence on my young mind ... and by the time I went to Orlando West High School, I was already beginning to question the injustice of the society ... and to ask why nothing was being done to change it ... It has been suggested that our aim was the annihilation of the white people of this country; nothing could be further from the truth. The ANC is a national liberation movement committed to the liberation of all the people of South Africa, black and white, from racial fear, hatred and oppression.

On the shop floor, too, militancy was spreading. In 1972–3 a wave of strikes had ended in violence, with the killing of 12 strikers in Johannesburg. By 1976 employers were suffering from so many unofficial strikes that they suggested that South Africa's industrial relations laws be reformed to permit legitimate black unions. A court of inquiry in 1979 recommended labour legislation to pacify black workers.

The same year the Federation of South African Trade Unions, FOSATU, consisting of 12 organizations, boasted 95,000 members in nearly 40 factories. The more militant Council of Unions in South Africa, CUSA, had 30,000 members and in 1982 set up the National Union of Mineworkers, which by 1984 had 100,000 members and was the most efficient union in South Africa. The wheel had turned full circle. Blacks once derided as indolent were now the powerhouse of much of South African industry, and their industrial might was to be flexed to full effect. Their lifestyles of past centuries had been transformed, and the tough industrial workers thus fashioned were to be one of the major elements in the downfall of the white overlords.

8
Afrikaner Caudillo

Few could have foreseen, at the time of Soweto, that the hard man at the top of the South African state would be toppled just two years later. But Soweto and its reverberations had gravely weakened John Vorster in the eyes of his fellow Afrikaners: social peace had been an illusion, and his dinosaur-like response inadequate. Just as the imposition of Afrikaans upon the blacks had been a sign of the almost hermetic, omnipotent arrogance with which the Afrikaner Broederbond clique believed they could impose their will on a nation of 30 million people – and it blew up in their faces – so Vorster, after so many years at the top, had come to behave as though he was above the law.

In 1973, he had appointed a brash young man, Dr Eschel Rhoodie, as secretary for information, with a large slush fund to launch a propaganda campaign on behalf of South Africa, placing a Goebbels-like faith in the ability of propaganda to blunt the ballooning overseas repugnance for the regime. Rhoodie set up a newspaper, the *Citizen*, under a cover, bought a British trade press publication organization, tried purchasing the London *Investors' Chronicle* and France's *L'Express* and *Paris Match*, and also made a bid for the *Washington Star*.

After a series of disastrous flops, this extraordinary use of government money was exposed in 1978 by the auditor general, one of Rhoodie's predecessors, allegedly at the instigation of National Party rivals of Vorster's designated successor, information minister Connie Mulder, whose protégé Rhoodie was. Two prominent politicians who loathed Mulder were the reform-minded and energetic Cape leader, P. W. Botha, and the foreign minister, Pik Botha. As the scandal escalated over the following months, Vorster instructed Mulder to deny that government funds had been used to buy the *Citizen*; this was to damage him fatally. Under the pressure, Vorster, puffy and ill, eventually resigned in September.

Mulder, head of the usually decisive Transvaal party caucus, controlling 80 out of the 172 votes in the party, pushed for the top job, although he had been badly discredited. P. W. Botha ran against him with his Cape Town support, and Pik Botha also stood, dividing the Transvaal power base. The former came out ahead with 78 votes to Mulder's 72 and Pik Botha's 22. On the second round, the front runner scored an easy victory.

* * *

It was a fateful choice. For the first time since 1948 the moderate wing of the Afrikaners had regained control of the government – although of course, unlike Smuts, Botha was himself a member of the Broederbond. He took office as a pair of clean hands, in an atmosphere of hope that the stubbornness, insensitivity and brutality of men like Malan, Strijdom, Verwoerd and Vorster were things of the past.

Indeed, the Broederbond itself had evolved after nearly 30 years in power. Its members, from being resentful outsiders, were occupying positions of power and influence throughout the land. The dogma of dispossession had given way to the pragmatism of prosperity. Its new chairman, Dr Gerrit Viljoen, was a man cast in a very different mould from his predecessor. Highly intelligent, cautiously reformist, a man aware of realities, this evolution within the Afrikaner secret society had helped to propel Botha to victory.

They were faced by a simmering black revolt that showed no sign of going away, and new and imaginative policies were needed. Botha, the intelligent, firm and much more open-minded Cape leader, seemed the man to provide them. More encouragingly still, he had the great advantage that, although liberal in Afrikaner terms, he was personally a tenacious man with a notorious temper and a famous wagging finger. As defence minister for 12 years, he was extremely close to the security establishment and could be relied upon to maintain public order and pursue a tough line against the guerrillas. He was a strong man, a de Gaulle, who could make reforms.

Yet in the end it was this tension between the political pragmatist and the devotee of the military establishment that proved his undoing. For, more than any prime minister since Smuts, he was the defence establishment's favoured man in the top job, and he much preferred to rule through 'the securocrats' than through the fount of his authority, the parliamentary party. Of the five prime ministers since 1948, he was the least closely bound to the Broederbond, to the core of Afrikanerdom, to its Transvaal heartland, and to the parliamentary party, where his Cape wing was in a minority. Yet in a supreme irony the Broederbond in the end outflanked him in seeking reform from which his own stubbornness and clique of military cronies had succeeded in isolating him.

Botha was not a reformer by instinct: his father had served in the Boer war, and his mother had been interned in a concentration camp, where two of the boy's brothers had died. As a minister, Botha had supervised the ravaging of District Six in Cape Town. But he was a pragmatist and, unlike Vorster, believed South Africa could survive only through adapting to the changed climate of the 1970s. However, his goal was the survival of white South Africa; there is nothing to suggest he ever accepted that the country would have to submit to black majority rule. Even when he came to see this as inevitable, he would not be the man to do it. He was installed not to preside over a surrender, but to save white South Africa through more flexible, intelligent policies.

Botha took office determined to replace the growing *immobilisme* of Vorster by going on the offensive. His military-style tactics, in response to the 'total onslaught' of the ANC, was 'total strategy'. It had five prongs. A shift from absolute political exclusion of the black community towards gradual political reform and the easing of apartheid in response to the shift in white opinion and in order to defuse post-Soweto racial tensions; an attempt to encourage the development of the black middle class as a counter to growing young black activism (this was actually to make irrefutable the black contention that they were ready and mature enough for power); a policy of trying to sell South African reforms abroad; the destabilization of neighbouring states in an effort to force them not to let the ANC operate out of their territory; and a tough-minded approach towards internal security.

It was a soft fist in an iron glove; and to begin with it worked. Hardline Afrikaners argued that Botha's reforms represented the beginning of a collapse; that a policy of unrelenting obduracy would have kept the blacks down, as it had in 1960. But that is to ignore the transformation of South African society since then; in particular the growth of an educated black middle class, an organized black industrial working class, and the transformation of the poor white Afrikaners themselves into a ruling class with a great deal to lose economically if the country degenerated into civil war.

Botha merely reflected the changes in South African society. He cannot be denied the credit for shifting Afrikaner politics – ossified for 30 years into an appalling state of arrogance, intolerance, sectarianism, totalitarianism and repression – back into the real world. In this he was reflecting a sea change that had also come over the whole Afrikaner tribe and its council of elders, the Broederbond. For last among South Africa's tribes, these people had tried to insulate themselves from the twentieth century, shroud themselves in their heroic voortrekker myths, pastoral ideals, and concepts of Calvinist predestination, cleanliness, purity and racial exclusiveness (based on exploitation, not extermination).

Now they were being forced for the first time to confront the reality of social and economic change in the twentieth century. The eighteenth- and nineteenth-century mould of attitudes in which Afrikanerdom was frozen was having to adapt to a new and not so simple era. Botha represented the awakening of Afrikaners from the slumber of the century since they were first robbed of the voortrekker republics by the British; an awakening from depressingly self-centred, resentful bitterness, a sense of inferiority accompanied by overweening arrogance, triumphalism and revanchism, to a more self-confident sense of reality.

It was hardly surprising that the awakening was clumsy, a stumbling about in an unfamiliar world. After years of subjugation and opposition, of the sense that they were second-class citizens in their own land, the Afrikaners had enjoyed three decades of total domination – and it softened and civilized them, just as adversity had hardened and embittered them. The changes in the Afrikaner outlook were slow, barely perceptible, but tangible by the late 1970s.

In another extraordinary respect, too, apartheid, as wicked a piece of social engineering, human-moulding and repression as any in world history, had had an ironic spin-off. After years of relentless propaganda, its own proponents had come to believe at least a part of it: where whites up to the 1950s had been prepared to voice the view that blacks deserved their lot because they were inferior, the line since had become that they were equal but different. Doubtless most Afrikaners in their hearts believed the blacks were still their inferiors. But that was not the justification for the apartheid doctrine of separate development.

As it became clear that the blacks were bound to have an increasing say in South Africa not as a marginalized people but as the majority, and that it was quite simply physically impossible as well as economically undesirable to bundle them out of the way to their homelands – the whites were increasingly dependent on them – Afrikanerdom had to adapt itself to the new circumstances. A combination of Afrikaner business, the defence establishment and the Broederbond itself reached the same conclusion.

A second great change in the Afrikaner mentality had occurred with empowerment. Now that they were at last the top dogs, and at least as prosperous – or more so – than the English-speaking establishment, they had drifted from their roots as spokesmen for wandering trekkers and poor whites to men with a fixed and sizeable stake in the land which was at risk if they did not confront political facts.

But there were more practical considerations too. The success of the Broederbond in business had made it less dogmatic and idealistic, more realistic about the real needs of the country. South Africa had to maintain peace and trade with the outside world if it was to prosper; it was beginning not to be able to sustain Afrikaner dogma and theology without regard to these considerations. In another field in which South Africa excelled and was becoming increasingly ostracized and isolated, the Broederbond had heard the concerns of the many local communities for whom sport had an almost god-like status.

However defiantly South Africa's leaders shrugged off the sporting boycott, the Broederbond could see the deep damage of such isolation in an area in which South Africans had always prided themselves. Young South Africans denied the chance to shine in international sport, and to support their teams abroad, were suffering a real deprivation – and the Broederbond noticed it at the grass roots.

* * *

A deeply poignant and untold story perfectly encapsulating the struggle between hardliners and enlightened whites at exactly this time, the brink of transformation or disaster, concerned a major South African school known as Bishops. In 1983 it welcomed as headmaster a towering personality, John Peake, a man who combined a distinguished career as an historian at Eton with a huge reputation for sporting prowess, particularly as an oarsman. His passionate anti-apartheid views (he had founded his own 'Africa class' at Eton, a hotbed of debate) and his force of personality were less well known to his new employers.

Peake was appointed principal of the Diocesan College in Cape

Town (always known as 'Bishops' after its founder, Bishop Gray, the first Bishop of Cape Town) in 1983. The school was founded in 1849, but had never yet had a South African Headmaster, and from the start there was strong prejudice against Peake in some quarters, not only because he was an Englishman, but also because almost all his teaching experience had been at Eton, where he was a housemaster. He would in fact have stood little chance of being appointed had he not spent a year in Johannesburg in 1967–8 at St John's College, at that time a notably liberal school under the leadership of the remarkable Deane Yates, later to found both Maru a Pula in Botswana and the NEST Schools in South Africa.

The council (governing body) which appointed Peake also contained some very liberal elements – Richard Luyt (ex-Chancellor of the University of Cape Town), Francis Wilson (Professor of Economics at UCT) and Alex Boraine (Progressive Party MP and later a leading figure on Desmond Tutu's Truth and Reconciliation Committee) – and at his interview the chief topic of debate was how Bishops should face the challenge of the, even then, rapidly changing South Africa.

This was particularly apt, since in a school 930-strong (college, prep and pre-prep) there were only 52 boys who were not white and only 7 who were black. These figures were fairly normal for the country's Anglican schools, but compared poorly with the situation in the Catholic schools, which had been ignoring government restrictions on non-white entry for many years.

Bishops was unquestionably one of the foremost schools in southern Africa, but like all its counterparts in the Republic at the beginning of the 1980s it was living in a time warp. Its previous headmaster, Anthony Mallett, had not taught in England since 1957, having just moved to Peterhouse in Rhodesia and then to Bishops where he had spent 19 years. Though he maintained high academic and sporting standards and running a school with a very considerable reputation, he had as a result experienced none of the convulsions which so transformed British independent schools in the late 1960s and early 1970s, nor had he seen the vast advance in artistic and cultural standards and facilities in these schools in the previous decade. Bishops in 1983 had no permanent orchestra, the theatre doubled as the gymnasium, no woodwork or design and only the most basic facilities for art. The director of music also ran the tennis, while the art master doubled as head of the cadet corps.

Peake thus faced a major challenge on two fronts and, possibly a little precipitately, lost no time in trying to implement changes. An appeal was launched with the enthusiastic backing and support of the Council and this proved so successful that a spectacular building programme was completed over the next few years. A new theatre, art school, sports hall, day boy house, sixth form centre, mathematics and computer block, squash courts, climbing wall, woodwork centre and 6 staff houses were all constructed in this period; the school site was quite literally transformed. At the same time Peake sought out sponsors for scholarships for black boys; and largely through personal contacts, especially with a good friend, the Norwegian consul-general, succeeded in bringing to Bishops a number of Xhosa boys from the local townships, virtually all from very deprived backgrounds. By 1988 there were 150 non-white boys in the school of whom 41 were black.

Among the more liberal thinking parents and old boys these changes were welcomed, but they proved very unpopular both with the traditionalists, who were still predominantly concerned with image and sporting success – especially in rugby, which had been introduced into South Africa by Bishops – and with the right-wingers, who regarded the new multiracialism with grave suspicion. John Wiley, an old boy and once a United Party MP, who had crossed the floor of parliament to become a Nationalist and later a member of P. W. Botha's government, wrote to the chairman of council on Peake's appointment demanding that a time limit should be set within which he would have to learn Afrikaans. He was a dogged opponent, and although he died in 1987, his two sons continued the fight, and became leaders in the political movement to oust Peake at the end. At the same time another old boy wrote to the head of the development appeal: 'A school is not everything in a boy's education and should not in my opinion try to be so. Let us rather stick to the tried and tested formula with plenty of maths, rugger and penal gardening. Let's cut out the frills and the sculpture. If boys are not talented at games they can still play or at least support their teams.'

In the face of this obscurantism, progress became increasingly diffi-cult for Peake, but he was also faced with considerable opposition from within the school, particularly among housemasters and senior staff. Moves to introduce Eton institutions such as the tutorial system somewhat backfired, while an assault on long-established school tradi-tion and practice, such as fagging and the initiation of new boys in often outdated rituals, and corporal punishment, now abolished, was strongly resented.

By 1988, despite the fact that the school was fuller than it had ever been and was flourishing in almost every sphere, the level of opposition was formidable and a concerted campaign was launched to get rid of Peake. At the Old Boys AGM in that year a very large crowd was brought together to hear Peake's review of the year. This was totally ignored and a series of speakers then rose to denounce not just his policies but even his personal habits in the most virulent terms.

In the light of this the council felt that he had become too controversial a figure and asked for his resignation. The incident exploded for several days on the front pages of the English and Afrikaner press. A financial settlement was agreed and Peake finally left in July. Interestingly, in 1999, a wholly different council invited Peake and his wife back to Cape Town to attend part of the school's 150th anniversary celebrations. This went very well and it was made clear on both sides that the reconciliation was complete.

Botha, the most military-minded president since Smuts, was to preside over a South Africa under attack on at least five fronts: externally, through economic sanctions, sporting isolation, and raids from the exile-based ANC; and internally, from growing trade union militancy and increasingly vigorous street protest. His government was the most turbulent in South Africa's turbulent history, bringing the country to the edge of racial war.

It all began on a note of hope. Botha's reform offensive was, for those who had lived under his four predecessors, a huge step forward. In 1983 he announced his programme in the shape of a 12-point plan. 'Petty apartheid' was gradually to be dismantled: segregation in public places and the buses were scrapped, the Mixed Marriages Act and the law prohibiting sexual intercourse between blacks and whites was repealed in 1985, and the hated Pass Laws, dating back to the beginnings of South Africa's colonial history, were at last repealed in 1986.

Limited as these reforms seemed to the outside world, they represented a giant leap in Afrikaner thinking away from the idea of exclusive white domination. In the case of the Pass Laws, they were a straightforward admission that the races could not be kept apart in the cities; in fact they amounted to nothing less than the abandonment of apartheid theory after nearly 40 years. The blacks were losing one of their most hated stigmas – the need to carry a passport inside their own country.

Botha's next reform was even more revolutionary for the white community: the establishment of a new tricameral parliament in which coloureds and Indians were given their own separate chambers. The idea derived from a commission set up under a Stellenbosch academic, Erika Theron, to report on the plight of coloured people. The report had also recommended the repeal of the Mixed Marriages Act and the Immorality Act's notorious Section 16, the abolition of 'petty apartheid', and the establishment of representation for coloureds. For Sampie Terreblanche, one of the commission's members, visits to coloured townships had proven to be a revelation. From then on he regarded apartheid as requiring drastic reform, if not abolition. For anyone at the very intellectual heart of Afrikanerdom to begin to doubt the creed of apartheid was tantamount to treason. But the process had begun.

With the creation of the tricameral parliament, in which the coloureds and Indians would have much less power than the white chamber, it was proposed that a new electoral college of all three would choose the new head of state, who would combine the office of prime minister and state president.

These new powers for the coloureds and Indians only served to underline the gross absurdity and injustice of denying the over-whelmingly largest racial group in the country any democratic representation. Were the Indians, so long despised by Afrikaners, now considered 'superior' to the blacks? Worse, under the new set-up, Botha would have unprecedented formal powers; he would now no longer be wholly dependent upon the white caucus in parliament.

This meant that South Africa for the first time had presidential-style government, rather than parliamentary government (inevitably the two lesser houses would in practice have virtually no power to control him) – a change which had huge implications for the crisis about to unfold, and which eventually led to Botha's downfall. In fact, it seemed that Botha, now elevating himself above parliament in a country which for all its faults had always had a deep-rooted parliamentary tradition, and governing increasingly through a cabal with tight links with the police, armed forces and intelligence services – the 'securocrats' – was becoming more of a traditional Latin American-style 'caudillo' than a civilian leader.

The Botha reforms were a calculated gamble. For on the one hand they incensed traditionalist Afrikaners and, on the other, in continuing wholly to exclude the blacks from national power and upholding the homeland concept and the township policy, into which the government now poured large amounts of money, they further incensed its most dangerous opponents – the blacks, not the coloureds or Indians.

But Botha was banking on two things: that the reforms would win him the support of moderate whites; and that they would win the gratitude of the coloured and Indian communities, enlarging the white laager against the black majority. In addition, so out of touch was South Africa with most of the outside world, he believed they would satisfy the government's major overseas critics. In fact, the aim was to strengthen the regime against the demand for majority rule – a point not lost on black leaders.

On the surface Botha's reforms looked ingenuously reasonable, securing the middle ground of South African politics. As he explained: 'The world does not remain the same, and if we as a government want to act in the best interests of the country in a changing world, then we have to be prepared to adapt our policy to those things that make adjustment necessary. Otherwise we die.'

In enlarging the franchise to include coloureds and Indians and scrapping many provisions of apartheid, he was moving the country back roughly to where it had been in 1910, before the moderate Afrikaner seizure of power under Louis Botha, and before it was hijacked and returned to the early eighteenth century by the apostles of apartheid. South Africa experienced another one of its jolting time-lurches. Yet the world had not remained the same over the preceding century; the attempt was bound to be doomed.

Botha was never made to appear more reasonable than by the avalanche of far-right white fury unleashed against him by Andries Treurnicht, head of the voortrekker rump, whose proselytizing of Afrikaans in black schools had largely been responsible for the Soweto uprising of 1976 in the first place. Treurnicht, who had succeeded Mulder as leader of the conservative opposition to Botha in the Transvaal, was a powerful and effective orator with a large blue-collar and farmer following. In 1983 he and 15 others rebelled once too often, and were expelled from the National Party. This appeared to be a rerun of the right-wing rebellion spear-headed by Dr Albert Hertzog in 1969, when he and others revolted against the Vorster government's 'soft' line on sport, only not to win a single parliamentary seat. But Treurnicht was altogether a more formidable figure.

Moreover, Botha faced a backlash from prominent world leaders, disappointed at his attempt to conserve 'grand apartheid' and continue to freeze out the blacks. When he announced a referendum for the new constitution in November 1983, the Afrikaner leader of the main opposition party, the Progressive Federal Party, which was mostly English-speaking, Frederik Van Zyl Slabbert, an impressive young Afrikaner academic with Harrison Ford good looks, promptly urged a 'no' vote. 'The tragedy of South Africa is that at a time when the voters have come to acknowledge the need for such reform, the National Party has come forward with a plan that is so defective and ill-conceived that, if implemented, it will set back the process of reform for at least a decade.'

Harry Oppenheimer, doyen of the rich liberal community, agreed with Slabbert. So did Anglican, Methodist and Catholic church leaders. The Dutch Reformed church split between those who supported Botha and those who supported Treurnicht. For a moment, with so much opposition, it appeared that Botha had blundered.

But in the referendum, 66 per cent of whites supported these limited reforms while 33 per cent opposed them. Buoyed by the results, Botha then sought the acquiescence of senior Indian and coloured leaders in the new dispensation. Two-thirds of these communities accepted, on the grounds that the reforms were at least a step forward. However, at the first election in 1984 for the new three-chamber system, only a third of coloureds voted, and only a fifth of Indians.

Yet the white referendum was the watershed for Botha, his moment of greatest triumph. The result, it seemed, isolated the far right – about which he was far more concerned than the liberals and the blacks. The issue now was whether he would build upon his boldness, and advance South Africa towards real reform. What he did not reckon on was that partial reform would ignite black opposition to the white regime more violently than ever before.

* * *

In the sphere of foreign affairs, Botha's policies were having mixed results. In 1980 the victory of Robert Mugabe's Marxist Zanu–Patriotic Front coalition, dedicated to the anti-apartheid struggle, further isolated South Africa, although their common border was small. Yet Botha appeared to cut off one possible source of ANC terrorism when he concluded the Nkomati Accord of March 1994 with President Samora Machel of Mozambique. Under this the South Africans agreed to stop helping the Mozambican guerrilla movement, Renamo, in exchange for the expulsion of the ANC from Mozambican territory. The agreement was only partially respected by both sides, however.

Botha concentrated South Africa's military forces in the west in a bid to continue to maintain the position in South West Africa against SWAPO, the black liberation organization there. Although South Africa ruled the territory under a League of Nations mandate, its successor, the UN, had voted in 1969 for immediate South African withdrawal, a position reaffirmed by the Security Council and the International Court of Justice.

The South Africans opted to stay. As defence minister, Botha had set out government policy in 1978: 'We are not prepared to hand over South West Africa to Marxism and chaos ... we are prepared to negotiate with the world. We will negotiate with the UN secretary-general, but if they expect us to hand over South West Africa to Marxism, we say there is no further point in talking.' Over the next few years, under a veil of secrecy, South African forces increasingly raided over the border into Angola to attack SWAPO bases. Forces engaged in 'hot pursuit' operations launched major strikes against both SWAPO and their MPLA supporters. Operation Smokeshell was followed by Operations Protea, Daisy, Askari and Treurwilger.

By 1985 SWAPO had been all but chased out of South West Africa; and the South Africans had the support again of the American state department in linking the holding of UN-supervised elections on the territory to Cuban withdrawal from Angola, both major American objectives, but also a quasi-legitimization of what the South Africans were doing both in South West Africa and Angola – even though the former flouted the will of the UN and the latter was outright aggression. Botha and his deeply loyal defence minister, General Magnus Malan, had come to feel satisfied with their activities on the western front.

Less satisfactory to the South Africans was the conduct of the diplomatic war being waged against apartheid, which had gradually been intensifying. The country had become a pariah internationally in terms of culture and sport. Botha's attempts to explain his reforms in Europe had been a fiasco. In sport, official obduracy had set the government against the interests of its own natural supporters, who were passionate sportsmen. To those who argued that politics should not interfere with sport, and urged an end to international sports boycotts of South Africa, the answer was clear: the South Africans, through segregating sport, had been the first to apply politics to it.

Nothing stung the Afrikaners more effectively, while doing less damage to the blacks, than sports boycotts. Those who argued that the boycott would merely serve to drive South Africa into laager-like isolation and stubbornness also soon had their answer: sport was the first area in which the grip of apartheid was prised open. Indeed, it was the first area in which the Broederbond winced under the unfavourable consequences of apartheid.

The sports policy dated back to the segregation imposed from 1948 onwards, which applied to spectators, clubs, and on the field. In 1965, Verwoerd banned a visit by New Zealand's All Blacks because the team included Maori players. He pronounced: 'Our standpoint is that just as we subject ourselves to another country's customs and traditions without flinching, without any criticism and cheerfully, so do we expect that when another country sends representatives to us they will behave in the same way, namely not involving themselves in our affairs, and that they will adapt themselves to our customs.'

The ban on the All Blacks set off a wave of retaliatory bans against South Africa around the world. Verwoerd's successor, Vorster, decided partially to relax it under pressure from furious Afrikaner rugby fans, who favoured the New Zealand All Black tour. This raised a storm of protest in National Party circles. But Vorster reiterated, 'inside South Africa there will not be mixed sporting events, irrespective of the proficiency of the participants. On this there can be no compromise, negotiations, or abandonment of principle'.

In order to secure white support for his decision, in 1968 Vorster banned the South African-born coloured cricketer Basil d'Oliveira, who had been selected by the British MCC to tour South Africa (not before MCC selectors had tried to keep him off the team in deference to South African concerns). Cricket was an English game, and Vorster was prepared to sacrifice this in order to gain the support of the Afrikaner rugby lobby. He declared bluntly, 'We are not prepared to receive a team thrust upon us by people whose interests are not the game, but to gain political objectives which they do not even attempt to hide. The team, as it stands, is not the team of the MCC selection committee but of the political opponents of South Africa.'

The d'Oliveira decision sparked off international sporting fury. African countries threatened to boycott the Mexico City Olympics if South Africa attended. The country was banned and in 1970 was expelled from the Olympic Movement altogether. African teams now started boycotting competitions to which the South Africans were invited, and then shunning countries which permitted tours of South Africa. In 1974, at Gleneagles in Scotland, Commonwealth countries voted to end sporting contacts with South Africa as long as apartheid remained in existence.

Faced by isolation, and by the spectacular success of the All Black tour and the defeat of the right in the 1970 election, Vorster decided he could afford to relax the policy. The Broederbond was called upon to draft a new one. Cautiously, it set out the grounds for a fresh approach in an internal consultation document.

> We have always believed that sport should not be mixed with politics, and politics must be kept out of sport. Throughout the world, however, the importance of sport in international affairs, for the prestige of the countries and the promotion of a cause, has come strongly to the forefront and politics are drawn more and more into sport.
>
> That the two issues can no longer be separated is obvious from recent developments on the international and the national level ... It is very clear that our enemies have gained much courage from their success [in isolating South Africa] ... They are full of confidence that sports isolation will help to bring the whites to their knees ... A total of 500 million people participate in sport ... and sport has indeed become a world power.

Eventually the Botha government and the Broederbond resolved that the authorities had no role in deciding the composition of teams – this should be left to the sporting boards, which ruled, in effect, that mixed clubs would be permitted. This provided the beginning of the end of isolation, with French and British teams visiting South Africa in 1980 and the Springboks travelling to New Zealand on a controversial tour the following year. Unofficially, mixed teams began to visit South Africa.

Yet is was not until the 1990s, with the fall of apartheid and the full integration of South African sport, that isolation was conclusively ended. The sporting experience showed, however, that South Africa was prepared to yield if forced to do so. Pressure could bend even the stubborn, intransigent Afrikaners.

9
The Rage

Botha's biggest challenge was yet to come. Up to 1985, he viewed the main threat to the country as arising from the ANC guerrillas operating from outside. These staged spectacular sabotage attacks, but never provided a real problem for the security forces; they were an embarrassment, not a military threat. In May 1983, a massive bomb went off prematurely outside the Nedbank building in Pretoria, killing the two bombers, as well as 12 civilians, and injuring some 180 people. The bomb seemed to mark a shift back to terror tactics aimed at innocent civilians, although the ANC claimed it had been a mistake. Paradoxically the government probably benefited from the attack, being able more credibly to brand its adversaries as heartless Communist terrorists. Indeed, the ANC seemed to be playing into government hands.

What came as a complete shock to the government was the sudden eruption within South Africa of mass black protest which was, at best, distantly coordinated with, rather than instigated by, the ANC. In 1983 the United Democratic Front was formed in protest against the new constitution; it consisted of an umbrella of black groups against apartheid. At a huge rally, its leader, Allan Boesak, president of the World Alliance of Reformed Churches, pronounced to resounding cheers, 'three little words, words that express so eloquently our seriousness in this struggle: "All, Here and Now". We want all our rights, we want them here and we want them now ... The time has come for white people in this country to realize that their destiny is inextricably bound with our destiny and that they shall never be free until we are free.'

Within a year, the organization consisted of 600 affiliates representing some 3 million people. A more militant, much smaller National Forum was set up by Black Consciousness radicals. Botha's response was to arrest 45 of the 80 senior UDF leaders, raid its offices and ban meetings, accusing it of links with the ANC and the Communist party. But such was its ground swell of support that the government hesitated to ban the UDF itself.

A further spark in the tinder of smouldering black resentment was lit in September 1984, once again at Sharpeville, when 6 people were killed in clashes with the police, and 3 'collaborators' with the whites were murdered by their fellow blacks, including the deputy mayor of the township, hacked to death on his doorstep. A month later, in retaliation, 7,000 troops searched 20,000 homes in Sebokeng township before moving onto Sharpeville and Boipatong.

They were only the harbingers of what was to follow. 1985 was the decisive year, the moment when the whites had first to confront the reality that mass black opposition would grow to a critical mass, and could no longer be bludgeoned into submission. It was the year, too, when Botha, so confident of the success of his combination of concession and repression, suddenly stared total failure in the face: the new constitution had merely incensed the blacks as never before, while infuriating many hard-line whites.

Seven years after taking office with a vigour that had put the crabby old bigots of apartheid to shame, Botha in one year saw all his efforts unravel and Afrikanerdom facing its greatest crisis since the beginning of the Boer War. Faced by a tidal wave of discontent, the president had the stark choice of standing in its path and seeking to fight it – or turning and running to keep ahead of it.

The breaking point was March 1985, when a 4,000-strong crowd at Port Elizabeth was fired upon by police equipped only with guns, not riot control equipment, killing 20 people. Archbishop Desmond Tutu, for some years Anglican primate of Cape Town and a vociferous critic of apartheid who had called upon churches to participate in the struggle and had urged international sanctions, was briefly arrested after holding a service to commemorate the dead.

But the killing sparked off a ferocious and savage retaliatory black campaign. Those who had collaborated with the whites were prime targets: black councillors were beaten and burnt to death. Already three massive weapons of black protest were being employed: strikes – beginning in October 1984, some 680,000 workers had downed tools; school boycotts – affecting some 400,000 people in 300 schools in the Johannesburg area alone; and rent boycotts. The ANC called on the people to 'render South Africa ungovernable'. This seemed, indeed, to be what was happening.

With the explosion in protest in March 1985, the army was rushed in to support the police. As the violence spread, in July 1985 Botha imposed a state of emergency across much of South Africa for the first time since Sharpeville 25 years before. The police were now armed with sweeping powers – but the violence went on: in Durban, the murder of a leading civil rights lawyer, possibly by a 'death squad', ignited the incipient internal black civil war between UDF supporters and the Zulu followers of Chief Mangosuthu Buthelezi. In an orgy of destruction, hundreds of buildings were burnt and 50 people were killed.

A march led by Boesak on Pollsmoor Prison, to which Nelson Mandela had been moved, was viciously broken up by police, leading to savage violence within the Cape Town area and the deaths of another 30 people. Within three months, some 14,000 had been arrested, 5,000 held in custody, nearly 700 killed and 20,000 injured. It was a quasi-insurrection, viciously suppressed. Nearly four-fifths of the dead were victims of the police. Many black victims were killed by death squads.

In those dark days the ANC-in-exile made a giant leap towards international acceptability. Although viewed as a 'terrorist' organization by Margaret Thatcher's Conservative government in the UK, it was invited to present its case to the influential House of Commons Foreign Affairs Committee, with its Conservative majority. On their pioneering visit both Tambo and Mbeki made a first, extraordinarily favourable, impression as anything but extremists.

The former British cabinet minister, The Rt. Hon. Norman St John Stevas MP, asked whether the ANC would renounce the use of force if it was permitted to contest an election as a democratic political party. Tambo was unequivocal:

> We would say this is what we are fighting for. This is what we are insisting on. We say that the government must be the government of the people of South Africa, it should be an elected government, elected by the people of South Africa, not by a small white minority. This is at the very heart of our story. Now the African National Congress is not a political party, it is a national movement and has within it people of all political persuasions. It is a national movement, but it seeks to establish in South Africa a democracy precisely so that the country should be run according to the will of the majority of the people who would seize upon an opportunity for elections to take place so that we elect a government of the people of South Africa.

Mbeki was even more direct, in response to a question of the author, in rejecting the conditions set by Botha for Mandela's release:

It is a very simple thing for Botha to instruct his gaolors to open the gates and let the prisoners out, but clearly Botha is not interested. The conditions he has placed, like the political prisoners having to undertake not to engage in political activity which is likely to lead to their arrest, are ridiculous when you have an apartheid system continuing because, if Mandela decides 'I am not going to carry this reference book any more' he is liable to arrest.

I asked: 'Would you be prepared to renounce the use of violence in exchange for the release of political prisoners, and in particular Mr Mandela?' Mbeki replied:

No. The point our President was making earlier was when the ANC was banned back in 1960 it was not because the ANC had decided on a policy of violence. The ANC was banned in 1960 as a result of ordinary political activity. Therefore, I am saying that we get into a situation of having to adopt armed struggle because everything is stopped. If Nelson Mandela was released, what should happen? Can Nelson Mandela stand up and say 'I am a member of the ANC, I carry out ANC policies?' He is liable to be arrested because the ANC is banned. The release of the political prisoners on its own would never be a sufficient condition for bringing about as peaceful as possible a solution of the South Africa problem.

Many other things would have to be done. The positions, for instance, taken at the Commonwealth Summit are important. I do not know whether the Commonwealth Summit put those conditions in any order of priority, or if they simply said the Botha regime must dismantle apartheid and actually implement a programme for that: political prisoners must be released, the state of emergency must be lifted, the ban on the ANC must be lifted and on all other political organizations. And if the Botha regime has said 'Okay, we are ready to dismantle apartheid and here are our actual practical measures to bring that about and we are ready to enter into negotiations as the Commonwealth said, negotiations which are going to lead to the formation of a non-racial and representative government', if all of that were seriously said by Botha, then of course there would be no need for violence, there would be no need for violence on our side.

* * *

Against this fearsome backdrop, Botha rose to confront the worst crisis of his political life with the astonishing revelation that his government was radically about to change its policies. It was billed by foreign minister Pik Botha as the 'Rubicon speech', after which South Africa would decisively cross the bridge towards a new beginning. Botha had assured no less a figure than the US National Security Council adviser, Robert McFarlane, of the importance of the change. Copies of the discourse had been circulated to South African embassies throughout the world.

Botha rose to address the public in Durban City Hall, with cameras beaming his words to a global audience of around 300 million people. To general astonishment, he launched a back-to-the-wall defence of the Afrikaner mentality. He would not lead 'white South Africans and other minority groups to abdication and suicide'. The world should not 'push us too far'. What few friends South Africa had abroad were appalled by this dismal spectacle

What on earth had happened? The explanation believed by most was that Botha had run scared at the last moment. The National Party had only narrowly won a by-election at Harrismith against Treurnicht's Conservative Party. Four more by-elections were pending. Also, economic sanctions had been sharply stepped up in previous weeks: France had announced a freeze on new investment; other European countries and the United States had recalled their embassies for consultation; and Chase Manhattan had unexpectedly called in its lines to South Africa.

Botha was said to be indignant, and had no wish to show that he was being pushed around. Yet pressure did usually have the effect of making the South Africans move, whatever they might say in public. The Conservative advance, while serious, was hardly a reason for changing course in mid-term. What seems really to have happened is that Botha, who as Cape leader was never all that strong within the parliamentary party, was warned by leading supporters, particularly in the Conservative Transvaal, to go no further or risk being unseated.

The Broederbond, whose views had evolved, was now led by the most enlightened president in its history, Gerrit Viljoen. As early as 1976, Viljoen made clear that conditions for the blacks must be improved – a radical departure for the organization:

For the great number of blacks living in the white areas to remain there for a long time, decent living conditions, effective self-government and maintenance of law and order must be ensured. The basic rules of human social engineering make it essential that acceptable procedures and structures for local self-government, leadership and expression of views should be created ... Blacks must get a measure of autonomy to maintain law and order and put down gangsterism in the black urban areas. We will have to get away from the old idea that life in locations must be made as uncomfortable as possible to encourage migration to the homelands.

No matter how successful the homelands are, there will still be hundreds of thousands of blacks in white cities' locations and certain minimum comforts are essential such as home ownership, a better physical environment, services like lights, water, sanitation, trading facilities, sport and recreation.

Unexceptional sentiments from a white liberal but astonishing from the mouth of the head of the secret society that had been the power-house of Afrikaner rule since 1948. Even under Viljoen, however, the Broederbond could not accept the dismantling of 'grand apartheid'.

Botha's own personal constituency, the National Security Council, which as president and commander-in-chief he ran as his kitchen cabinet, advised him that it was still possible to crush black protest. Military intelligence was more guarded, and could see the problems ahead. Faced by such a formidable body of advice, Botha decided to abandon his reform, which at that stage would have involved the creation of a new black advisory chamber, the scrapping of the Pass Laws, and even possibly the release of Nelson Mandela on humanitarian grounds.

He missed an opportunity of historic proportions. If Botha had gone ahead with a more radical Rubicon speech, he would have swung the weight of the presidency behind reform. The majority of the white community would have followed him, although the Conservative Party would certainly have seen new recruits. It might have been possible to begin negotiations with the UDF and ANC-in-exile, as well as Mandela in prison, five years before this in fact occurred. But the argument that seems to have swayed him was that, faced by so major an explosion of black rage, the government could not afford to be seen to bend.

South Africa was in a nearly revolutionary condition: if the whites gave way under the impact of the first offensive, the blacks would assume they were stronger than they actually were, and would demand a full-scale surrender. Botha believed it was necessary for the regime to prove that it had the monopoly of power, the ability to crush this uprising; then talks could start. Botha was advised both by his national security advisers and the Afrikaner establishment that it would be fatal to make concessions under pressure: better to negotiate from a position of strength. With that, however, ended any chance of understanding in the outside world for the 'reforming' Botha government. He was seen, far from being an agent for change, as an irascible, obstructive and increasingly vicious exponent of the old Afrikaner mentality.

Yet even as he bowed to the political pressures upon him, there were those in Afrikanerdom who reckoned that the game was up. Sampie Terreblanche, for example, cites the Rubicon speech as the moment that he gave up all hope of reform from the Botha government. More significant, Frederik (F. W.) de Klerk, who in 1982 became the youthful 46-year-old party leader in the Transvaal, the key Afrikaner state, had been given charge of the repeal of the Mixed Marriages Act and the offending section of the Immorality Act. He concluded that 'grand apartheid' had failed – something that was anathema still to most of his party. He later expounded the view that he was in no sense viscerally opposed to apartheid; he had simply come to the pragmatic conclusion that it couldn't work ('like Communism', as a perceptive Afrikaner observed).

Botha may himself have come to the same conclusion; certainly he was opposed to the Pass Laws (which in fact were scrapped the following year). Without the Pass Laws, which had regulated black access to white urban areas, the whole concept of apartheid had crumbled away; along with the ending of petty apartheid it was a thundering acknowledgement that the races, in a modern urban society, could not be separated after all. In theory, 1985 marked the end of apartheid, the great dream of the voortrekkers and their Broederbond successors of a pure, separate white state constructed on the labour of the blacks.

But Botha dared not admit so publicly. Moreover, acknowledgement of the failure of apartheid, while a big step, was still a long way from accepting the need for black majority rule. One of the key diplomatic observers of events makes it clear that 'I never believed Botha could make that jump. He was determined to resist black rule, real reform, the release of Mandela, at all costs.' As in the Boer War, defeat in the field was followed by years of bitter guerrilla resistance before the

Afrikaners would finally surrender. But the turning point had been reached. Botha had decided to obey the military maxim: under attack, advance; only in victory could he afford to make concessions. After Botha's stand, he narrowly won four of the five by-election seats – although the white right was the least of his worries. The country was now facing a showdown – the forces of order against a quasi-insurrection. Only if Botha could have controlled the insurrection would he have been justified in the eyes of his own constituency in his tough new approach. Otherwise he would merely be adding fuel to the flames.

In November 1985 I had this graphic exchange with the impressive leader of the Progressive Federal Party, Dr Van Zyl Slabbert. I asked him whether he thought South Africa had passed the point of no return. He replied:

No, I do not at this stage. I have three informal thresholds beyond which I would say we can move into a situation of enduring conflict and siege. One is the extent of isolation from the rest of the world. Whatever else can be said, I think generally speaking the South African government is sensitive to the West and what it represents in terms of its values, its philosophy and so on. If the perception there grows, say, among an extreme faction, that the world has cut us off and we are totally isolated, then we could move into what I would call an unsalvageable situation.

Of the other two thresholds, one would be the extent of black violence, if that violence should spill over from the black townships into the so-called white areas, for example, a white school or school bus, or petrol bombs are thrown indiscriminately in shopping areas. If that happens, then I think we move into a very difficult period. The third one is the reaction to that which would be white violence. However deplorable the scenes of brutality you have seen on your television screen may be, the point has to be made that the government have not yet begun to use the instruments of violence at its disposal if it should really want to escalate that violence – I am thinking here of bombs, of automatic weapons, of helicopter gun ships, that kind of violence on the scale one sometimes sees in the Lebanon. Then we would be in the situation you described, but we are not there yet. I hope we can still avoid that.

As far as the by-elections were concerned, he told Sir Ivan Lawrence MP:

I think one should not over-estimate the recent by-elections. If one had to spell out the circumstances in which one would expect the right wing to flourish in electoral circumstances, I cannot think of more favourable circumstances than we have had over the last six months. One should argue, why did they not win more seats instead of just scraping home in the one they got, Sasolburg? I do not think the right wing poses an electoral threat to the government to the extent that you can say it could only take over the government by winning 85 seats, and that is impossible. I cannot see it. The right wing does pose a violence threat. I think the possibility of right-wing violence makes it a very difficult factor. But if one talks about the ability and the capacity of the government to move, I think it has not used that ability in any way that it can if it wants to.

In other words, if one takes the Human Science Research Council's report on white attitudes, it shows that 60 per cent of whites are prepared to accept some power-sharing compromise. That is a significant statistic. It also shows two-thirds of the whites expect a fully integrated South Africa in fifteen years' time. So you have an attitude of mind there that can be very effectively exploited by the government if it wishes to move systematically on the level of reform; but what will not contribute to the mood or climate for reform is if the government does so in an ambiguous, unsystematic way, which increases anxiety and feeds fears that the situation is running out of control. So my answer is that the government can in fact with the support that it has got move much faster than it is actually moving at the moment.

Slabbert's colleague, C. W. Eglin, argued that apartheid was dead:

The one thing that has happened is that apartheid is no longer the pattern for the future even in terms of the government's thinking. So the government has moved away from the concept of the bantustans being the total political answer, away from the concept of no power sharing to some form of power sharing, away from the concept of white exclusivity to some form of inclusiveness. As Dr Slabbert has pointed out, it is one thing for the government to move away but it does not appear to have a very clear vision of the future. I think in that sense at the moment it seems to be trapped between the past and the future. It is possibly because it has got no clear perception of what it puts in place of what it has undone that it is hesitating at the moment and at the same time in this particular state it sees violence, it sees pressures. I think in these circumstances it applies the brakes because of the uncertainty it has about the future. So I do not think the restraint of the right is preventing it from moving, it is the lack of perception of the future that is possibly the reason.

Astonishingly, this was buttressed by South Africa's reformist ambassador to London, Dr Denis Worrall, replying to Nigel Spearing MP some months later:

> If one means by 'apartheid' racial discrimination and segregation then the fact is that we are very far advanced already in eliminating apartheid from South Africa. The government have said if apartheid means domination of any particular group or race of the society, denial of human dignity on the grounds of colour, and unequal treatment before the law, etc., then it rejects apartheid. You will be aware that there are many areas of life in South Africa – sport, industrial labour relations, public amenities and facilities – where, in fact, segregation has been removed. That is one part of the process. The other part of the process of moving away from apartheid is achieving a fully representative government for South Africa, where the government is representative not simply of the non-black groups but, in fact, is representative of all of the South African people; that is a more difficult task. That is, in fact, what the end of apartheid signifies and that is, in fact, what the government is moving towards.

The government now really turned the heat on black protest: by the end of the year, 824 people had died and more than 2,600 had been injured; the overwhelming majority were victims of the police. But the blacks continued to fight back. For the government the worst news was the decision at the end of 1985 by the Federation of South African Trade Unions (Fosatu) to merge with several others, including the National Union of Mineworkers, spear-headed by an extraordinarily articulate, able and tough-minded secretary-general, Cyril Ramaphosa, into Cosatu, the half-million-strong Congress of South African Trades Unions.

The organization was multiracial, and its creation caused the old white trade union organization, the Trades Union Council of South Africa, to collapse the following year. The blacks had secured the adhesion of white members in their struggle for higher pay and better conditions. Cosatu was able to organize its members into staging the highest number of strikes for a decade, working in close coordination with the UDF and the ANC outside the country for political, as much as narrow trade union, ends. On May Day 1985, 2.5 million people stayed away from work.

The employers tried to fight back; one major NUM fight ended in defeat, with 50,000 miners being dismissed. But the sheer number of strikes wore the economy down. The government fought back in 1986, arresting 2,700 trade unionists in 1986. Over the year there were nearly 800 strikes – a record.

The government also drew up a Labour Relations Amendment Act allowing employers to sue for loss of profit resulting from industrial action, and to impose restrictions on strikes. Early in 1988 the government also banned unions from engaging in non-union – that is, political – activities; the law came into force in September of that year.

* * *

By the middle of 1986, the government had lost control of many of the townships. The security forces could, of course, enter any of them in strength at will; but on a regular, day-to-day basis, the townships were left to look after themselves as the police withdrew or stayed inside their armed compounds. The black councils that were supposed to administer the townships had long since crumbled away under intimidation. Instead, 'semi-liberated zones' were set up, policed by street committees; when these were controlled by disciplined UDF cadres, the townships were well-run and crime practically eliminated.

In other areas, however, punishments were meted out with savagery towards dissidents and informers, and in others still, outright gangsterism and protection rackets took over – in turn leading to a backlash from older, more law-abiding blacks who set up vigilante groups to fight the new extremists. Often these were based on tribal tension, usually between ANC supporters and the allies of the Inkatha Freedom Party, led by Chief Mangosuthu Buthelezi, whose henchmen controlled the all-male hostels in the townships into which Zulus were packed. From their hothouse dormitories they frequently embarked on sprees of violence like their celibate ancestors under Shaka.

The police and elements of the security forces were increasingly accused of collaborating with Inkatha militants. In the dismal

Alexandra township north of Soweto, outright street warfare broke out between vigilantes and 'comrades' – young activists. Troops and police in armoured cars had to be sent in. The blacks were battling among themselves, as if in a war they had already won, for the spoils.

Nor was violence confined to the townships. The real black underclass in South Africa were not the township dwellers, but the millions shoved away in the self-governing 'homelands' out of the sight and out of the minds of educated South Africans. The Carnegie Inquiry into poverty and development in South Africa, a massive academic investigation during this period, made shocking reading: more than 90 per cent of the country's poor lived in rural areas, with 9 million people in the homelands living below the poverty line and nearly 1.5 million having no income at all. Average family income in the country was half that of black families in the cities.

The homelands were appallingly overcrowded: in Kwazulu there were 76 people per square kilometre, compared to 22 in white Natal; in Lebowa, Gazankulu and Kangwane, the figures were similar, while in Bophuthatswana the ratio was a more acceptable 29. In white-dominated Transvaal it was only 11 per kilometre (admittedly Transvaal was mostly rough pasture compared to the lush black lowlands). The whites had simply shoved the black majority into densely populated rural slums while they roamed free through most of the countryside, using temporary mass black labour for their industries.

Apartheid collapsed – as much as from any other reason – because of the huge pressure this rural poverty imposed, driving blacks to defy the law and squat on the outskirts of cities in squalid shantytowns. The extent of violence in the rural areas is hard to assess; but with unemployment and inflation at record levels, impoverished blacks fought the whites and each other. Boycotts and attacks on buses escalated; in an incident at Winterveld in Bophuthatswana 11 people were killed fighting police. Thirty were murdered after rising against the government of Lebowa. In January 1986, a similar number died in fighting between the Sotho and the Ndebele. The rural tensions were not instigated by the UDF and were peripheral to the struggle in the cities; but they were damning proof that apartheid was breaking down in the countryside as well.

* * *

Another turn of the screw was the now serious effect of international economic sanctions. The Botha reforms had failed to make much impact on South Africa's crisis; and the spiral of violence in 1985, followed by savage repression, intensified the external pressure on South Africa. Perhaps the worst psychological blow was the decision by South Africa's debtors', the Paris Club, for purely political reasons, not to roll over the country's relatively modest debt the same year.

In this they followed the lead of Chase Manhattan. For the South Africans, virtually isolated, with no ready source of outside capital, and yet deeply committed to financial probity, the blow, combined with the outflow of capital from the country, was potentially lethal. As one senior Afrikaner economist puts it, 'The ANC did not realize just how vulnerable the government was at that moment. The ANC deeply distrusted the banks because Chase Manhattan, in particular, had moved in after the Sharpeville massacre of 1960 to replace the country's traditional creditors who had pulled out. But the country was on the verge of financial collapse. All the ANC had to do was to put pressure on the banks and the government would have fallen.'

Instead, a prominent Swiss financier, Dr Leutwiler, was sent for during eleventh-hour talks with Botha. Leutwiler, who refused to see Mandela because of his 'Communist' connections, was in fact a close friend of the British prime minister, Margaret Thatcher, who did not favour economic action against South Africa, and there must be suspicion that she put pressure on him to reach a deal at all costs; this happened, although many of his fellow bankers distrusted him. Botha, under pressure, made iron-clad commitments to immediate reform – which he then failed to keep. But by then the immediate danger was past.

South Africa had now twice failed to take action to avert disaster – first in August 1985, at the time of the Rubicon speech, and then later in the year, this time as a result of a failure of ANC leadership. Had the banks failed to renegotiate the loan, the government might have been forced into direct talks with the ANC far sooner. But it was not to be.

Meanwhile, disinvestment by the multinationals proceeded apace: General Electric, General Motors, IBM, Coca-Cola and Warner Communications all pulled out. Banks and pension funds stopped supporting companies with South African connections. In the United States, Congress banned new investments and loans to South Africa, and barred imports of agricultural products, as well as uranium, coal, textiles, iron and steel. South African Airways was denied landing rights in the United States. All this took place in defiance of President Reagan's policy of 'constructive engagement' with South Africa.

One Commonwealth conference after another was derailed by attempts to impose comprehensive mandatory sanctions against South Africa, staved off with great difficulty by British prime minister Margaret Thatcher, also acting against the advice of her own Foreign Office. In Europe, the campaign for sanctions was gaining momentum. The economic pressure was beginning to hit home. In the first half of 1988 alone nearly $3 billion flowed out of the country, principally as 'the result of the country's strained international relationships', according to the Central Bank governor. In 1986, the economy contracted by 2 per cent, while unemployment began to spiral, reaching 3 million of the black population.

Between 1985 and 1990, according to another estimate by the Chamber of Mines, the total cost of sanctions and disinvestment was a staggering 40 billion rand – not enough to bring the economy to its knees, but enough to hurt badly. Trade sanctions did harm, but were not decisive. 'The important thing was the outflow of capital', says one leading Afrikaner economist. There can be little doubt, though, that the economic pressure on South Africa converted a large part not just of the English-speaking, but the Afrikaner, plutocrats to the view that there had to be a negotiated settlement – which in turn increased the pressure upon Botha.

* * *

It is hard to exaggerate the seriousness of the situation in the declining months of 1985. The Botha regime had very nearly fallen; if it had been forced to negotiate with the blacks, it might have survived – or it might have been replaced by an even more obdurate government. Certainly on the white side many were prepared to resort to all-out war against the blacks. On the black side, with the scent of victory in the air, there was an attempt to move in for the kill. All-out civil war beckoned.

As Walter Sisulu, Mandela's closest imprisoned comrade and nominal chief, put it, in an astonishing admission to the journalist Anthony Sampson in January 1996, if Mandela had been released in 1985 'You would not have avoided actual civil war in that situation ... that delay was necessary, for [the Afrikaners] to sober up. They were the danger. In 85 the feeling in jail was "let's have it" – even if we were not quite ready. Let's take the bull by the horns. (Mandela too.) There was no question of saying no, to give us a little bit more time.'

Part II
Rainbow Bridge

10
Romancing the Prisoner

In November 1985, at the age of 67, Nelson Mandela was admitted to the Volks Hospital in Cape Town for surgery for an enlarged prostate gland. His wife, Winnie, was permitted by the authorities to fly to see him before the operation. She boarded the same flight as Kobie Coetsee, South Africa's new minister for justice, the police and prisons. He represented a younger, more open-minded type of Afrikaner, above all one who understood the inevitability of change.

Coetsee had been a close friend of Piet de Waal, a former fellow student and tennis partner at the University of Orange Free State who had become a lawyer in the remote farming town of Brandfort. By chance, it was to this community that Winnie Mandela had been exiled in 1977, after the Soweto riots the previous year; the flamboyant Winnie became a close friend of de Waal's wife, Adele.

Although Piet himself was a cautious conservative, as the only lawyer in town he was obliged to represent her, and was later to admit, 'she became a friend of mine also. It began at a professional level, but I also got to know her as a person. I learned quite a few things from knowing her, and came to understand her point of view.' Winnie regarded Adele as her 'white sister', and was deeply upset by her death in a car crash in 1990.

De Waal was in regular touch with his old friend Coetsee, who showed more than a casual interest in his famous client. 'Whenever Kobie phoned about matters to do with his farm he would ask, "How are things going with your client?" I would give him a report on what she was doing, but then, gradually, I found openings to tell him the government should reconsider its attitude to the Mandelas ... I would say, "Look man, this banning order is achieving nothing. If she wants to say inflammatory things they still get reported overseas anyway, so what's the point?"'

De Waal urged Coetsee to make contact with Mandela himself. Coetsee all along was keeping a watching brief on Winnie, with a view to using her as a conduit to her husband. On the plane to Cape Town he stopped by her seat and voiced his concern for Mandela; after take-off she strode down the aircraft into first class and urged Coetsee to visit Nelson in hospital. It is open to doubt if this encounter was quite as spontaneous as it seemed: the first contact between a senior Afrikaner minister and South Africa's man in the iron mask, representative of the feared and hated ANC, was unlikely to have been the result of a spur-of-the-moment decision taken as a result of a chance encounter on a plane.

* * *

Coetsee became minister of justice in 1980 and had long concluded that the time was ripe for a new approach to the plight of Mandela, incarcerated on Robben Island off Cape Town since 1963, and the former ANC leaders who had joined him there – Walter Sisulu, Ahmed Kathrada, Raymond Mhlaba and Andrew Mlangeni. 'I was convinced that Mandela and his colleagues would have to be released sometime and that they should be prepared for that.'

In March 1982, the Robben Island five were transferred to Pollsmoor maximum security prison in Cape Town, and held in a spacious communal cell on the roof. For Mandela the experience was cathartic. 'I looked back at the island as the light was fading, not knowing whether I would ever see it again. A man can get used to anything, and I had grown used to Robben Island. I had lived there for almost two decades and while it was never my home – my home was in Johannesburg – it had become a place where I felt comfortable. I have always found change difficult, and leaving Robben Island, however grim it had been at times, was no exception. I had no idea what to look forward to.'

While in Pollsmoor the 'politicals' had been given what was in effect the prison's penthouse: a spacious room on the third and topmost floor. 'We were the only prisoners on the entire floor. The main room was clean, modern and rectangular, about fifty by thirty feet and had a separate section with a toilet, urinals, two basins and two showers. There were four proper beds, with sheets, and towels, a great luxury for men who had spent much of the last eighteen years sleeping on thin mats on a stone floor'.

Mandela promptly indulged in his favourite activity, in grand style for a prisoner. He was supplied by the prison service with 16 huge oil drums, which were chopped in half, each being filled with soil, 'creating in effect thirty-two giant flowerpots'. There he grew onions, aubergines, cabbages, cauliflowers, beans, spinach, carrots, cucumbers, broccoli, beetroot, lettuce, tomatoes, peppers, strawberries and much more – some 900 plants altogether.

Mandela and his colleagues believed the intention behind their transfer to the mainland was to isolate them from the bulk of imprisoned ANC supporters on Robben Island. Coetsee later insisted that it was to initiate a secret dialogue in more comfortable surroundings. In fact the South African government's aim had always been to drive a wedge between Mandela, with his huge moral authority, who had been insulated from the world and was in the palm of the government's hand, and the leaders of the ANC outside the country.

Coetsee's hard-line predecessor, Jimmy Kruger, told Mandela, 'we can work with you, but not your colleagues. Be reasonable.' Coetsee had gone one stage further, permitting outsiders – for example Lord Bethell of the European parliament, and Samuel Dash, a Georgetown professor – to visit Mandela in Pollsmoor, as well as a pair of conservative American journalists.

On 31 January 1985, Botha produced his trump card. Mandela was offered his release if he 'unconditionally renounced violence as a political instrument' – that is, disowned the ANC's armed struggle. Mandela replied in eloquent, measured and contemptuous tones. His message was delivered by his 24-year-old daughter Zinzi, the only member of the family not subject to a banning order, at a huge meeting in Soweto's Jabulani stadium to honour Archbishop Desmond Tutu for his award of the Nobel Peace Prize:

> I am a member of the African National Congress. I have always been a member of the African National Congress and I will remain a member of the African National Congress until the day I die. Oliver Tambo is more than a brother to me. He is my greatest friend and comrade for nearly fifty years. If there is anyone amongst you who cherishes my freedom, Oliver Tambo cherishes it more, and I know that he would give his life to set me free ...
>
> I am surprised at the conditions that the government wants to impose on me. I am not a violent man ... It was only ... when all other forms of resistance were no longer open to us, that we turned

to armed struggle. Let Botha show that he is different to Malan, Strijdom and Verwoerd. Let him renounce violence. Let him say that he will dismantle apartheid. Let him guarantee free political activity so that people may decide who will govern them ...

It was dignified and all the more poignant for being delivered by an inexperienced young woman.

In fact the Botha offer had been the product of a remarkable piece of political naivety. According to Coetsee, the president thought 'this was a brilliant solution because if Mandela refused, then the whole world would understand why the South African government couldn't release him'.

Coetsee rejected this view. 'I had studied the man and knew he would never accept this. There was no way Mandela was going to renounce the ANC's armed struggle for which he had spent all these years in prison. We had to put it in a positive way, asking him to commit himself to a future peaceful purpose rather than asking him to renounce the past.'

Mandela's rejection was not, however, the militant brush-off of a thoroughly silly offer many had feared. As Mandela himself admitted, 'I wanted to reassure the ANC in general and Oliver Tambo in particular that my loyalty to the organization was beyond question. I also wished to send a message to the government that while I rejected its offer because of the conditions attached to it, I nevertheless thought negotiation, not war, was the path to a solution. Botha wanted the onus of violence to rest on my shoulders and I wanted to reaffirm to the world that we were only responding to the violence done to us.'

* * *

Eight hours after the contrivance of his chance meeting with Winnie Mandela, almost certainly with Botha's full authority, Coetsee called on Mandela. It was the first historic meeting between a senior minister and one of the leading – and certainly the most famous – members of the ANC. Coetsee, along with the prisons commissioner, General Johannes Willemse, met Mandela clad in a dressing gown.

As Coetsee recalls it, Mandela immediately dominated the conversation through his charm:

He acted as though we had known each other for years and this was the umpteenth time we had met. He introduced General Willemse and me to the two nurses, and chided me for not coming to see him sooner. I remember he made a little joke about this being his ward and me being his warder. He took complete command of the situation. He was like the host. He invited us to sit down, and, 'General Willemse, are you comfortable and is there anything we can do for you?'

I had read a lot about him – all his speeches and all those reports that came across my desk every day – and I was fascinated at what kind of man he must be to have attracted all this international attention and have all these honorary degrees and awards given to him. When I met him I immediately understood why. He came across as a man of Old World values. I have studied Latin and Roman culture, and I remember thinking that this is a man to whom I could apply it, an old Roman citizen with dignitas, gravitas, honestas, simplicitas.

Mandela was equally surprised and guarded about Coetsee:

that morning he dropped by the hospital unannounced as if he were visiting an old friend who was laid up for a few days. He was altogether gracious and cordial, and for the most part we simply made pleasantries. Though I acted as though this was the most normal thing in the world, I was amazed. The government, in its slow and tentative way, was reckoning that they had to come to some accommodation with the ANC. Coetsee's visit was an olive branch.

On his discharge from hospital, Mandela was transferred away from his ANC colleagues to isolation on the ground floor. The objective was clearly to prevent him being restricted by his old friends as he began a dialogue with the government. The authorities had probed whether he was prepared to act alone, and he had responded with a cautious yes – which was extremely dangerous from the ANC's point of view.

To the South African government, the chance of securing Mandela's detachment from the ANC was too good to miss. At the least they might start the process of dialogue with the organization; at best they might split and sow confusion in the movement's ranks by separating the ANC's most famous member from the movement itself. Mandela's own sense of mission, leadership, indispensability – and, yes, vanity and self-sufficiency – appeared to lend itself to this manoeuvre.

In the most significant passage in his memoirs he writes,

My solitude gave me a certain liberty, and I resolved to use it to do something I had been pondering for a long while: begin discussions with the government. I had concluded that the time had come when the struggle could best be pushed forward through negotiations. If we did not start a dialogue soon, both sides would soon be plunged into a dark night of oppression, violence and war. My solitude would give me an opportunity to take the first steps in that direction, without the kind of scrutiny that might destroy such efforts.

We had been fighting against white minority rule for three-quarters of a century. We had been engaged in the armed struggle for more than two decades. Many people on both sides had already died. The enemy was strong and resolute. Yet even with all their bombers and tanks, they must have sensed that they were on the wrong side of history. We had right on our side, but not yet might. It was clear to me that a military victory was a distant if not impossible dream. It simply did not make sense for both sides to lose thousands if not millions of lives in a conflict that was unnecessary. They must have known this as well. It was time to talk.

For the man who had persuaded the ANC to take up arms in 1961, this was remarkable indeed. He acknowledged that the 'decision to talk to the government was of such importance that it should only have been made in Lusaka [the ANC headquarters]. But I felt that the process needed to begin, and I had neither the time nor the means to communicate fully with Oliver. Someone from our side needed to take the first step, and my new isolation gave me both the freedom to do so and the assurance, at least for a while, of the confidentiality of my efforts.' This was a naked admission that he had decided to brush aside the objections of his colleagues in charge of the guerrilla war and take leadership into his own hands.

It was a drastic step for one isolated man at the mercy of his white enemies to make. When he was allowed to see his prison colleagues a few days later, he informed them, to the irritation of two of them, that he was pleased to be separated from them. 'Perhaps something good will come of this. I'm now in a position where the government can make an approach to us.' Mandela, cut off from them, would now be treated royally by his captors, one man negotiating with the whole colossal apparatus of the South African government. He – not even the leader of the ANC – had decided to strike out on his own and negotiate. He was openly dismissive of his fellows:

I chose to tell no one what I was about to do. Not my colleagues upstairs nor those in Lusaka. The ANC is a collective, but the government had made collectivity in this case impossible. I did not have the security or the time to discuss these issues with my organization. I knew that my colleagues upstairs would condemn my proposal, and that would kill my initiative even before it was born. There are times when a leader must move out ahead of the flock, go off in a new direction, confident that he is leading his people the right way. Finally, my isolation furnished my organization with an excuse in case matters went awry: the old man was alone and completely cut off, and his actions were taken by him as an individual, not as a representative of the ANC.

That last disclaimer was ingenuous; if Mandela collaborated, the ANC would be badly wounded. It seemed that white South Africa was about to secure one of its most significant successes. Mandela himself, deluded by his position in history, could be induced to become an Uncle Tom, another Bishop Muzorewa. For the ANC outside, it was a desperately worrying moment.

* * *

But one factor weighed even more heavily with the ANC leadership in Lusaka: they too had decided it was time to talk. The balance of power within the movement will be examined in a later chapter. In general, though, the high command in Lusaka under the control of Tambo, Thabo Mbeki and Aziz Pahad, although trained in Moscow and receiving Russian support, were much more pragmatic than the commanders of the guerrillas in the field, many of whom were Marxist-indoctrinated and saw the struggle as a class one as much as a racial one.

Tambo and Mbeki were increasingly concerned that control of the movement might slip into the hands of the young radicals, which was a powerful incentive for them not to allow South Africa to drift into civil war. In addition, there were acute fears at the ANC high command in Lusaka that Mandela might indeed be prepared to do a separate deal with the authorities. They knew Mandela had been cut off not just from the ANC outside South Africa but his prison colleagues also; he might have been intimidated or drugged, or have lapsed into mental instability, for all they knew.

He had long sought to talk to the government, and they were now

talking to him. (For their part, the South African security organizations believed that important sections of the ANC wished to see
Mandela dead.) Mandela had taken care to open a single line to
Lusaka, in the shape of George Bizos, his portly, 57-year-old legal
adviser, whom he met after the Coetsee encounter. 'Nelson was
worried that news of his meeting with Kobie Coetsee might get out
and reach the ANC leadership in exile, and that they might think he
was doing deals without their concurrence. He asked me to try to get
to Oliver Tambo in Lusaka and assure him that nothing would happen
without their approval.'

Bizos went to see Coetsee to inform him of his impending visit to
Lusaka, partly in order to cover himself in case he was accused of clandestine contacts with the ANC, but partly because 'I was suspicious
that they were trying to use him as part of a plan to split the internal
and external wings of the ANC and have him lead the internal wing.
I still believe that was their plan at the time, but they had underesti-
mated Nelson's intelligence and integrity. I didn't think Nelson would
fall for it, but he was unable to speak publicly for himself, and I was
worried that they might be able to do things that would compromise
him and cause confusion.'

In fact Mandela was not going to play the game by South Africa's
rules, but nor was he going to play by Tambo's; he was striking out on
his own, determined to initiate the process and seize the initiative
from Lusaka – an extraordinarily high-risk strategy. Bizos met Coetsee
in another bogus prearranged chance plane encounter (because of the
difficulty the hard-line security services had in bugging aircraft) and
they argued for four hours.

Then Bizos flew to Lusaka to meet Tambo, who was 'elated at the
news I brought him. He told me they had indeed been concerned;
they didn't know how ill Mandela was and they were worried that he
might be tricked into a deal, but I assured him Mandela was in good
health and in full control of the situation. His message to them was
that they shouldn't worry, that he wouldn't do anything without
their concurrence.' In a second meeting in February 1986, Tambo
confirmed that 'they had full confidence in Mandela's ability to
handle the situation. I should tell Mandela to carry on, that he had
their full support.'

Bizos returned to reassure Mandela, and then to meet Coetsee again,
to assure him that 'there was a serious desire to start talking to the
government. I also told him – and I don't know how pleased he was
to hear this – that there were no differences between Mandela and the

outsiders, and that, whatever agreements were reached, the ANC in exile would support Mandela.'

How genuine was Tambo's trust in Mandela? Diminutive, energetic, eloquent, the former had been the ANC's real leader for more than two decades, tirelessly supervising the guerrilla struggle, the negotiations with foreign governments, the interminable political wrangles. He had not seen the reflective, gracious, calculating Mandela in 22 years, since their early heroic struggles against apartheid. Mandela's frequent public expressions of friendship for Tambo might have seemed patronizing, if they were not so necessary. Yet the latter had no choice but to support the initiative launched by the world's most famous political prisoner.

One of the ANC's worst internal enemies, Chief Buthelezi's largely Zulu-based Inkatha Party, played up the differences between Mandela and Tambo in response to a question from the author on the House of Commons Foreign Affairs Committee. In view of later revelations about the extent of Buthelezi's collaboration with the government, this may have reflected Inkatha's attempts to woo Mandela away from Tambo and conclude a separate peace. Buthelezi said:

> It depends what 'moderate' means. But I would think that I have always respected Mr Mandela because of his patriotism and because his politics have always been realistic and he has never despised ordinary people. We know Inkatha is supported by ordinary black workers and peasants, and very often many people look down on them and think they are just the scum who must be dictated to. So I would think that one good example which shows the difference between the External Mission leaders and Mr Mandela, is the fact that Mr Mandela does not consider me to be political dirt to the extent that in the past we have exchanged very warm letters – even recently. In the *Sunday Times* yesterday they published a letter he wrote to me from Pollsmoor Jail which was very warm, quite contrary to the attitude of those in Lusaka with Mr Tambo. The attitude is completely different from that.

If Tambo had signalled disapproval, Mandela would have gone ahead anyhow; he almost contemptuously brushed aside the objections of his nominal boss in prison, Walter Sisulu, who told him, 'in principle, I am not against negotiations. But I would have wished that the government initiated talks with us rather than our initiating talks with them.'

Mandela replied that if he was 'not against negotiations in princi-ple, what did it matter who initiated them?' By agreeing to the Mandela initiative, Tambo might at least retain some influence over the prisoner at Pollsmoor. But he and his fellow ANC leaders were desperately worried. Among the hard-line Marxists at the base of the organization, there was no knowledge that Mandela was actively seeking talks with the regime. Yet there were those who regarded him as a potential traitor.

Sisulu later commented, 'I was not worried. I'd worked with Madiba [Mandela] for many years ... I knew that he is a fighter, very stubborn too. He was not going to be persuaded in a wrong way. My worry was the thinking of our people, beginning to doubt Madiba ... that he is now isolated and not a man who is ultra-leftist ... I didn't think so. I had the confidence, that he would be able to discuss and overcome whatever problems faced him.'

But Sisulu was deeply suspicious of the government's intentions. 'The idea was certainly to make him a real moderate ... He originated the discussion. When he raised it with us my line was: it may be too fast. Let the feeling come from the other side. Kathy agreed with me. All the others said no. I knew [that the government wanted to sepa-rate Mandela from Tambo]; that the reason for his separation was that he would not be influenced by any other front. They were also under-estimating the ability of the man to look at the situation. We knew that Tambo thought it was the right time for discussions.'

The need now for Tambo was some vehicle of direct contact between the ANC-in-exile and the government. Clearly Tambo could not rely on a psychologically pressurized political prisoner to negoti-ate directly as the ANC's sole representative with the South African government. Moreover, Mandela had no mandate from either the ANC's conservative elite or its radical wing, nor had had any contact with either for two decades, nor even any detailed knowledge of their activities beyond the few selected publications he had been allowed to read in prison. He was a loose cannon on the ANC ship – of such immense international and legendary domestic weight that he could potentially wreck it.

As for Tambo, he had smuggled a note to Mandela. This was brief and to the point: 'What, he wanted to know, was I discussing with the government? Oliver could not have believed that I was selling out, but he might have thought I was making an error in judgment. In fact, the tenor of his note suggested that ... I replied to Oliver in a very terse letter saying that I was talking to the government about one thing only: a meeting between the national executive of the ANC and the South African government.' Thus was the real, day-to-day leader of the ANC acidly slapped down by a colleague sufferingly detached from the struggle.

Any separate agreement would have to be rejected by the ANC high command in Lusaka. Then the Pretoria regime would be able to claim that the world's foremost political prisoner was prepared to accede to a negotiated settlement while the ANC 'terrorists' had rejected one.

Tambo now had to open his own channel of communication to Pretoria. But how could he? The government flatly rejected negotiations with 'communists and terrorists'. Anyone seeking such negotiations was considered not just a traitor by the white establishment; he was liable to have his passport withdrawn and be treated as a criminal. There was no contact of any kind between the ANC high command and white South Africa; they were enemies, at war. ANC leaders were liable to be killed if they encountered official Afrikaners.

* * *

For Tambo the prospect at the beginning of 1986 was dire in the extreme: the Botha government had clearly initiated an attempt to detach Mandela from the ANC outside South Africa; which the prisoner of destiny, seeing his moment of history slipping away, was disposed to play along with. Meanwhile the armed forces continued to keep the guerrillas at bay. Tambo knew this could not but increase the resistance to the regime.

As the struggle intensified, and hostility grew on both sides, the extremist, Marxist wing of the ANC would be strengthened and power would ebb away from the old 'historical' leaders. South Africa could then slide into a real war involving possibly millions of lives. The armed forces on one side were too strong, the numbers on the other too overwhelming for it not to be protracted and bitter.

Few men on earth could have been as apprehensive as Tambo at the beginning of 1986, the watershed year in South Africa's history. He desperately wanted to talk to the other side. But there was no one to talk to.

He could little have suspected that a conduit would shortly present itself in the shape of one of Britain's best-known conservative international business concerns with major interests in South Africa; or that, on the Afrikaner side, there were those who despaired of Botha's primitive divide-and-rule approach and recognized that any deal that did not involve the ANC outside South Africa – which, loosely, controlled both the guerrilla offensive and the more peaceful UDF political umbrella front – would be no deal at all.

Mandela was one extremely strong-willed man in prison. The ANC consisted of hundreds of thousands of guerrillas, activists and supporters. To secure peace in South Africa, the government would need the agreement of the latter, not the former.

11
Punch, Counterpunch

The ferocity of Botha's repression was probably what permitted the government to survive the fraught summer of 1985–6. By autumn, with the visit of the 'Eminent Persons' Group', established by the Commonwealth in a last-ditch attempt to avoid the imposition of comprehensive and mandatory sanctions, Botha was just beginning to feel hope that he could ride out the storm. In March he lifted the state of emergency, during which 750 people had died and 8,000 had been arrested. In May he effectively scuppered the Commonwealth initiative through his raids on Botswana, Zambia and Zimbabwe. A month later he reimposed the state of emergency more savagely than ever before. Hundreds were detained, journalists were banned from reporting in areas of unrest, and sweeping powers were introduced to ban opposition activity.

A senior Afrikaner observed that in this, Afrikanerdom's greatest crisis since the Boer War, the behaviour of its leader was nothing if not erratic: 'Botha was a strange man. Chris Heunis [the architect of the constitutional reform] was the President's closest adviser. Up until about 1983 there was method in his madness. After that a kind of Madness of President Botha – like the Madness of King George – gripped him, which had nothing to do with the stroke he eventually suffered. He kept reinventing himself.'

One constant trend of Botha's rule was his increasing isolation, which was connected with the crisis in South Africa. As the emergency deepened, as the country became a police state increasingly in the hands of the security forces, so he dispensed with his democratic power base. The former defence minister ruled through the security council, rather than the cabinet or parliament. A National Security Management System was set up, comprising 12 Joint Management

Centres in major cities; beneath them were 60 JMC subcentres and more than 400 mini-JMCs; this was part of the 'total strategy' reply to the 'total onslaught' strategy of the ANC.

In effect, a parallel administration of the army and police, independent of elected bodies and directly advising the president, had taken over the running of the country. South Africa had become a Latin American-style dictatorship, run by a civilian, Botha, who preferred to rule through the military with which he was thoroughly at ease. The president even evolved a philosophy of 'co-optive dominance' – giving orders directly to such groups as homeland leaders, business leaders and coloured leaders.

As the country's first executive president and commander-in-chief – not just parliamentary leader – he ruled arbitrarily, from the top down: the cabinet and parliamentary party expected to be told what to do, and to carry out his orders, not to impose their will upon him, or constrict him. In a country with a parliamentary tradition, he was its first dictator, ruling through the military. He was never happier than when ordering military actions – such as the raids into Botswana which forced the government there to tell the ANC to withdraw its bases, or the strike into Lesotho that led to the South African-backed military coup that toppled its chief, Leabua Jonathan, in January 1986 – after which the ANC representatives there were expelled. South African raids continued into Mozambique, to disrupt railways, as well as into Zimbabwe, Botswana and Zambia, to persuade those countries to withdraw their support from the ANC. Meanwhile, cautiously, South Africa continued to push into Angola and to provide support for Savimbi's UNITA movement.

In April 1986, the month after the state of emergency was lifted, Winnie Mandela, perhaps suspecting that moderate black leaders had made a private agreement with Botha to lower the political temperature, deliberately wrecked it with an inflammatory speech at Krugersdorp.

> The time of speeches and debate has come to an end ... [1986 will see] the liberation of the oppressed masses of this country. We work in the white man's kitchen. We bring up the white man's children. We could have killed them at any time we wanted to. Together, hand in hand, with our sticks and our matches, with our necklaces, we shall liberate this country.

At that time, 'necklacing', filling rubber tyres with petrol, jamming them over the heads of victims and pinning their arms to their bodies, then setting light to them – was spreading as a particularly vicious practice in the developing civil war in the townships. Winnie's call to arms was followed by mass boycotts of white shops. Blacks were intimidated by having cooking oil poured down their throats if they bought white goods, which were confiscated if found. It seemed that the furies had flared up again as soon as the state of emergency was lifted. The Crossroads squatter camp became the scene of serious fighting and house burning. Some 30,000 people were left homeless in a few days. Vigilante attacks broke out against ANC supporters – and there were strong suspicions that the government was behind them in an attempt to force the move to the new Khayelitsha black township. In Alexandra township near Johannesburg, violent clashes erupted between ANC supporters and the security forces.

Mbeki, then visiting London, made it clear that terrorism against innocents was not the policy of the external ANC. In response to a question from Sir Jim Lester MP he said:

> First of all, there is the very clear position of the leadership of the ANC that we should not carry out military operations against civilians, whether black or white; secondly, that none the less, despite that, in the conduct of military operations you could never guarantee that there would not be civilian casualties. It can happen, regrettably, but you cannot honestly and genuinely say you are conducting a military struggle and expect there not to be civilian casualties. That must not, however, be the object of the attack, that you plan an operation against civilians.
>
> Certainly, therefore, in the light of the worsening situation in the country the leadership of the ANC has said to the leadership of our army that they should stick to the position of not going for civilian casualties, but that it cannot be the absolute rule that you cannot attack an army barracks with 200 men because one civilian is going to be hurt. The particular operation that is referred to in 1983, of course, is the one at the South African Air Force Headquarters, but the majority of the people who were killed or injured in that were army/air force officers. Even the Botha regime, in the end, could not deny that; but certainly there were civilian casualties also. You could, therefore, say that operation, and others since then, have had that element of having to accept the necessity for civilian casualties.

* * *

By the winter of 1986, Botha, for the first time in 18 months, was beginning to feel confident again. The country was still in turmoil, but under the ferocity of the repression, the wave of protest was beginning to buckle. He believed he had turned the tide through keeping a steady nerve. The wave of revolution was receding.

He could even afford to proceed with his gradual political reform. Hotels and restaurants were allowed to serve all races, blacks were permitted to set up businesses in city centres. Africans were granted freehold property rights in townships outside 'white' cities. These might have seemed piffling reforms in the face of a revolution; but they also marked the continuing collapse of the whole elaborate structure of apartheid. Apartheid was crumbling; white rule was not yet dead.

At about the same time Mandela sought, and secured, a second meeting with Kobie Coetsee in prison, and Young agreed to Tambo's request to set up a direct channel of communication between the ANC high command and the Afrikaner community. Both Mandela and Tambo had been deeply sobered by what seemed to be a black revolution getting out of control: the euphoria of the year before had gone.

The blacks, spear-headed by Winnie, had threatened to surge forward and stage an uncontrollable revolution that would sweep away elders like Mandela, Sisulu and Tambo; the whites meanwhile had responded with savagery and were not about to be overthrown. If the blacks kept up the pressure there would be no alternative to an appalling and prolonged racial war which the blacks, to begin with, could not win. Equally, for all their bravura, the whites regarded the prospect of civil war with dismay, knowing that in the long run they could not prevail.

An extraordinary dialogue was now about to begin: the black moderates needed the whites to douse the revolutionary brushfire before it got out of control and burnt moderate whites and blacks alike; the whites needed moderate black support to restrain their followers – in exchange for a recognition that majority rule would eventually be installed. As Sampie Terreblanche, an outspoken Afrikaner critic of Botha's, put it, 'The two sides would only get around the table if both were on their knees. The National Party was on its knees; and the ANC was fired up by the winter of 1986 – they were keen for results, which had not materialized after a year of ferocious struggle. They were a bit desperate.'

With apartheid all but in ruins, Botha was still veering away from the inevitable endgame: direct negotiations about a possible transfer of power. His idea of a National Statutory Council for Africans as a constitutional chamber was stillborn; they wanted nothing short of majority rule. Botha is said to have told close associates that he would not be the man to give them majority rule – as though he knew already that the game, in practice, was up.

Behind the mantle of censorship, repression was vigorously enforced through the second half of 1986. After the new state of emergency was imposed, resistance continued: on 11 June, the anniversary of the Soweto riots, more than two-thirds of black workers downed tools. The following day Cosatu held a one-day strike throughout the Transvaal and Eastern Cape. The consumer boycott was supplemented by a rent boycott.

Meanwhile, behind the cloak of censorship, the security forces continued to strike back hard: some 20,000 people had been detained by the end of August, about 3,000 of them under the age of 18. Under the government's iron hand, the violence and bloodshed began slowly to abate in the summer of 1986–7. It seemed that once again the government was regaining control, and that the ANC had overreached itself. In the early months of 1987, South Africa seemed to be settling into a long, grim war of attrition with neither side willing to give way, but the ambitions of the ANC checked for the moment.

Cyril Ramaphosa told the author that the first moment he felt 'it was possible to have freedom in our lifetime' was during the mineworkers' strike in 1987, which lasted 21 days. 'We felt the power surging in our veins, and felt it was possible.' But he is certain that 1987 was the wrong moment – a remarkable and surprising admission for the most powerful leader of the internal resistance. 'The combination of forces wasn't right – we would have snatched defeat from the jaws of victory.'

Mandela attempted to resume his blocked channel of communication in June 1986, the same month that the state of emergency was declared, on the grounds that 'often the most discouraging moments are precisely the time to launch an initiative. At such times, people are seeking a way out of their dilemmas.' In a phrase he was fond of, the darkest hour of the night comes before dawn.

He requested an interview with General Willemse, the commissioner of prisons. Mandela was eventually taken to the general's residence in the grounds of Pollsmoor prison, where he asked for a further interview with Coetsee 'in order to raise the question of talks between the government and ANC'. By another of those strange, stage-managed coincidences, Coetsee was in Cape Town at that moment and could see Mandela straight away. Mandela was spirited across town with only a single police escort car.

Coetsee greeted him cordially at his residence and asked him bluntly under what conditions the ANC would suspend the armed struggle, whether Mandela spoke for the movement as a whole, and whether he would consider constitutional guarantees for minorities in the new South Africa – in particular the whites. Mandela was astonished that Coetsee should even be considering the prospect of a black-dominated South Africa.

But it was the second question that was the more important: it showed that Coetsee, at least, regarded the attempt to detach Mandela from his colleagues outside South Africa as doomed, merely a prolongation of their struggle. Mandela's adherence to a separate deal would weaken the ANC; but it would not stop the bloodshed; indeed it might intensify the fighting as the guerrillas in the field began to reject the moderation of their older leaders. Mandela asked Coetsee to relay to President Botha and the foreign minister, Pik Botha, his request for a direct meeting. Coetsee promptly agreed to do so. Nothing further happened: whatever the minister's private views, he could not prevail upon his bosses to talk.

In delightful sunny weather before Christmas, Mandela was suddenly taken out in the first of many excursions around Cape Town, as a kind of decompression process after his long years in prison. As he wrote movingly:

> It was absolutely riveting to watch the simple activities of people out in the world: old men sitting in the sun, women doing their shopping, people walking their dogs. It is precisely those mundane activities of daily life that one misses most in prison. I felt like a curious tourist in a strange and remarkable land.
>
> After an hour or so, Colonel Marx stopped the car in front of a small shop in a quiet street. 'Would you like a cold drink?' he asked. I nodded, and he disappeared inside the shop. I sat there alone. For the first few moments, I did not think about my situation, but as the seconds ticked away, I became more and more agitated. For the first time in twenty-two years, I was out in the world and unguarded. I had a vision of opening the door, jumping out, and then running and running until I was out of sight. Something inside me was urging me to do just that. I noticed a wooded area near the road where I could hide. I was extremely tense and began to perspire. Where was the colonel? But then I took control of

myself; such an action would be unwise and irresponsible, not to mention dangerous. It was possible that the whole situation was contrived to try to get me to escape, though I did not think that was the case. I was greatly relieved a few moments later when I saw the colonel walking back to the car with two cans of Coca-Cola.

But, to his intense frustration, as the fighting in the townships worsened, nothing further happened, and the weeks dragged by, then months. Coetsee began occasionally to call on Mandela again. It is not clear what was discussed, or how specific these meetings were. Mandela himself gives no clue. Deprived of any contact with him, the ANC's leaders were deeply anxious he might give the game away. Only the very occasional visit by George Bizos furnished a link between Mandela and the ANC leaders in Lusaka.

Botha now had the ideal opportunity to make concessions from a position of strength. First, though, he had to secure re-election from the whites in May, 1987. Events here again played into his hands: the previous year, Frederik Van Zyl Slabbert, leader of the moderate Progressive Federal Party, had met ANC leaders in Dakar, a move which shocked South Africa. Given levels of violence, white voters were appalled. Shortly afterwards, claiming that reform was impossible within the system, the energetic and idealistic but temperamental Slabbert resigned both the party leadership and his seat in parliament. Meanwhile three prominent National Party supporters, taking their lead from the moderate and politically astute South African ambassador in London, Denis Worrall, who found it impossible to defend the regime any more, stood against National Party candidates.

The election resulted in a resounding defeat for the Progressive Federal Party, which lost many of its English-speaking supporters to the National Party, seen now as a middle-of-the road bastion against black rule and white extremism. The Conservative Party under Treurnicht became the official opposition, picking up right-wing Afrikaner votes from the National Party. Worrall narrowly failed to defeat Chris Heunis, Botha's *éminence grise* and the powerhouse behind the limited reforms. Botha had every reason to feel satisfied: he had withstood the storm and had taken the white community with him. Now was the time to start talking to the enemy.

* * *

Shortly after the election, Botha suffered an unexpected and serious setback: in mid-1987 he had responded emotionally, and without much justification, to an appeal by his old ally Jonas Savimbi in Angola to try and stop Angolan and Cuban troops capturing the town of Mavinga in Cuando Cubango province, which they intended to use as a forward base for capturing Unita's stronghold of Jamba.

The South Africans had become used to easy victories in Angola. They were entirely unprepared for the ferocity with which the Angolans and Cubans fought back when they attacked the town of Cuito Canavala. The fighting was to rage on from September 1987 until April 1988. Nearly 500 of the enemy were killed, while the South Africans claimed only to have lost 31 men (more than 140, according to the Angolans). But an entire South African armoured division had been trapped.

At that point the South Africans decided that they were going too deeply into Angola and feared a Vietnam-like quagmire. Similarly, it seemed that the Cubans had at last had enough – and were being prodded to withdraw by the new Soviet leader, Mikhail Gorbachev. The Namibian conflict was at last coming to an end. That same year, 1987, the minister of justice, Kobie Coetsee, told Nelson Mandela that talks between him and the government would now begin. Simultaneously, the first of the meetings in Britain between ANC leaders and senior Afrikaners – at least one of whom, Willie Esterhuyse, was plugged directly into Botha's private office – began in October 1987.

12
Most Secret Conduit

The only channel of communication between the two sides, other than that between Mandela and Coetsee, was Consolidated Goldfields' Michael Young, who on Tambo's prompting had embarked on his one-man mission, showing extraordinary persistence, against a backdrop of intransigence, burning townships and wailing sirens. Young had been asked to set up a channel of contact by the real leader of the guerrilla struggle. It was rather like trying to act as an intermediary between the British and the Germans at the height of the Second World War.

As Consolidated Goldfields was treated with intense suspicion by the Afrikaner community, who regarded it as a pillar of the English community – albeit, unlike Harry Oppenheimer's Anglo-American corporation, with its liberal aspirations, a highly conservative one – this would not be easy. Moreover, any such approach risked being discovered by the South African security apparatus. He had to make a blind date with prominent Afrikaners, in secret, not knowing if he would be betrayed and sent packing by security services determined to stop contacts between the ANC and the white South Africans.

Young first sought advice from Fleur de Villiers, a former journalist and consultant for Consolidated Goldfields in Britain. The latter suggested two people as moderates within the Afrikaner establishment: Sampie Terreblanche and Willie Esterhuyse, both prominent in the University of Stellenbosch, which for decades had acted as a kind of finishing school for the South African political establishment. Terreblanche proved to be something of a disappointment: because of his known disillusionment with government policy, his contacts had grown rusty and he had few names to put forward, although he agreed to participate in the discussion.

Esterhuyse, by contrast, was enthusiastic. On the idyllic, secluded campus of the university, after long and thought-provoking discussions, he came up with a list of names he thought might be open to such an approach. Top of the list was no less a figure than Pieter de Lange, the current head of the Broederbond.

Because of Esterhuyse's introduction, de Lange received Young politely, but gave him a non-committal hearing, refusing to participate directly in talks with the ANC. It turned out that de Lange was facing re-election as chairman of the Broederbond and was fearful of prejudicing his chances by so bold a move. However, this pillar of Afrikanerdom agreed to give Young an introduction to a friend of his, the ex-Broederbond leader and minister of constitutional affairs, Gerrit Viljoen, who, he claimed, recognized the need for change. Young left the meeting not a little crestfallen: his request had been politely rejected, and his initiative might now be reported to the South African intelligence services.

Esterhuyse had next given him an introduction to Tjaart van der Walt, rector of Potchesftoom University, and closely linked to the Dutch Reformed Church. Here Young was given a warm reception, but another gentle refusal. Young's instinct was that he was being warned off by the authorities. He tried once again, approaching Johan Heynes, Moderator of the Dutch Reformed Church, the bastion of Afrikaner Christianity. He was received in the latter's spacious residence in Pretoria, listened to with attention, but told that the church could not become involved in politics.

It seemed that Young was knocking at a closed door. He returned to his hotel that evening disappointed and depressed. Next on the list was Marinus Weickers, professor of constitutional law at the University of South Africa, who had been instrumental in drafting the new national constitution then being negotiated. To Young's delight, Weickers, a much more open-minded man, responded readily and agreed to take part.

The last port of call suggested by Esterhuyse gave Young even more reason for trepidation: Willy Breytenbach, a senior civil servant who was reported to have close connections with senior members of the military establishment. Almost certainly the security forces had by this time been alerted to Young's mission; but this was to approach one of their advisers direct. To his relief and surprise, Breytenbach agreed to attend.

The young enthusiast had persuaded four senior Afrikaner intellectuals to attend the first face-to-face talks with the ANC in history.

None of them held any official role. Three were academics and one worked for the civil service. Yet it was a beginning. All were well connected; and they were prepared to meet the leaders of the 'communist and terrorist' ANC on neutral ground in Britain.

Young's worst problem lay in relaying the good news to the ANC. He decided to bypass the ANC's London office, which was thought to be heavily infiltrated by both the British and South African security services. He made contact directly with the ANC in Lusaka. However, the Lusaka telephone system was itself bugged by the South African security services as well as the Zambian ones. It soon became apparent that taps had been put in Willie Esterhuyse's phone as well.

Young and his new South African contacts began to find it difficult to talk directly over the lines: they would have to wait for the meeting itself. The main concern was not that the South African government itself might object to the proposed talks, but that their allies in the security services would – and might seek to sabotage them by underhand means. The risk for all was considerable: their professional reputations, their liberty, and conceivably their lives might be at stake.

* * *

The Compleat Angler at Marlow, in England, is the kind of delightful, quaint, olde-English rustic retreat now largely overwhelmed by large-girthed Americans out spotting that increasingly rare English breed – a brace of Agatha Christie old ladies in tweeds, buttoned up blouses and sensible shoes, plotting to strip ungrateful relatives of their inheritances. The hotel was also ideally suited for Young's purposes in organizing the first-ever meeting between senior Afrikaners with government connections and exiled ANC leaders: it was the most improbable place conceivable for such a venue – and the talks had 'above all to be secret' to protect both sides.

There, on a pleasant October morning in 1987, in what Terreblanche describes as a 'secret cellar room' overlooking a weir with swans dabbling picturesquely in the water, the three white South Africans – Esterhuyse, Terreblanche and Breytenbach (Weickers did not attend after all) – met the ANC delegation headed by Aziz Pahad, head of the ANC's London office, Harold Walpe, an avowed Marxist, and Tony Trew. All three were senior members of the national executive (the 'higher organ', as it was somewhat comically called).

Young says that there were 'enormous tensions' as they met for the first time. 'It was like the Pope shaking hands with the devil.' They sat down at the small table. Conversation was tense and disjointed, and Young had to be 'forceful' in controlling the discussion. More than mere politics and race divided them. The whites were well-heeled, well-fed, at ease with their surroundings. Pahad, living in North London, was the most urbane of the ANC members. They were poorly dressed and fed after years of living life on a shoestring as political exiles. The Americans and old ladies sipping tea looked askance as the delegates entered the hotel.

Within a day, both concur, the two sides had noticeably relaxed. They found there was much more to talk about than they had expected. Neither was unreasonable; instead they proceeded to find common ground. Young ensured that the discussions were deliberately vague, and ranged over major issues without touching on specifics, each side seeking to understand at roughly what point the other conceived South African history to have arrived. Their only conclusion was that they must meet again at a senior level, and with a more specific agenda. Almost certainly both sides saw this as the beginning of a secret negotiation, but neither acknowledged as much. There is no written record of the meeting – in keeping with its secret and tentative nature.

The participants, before arrival in London, had been given no idea of the venue. These precautions were shown to be necessary. Young was soon aware that he was being followed, usually from his office, and sometimes being watched outside his home by a man 'in a trench coat' – such was the crudeness of the Bureau of State Security. Young owned a hotel in London and lived in a flat opposite. He was sure that his watchers were trying to make it clear they were present, to intimidate him. They parked a car opposite the hotel and would stare at his apartment, occasionally changing the vehicle's position. His three tails took it in shifts, taking photographs and generally making themselves visible. They observed that on one occasion Helen Suzman, South Africa's veteran liberal leader and an old friend of Young's, visited the hotel. Young says he eventually informed 'Lynda Chalker about this and their actions ceased' – presumably after discreet protests from the British government to the South Africans. He was careful on the telephone in case his lines were tapped, although he had no firm evidence of this. He found the surveillance 'disquieting and physically threatening'. When in South Africa, he was to receive menacing telephone calls – 'we know what you're up to' – which concerned him.

Esterhuyse received actual threats on his return and was given instruction by security officials on how to look under his car for bombs. Over the next three years, the need for vigilance remained constant: in 1988, when Esterhuyse met Mbeki for a private meeting in Michael Young's office at British American Tobacco, the Stellenbosch academic signalled to the ANC leader that the room was bugged, and they had to adjourn to the Prince Albert pub next door.

* * *

That had been a first encounter between ANC leaders and senior Afrikaners. After the initial tension, these men, who up to then had regarded each other as murderer and oppressor respectively, and whose followers had been geared up to fight to the death back home, had been pleasantly surprised by the basic reasonableness of the other side. But what had actually been achieved? Handshakes and the discovery that the others were human after all in the comforting glow of a small English hotel in mid-winter, so different from their homeland in midsummer. A significant measure of common ground between strikingly opposed political positions.

Young could point to nothing specific. But that, to him, had not been the intention. Just the fact of the meeting was enough. He flew back to South Africa in late November 1987, uncertain as to how he would be received by the authorities, who now knew of the talks. But he was undisturbed as he went about his business. There he found that Esterhuyse had done something quite astonishing. He had approached Dr Neil Barnard, director-general of the National Intelligence Service – South Africa's equivalent of the CIA – and told him of his Marlow meeting.

That Botha, who bitterly opposed any private contacts with the ANC, now knew of Young's mission was certain; that he accepted that the talks should continue was extraordinary; that the Old Crocodile would himself give the talks his imprimatur was astonishing. The truth was that government policy, since the reimposition of the state of emergency 17 months before, had been leading South Africa only to racial conflagration; and the Afrikaners needed a way out. The president had decided to talk: cautiously, secretly, indirectly. The government had to determine whether or not the external ANC – the most important party to the talks – was commanded by reasonable men after all – contrary to decades of the government's own propaganda; and whether the leadership could deliver the men in the field.

Even Botha had accepted that it was necessary to explore a way out of the war (on, of course, his own terms). Even he had accepted that it was not enough to seek to prise Mandela away from the mainstream movement, because he could not deliver peace either in the country or in the townships. Instead, the strategy had changed: Mandela's symbolic importance and qualities of leadership might be used to blunt the terms demanded by the ANC radicals – but not to split the movement.

Esterhuyse's description to Young of his conversation with Barnard was a trifle disingenuous. Barnard had asked to see Esterhuyse on his return, knowing full well about the meeting from the telephone tapping, if no other source: 'He told me the government wanted an informal contact with the ANC and he asked whether I would be willing to report to him on the discussions we were going to have.' He wanted to be kept informed of the talks. To Esterhuyse's relief, he realized he was being asked to act as an informer, but agreed to do so if he could tell the senior ANC people present. Mbeki was later to confirm that Esterhuyse kept his promise: 'He squared with me right at the beginning. I knew all along that he was talking to Barnard – and that Barnard was reporting to P. W. Botha.'

In fact the ANC side was secretly delighted: they would not just be just talking to a group of disaffected Afrikaner intellectuals, but indirectly to the government itself. A channel had been opened up to the very pinnacle of the whole, fearsome repressive apparatus in South Africa – to President Botha and his shadowy intelligence chief. The next talks would not just be a tense exchange of pleasantries after all, but hard negotiations on the main issues concerned, at just one remove, at the highest level between the two sides.

For the ANC this was a splendid prize – the opportunity for the men who actively commanded the guerrillas to talk to the enemy. The risks of the guerrillas in the field finding out what their leaders were doing were great. But the risks were even greater for Barnard, and it must be conceded, for Botha himself: if news of the talks leaked out, the entire credibility of his tough-minded approach would be undermined. By working through intermediaries, of course, the South African government could quickly disown them in the event of discovery; but the connection might leak out, because the ANC side had been told of it by Esterhuyse.

The success of this frail line of communication depended absolutely on secrecy; and that had to be not the least of Young's concerns, as the talks' compere. For him the news that Botha himself had secretly approved the talks was a massive breakthrough. From that tiny beginning at Marlow, real negotiations were now possible between sworn enemies. The flag of truce had been raised in the unlikely setting of the countryside of the south of England.

Now Young would have to ensure that, in particular, news of these improbable gatherings did not reach the lower echelons of the formidable South African security apparatus, which was infested with diehard Afrikaners who would have been appalled by the action of their boss, Barnard, and even of Botha. Young's sense of achievement was further enhanced when Van der Walt, who had refused to attend the first time, expressed support for the initiative, as did Naas Steinkam, president of the Council of Mines, an extremely prominent representative of the South African business community, and Marinus Weickers, professor of constitutional law at the University of South Africa. De Lange meanwhile was this time much warmer in receiving Young, while still refusing to attend for electoral reasons. The Afrikaner establishment had at last approved the process – now that Botha had given it the nod.

* * *

What Young did not know was that the government had decided to embark on parallel talks with Mandela. Astonishingly, the prisoner, after his two talks with Coetsee, decided not to inform his colleagues in the ANC abroad; as he admitted frankly: 'sometimes it is necessary to present one's colleagues with a policy that is already a fait accompli'. He had been asked to negotiate directly with a committee consisting of Coetsee, Willemse, Fanie van der Merwe, director general of the prisons department – and the ubiquitous Barnard, with the full knowledge of President Botha.

Mandela was, for once, embarrassed. 'I could justify to my organization discussions with the other officials, but not Barnard. His presence made the talks more problematic and suggested a larger agenda.' The others were all involved with the prison system, so Mandela could claim that all he had been doing was discussing prison conditions. But Barnard was the head of South Africa's equivalent of the CIA, and was also involved with military intelligence.

He slept on the problem and the following morning agreed to Barnard's presence on the grounds that he was a key player on the State Security Council 'and was said to be a protégé of the president. I thought that my refusing to see Barnard would alienate Botha, and decided that such a tack was too risky. If the state president was not brought on board, nothing would happen.'

Mandela sought a meeting with his four Pollsmoor colleagues. The government, alarmed lest he be dissuaded by them, refused – even though he had said he was prepared to talk directly with four senior South African officials. Eventually they permitted Mandela to see the prisoners one by one. Mandela vaguely told each that he was preparing to talk to the government, without informing them he would be facing an extraordinarily high-level group, one plugged directly into the president's office.

Walter Sisulu grumbled. Raymond Mhlaba and Andrew Mlangeni were in favour. The fourth, Kathy, was vehemently opposed. Tambo's objections, which were smuggled into Mandela from outside, he brushed angrily aside. The man of destiny was not going to be inhibited by anything so minor as the views of his colleagues.

He was confident he could take on the best brains in the South African government and out-negotiate them. He did not know that another channel of communication had been set up, with the ANC as a whole, in parallel to his talks, watched over by the same man, Barnard, with the president's approval. When they met for the first time, Mandela found Barnard 'exceptionally bright, a man of controlled intelligence and self-discipline.'

* * *

Between the first encounter at the Compleat Angler and the next, at Eastwell Manor in Kent in February, 1988, South Africa was relatively quiescent. Black power had been worn down by the sheer economic need to continue daily life. Many of the townships were no-go areas. In Pietermaritzburg and other parts of Kwazulu-Natal, fierce fighting broke out between UDF supporters and supporters of Inkatha. A compromise was being reached between the government and the unions over the proposed Labour Relations Amendment Act. But the pressure for the moment was off.

South Africa began to return to a semblance of normality. Botha had been given the breathing space necessary to try and advance the country towards a settlement without pressure from internal unrest, violence, international outrage and white panic pressing down on him quite so strongly. In this climate a first, gentle gesture was made by the government in November: the release of Govan Mbeki, one of the most famous and hardline of the Rivonia trialists and a frequent critic of Mandela in jail. He remained banned from political activity. His son was the external ANC's deputy leader, Thabo Mbeki.

The ANC itself held a conference in Tanzania to mark its 75th anniversary, which was attended by delegates from more than 50 countries. Tambo declared that the armed struggle would now intensify. Against this more peaceful background (although one more worrying for the ANC) the second encounter between Afrikaner and ANC leaders in exile took place – just three months before Mandela was sucked directly into negotiations with senior government officials. The Eastwell Manor meeting was held against the inauspicious background of a sudden ban by the government on 17 anti-apartheid organizations, including the UDF. Cosatu was barred from engaging in any non-trade union activity. The government was growing bolder. Botha felt he was in control of events again.

Between 21 and 24 February 1988, in the grand surroundings of the Eastwell Manor Hotel, Kent, England, Young welcomed the two delegations to what were to become the first direct negotiations between the ANC and the Afrikaners. This time the ANC players were drawn from the very top: Thabo Mbeki, regarded as Tambo's likely successor and director of information of the ANC, headed their team, which otherwise consisted of the three others who had attended the meeting at the Compleat Angler. Esterhuyse was the white delegation leader once again, accompanied by the two prominent academics as well as, for the first time, Weickers, the constitutional expert, and Willem Pretorius, representing business interests.

The initial atmosphere was much less tense: the two sides showed more business-like courtesy than defensiveness in outlining their respective positions. 'It was terribly cold. We had to huddle around the fire close together with whisky,' said one. Both sides went through the ritual of denying that they had any mandate to negotiate; and both sides proceeded to do just that, but on the broadest and most central theme. Young's rather broad framework was entitled 'creating the climate for change', but the subjects they tried to find some common ground upon were anything but bland.

First, though, the Afrikaner side embarked on a small and rather comical face-saving exercise. The government could not relax its requirement that the ANC declare a cessation of violence before a dialogue could begin – and this, of course, was not a dialogue. But the authorities realized that the ANC alone could not end the violence, particularly in Pietermaritzburg, between the different black communities. Therefore, the government was prepared for a dialogue without a cessation of ANC violence. They had given up one of their most crucial conditions – while still pretending that they had not, and that this was not a negotiation, for public consumption, should news of the talks leak out.

Mbeki, surprised and pleased and refraining from making capital out of this concession, then outlined the core demands not just of the ANC but of all black organizations in South Africa: the release of political prisoners and the unbanning of proscribed organizations. The Afrikaners retorted that although the government understood this, it was nervous of the right-wing Conservative Party sharply increasing its support if such action were taken.

Mbeki then made two significant proposals obviously approved by the ANC leadership in advance. He argued that the right would only be strengthened if rioting and disorder accompanied the release of political prisoners; if ANC leaders were allowed back into the country to control their followers, there would be no rioting or disorder. Alternatively, if the government continued to reject the idea of ANC leaders returning to South Africa for fear this would provoke the Conservatives, then his father, Govan, at 78 the oldest of the ANC leaders and in fact a Communist, who was about to be released, would mediate to ensure there was calm. The ANC side emphasized that it believed that, as the banning orders were revoked and political prisoners released, things would get calmer anyway.

In fact, they were making their own concession of principle: they could not budge from the attitude that they would not order a cessation of violence in exchange for the release of political prisoners; but they were tacitly offering a diminution of violence in return for the release. The choice of Govan Mbeki was an interesting one: once released, he would enjoy a prestige no other opposition leader inside South Africa possessed. Moreover he had the impeccable militant credentials needed to calm the black radicals.

The risk was that he might prove unacceptable to the whites; he himself was bitterly opposed to any dialogue. Indeed he had quarrelled with Mandela just a few weeks before the Eastwell Manor meeting, when the latter visited him in prison to tell the grizzled old man of his impending release and to admit that he was having talks with the government. As the veteran Communist complained, 'I was not very happy about the fact that he seemed either not to have sufficient confidence in me to tell me the full story, or, alternatively, that the other side might have come to some arrangement with him which he felt he couldn't break.'

Yet Thabo Mbeki clearly believed his father alone would have the authority to calm the township radicals if the Lusaka leadership was kept out. There may have been another motive: to suggest that the ANC leadership abroad had more faith in the old man than in Mandela himself; indeed, perhaps, as a blatant power play, he imposed the external moderates on the negotiating process, in place of either Mandela or the internal radicals. Either way, it was hardly a suggestion to please the whites. As Young remarks with understatement, 'It was clear to me that the exchanges concealed much mistrust as to motives.'

Esterhuyse and the whites, with equal civility, asked what the ANC would do in exchange for this major concession: for example, they asked, not unreasonably, whether they would recommend the resumption of international sporting links. Mbeki hedged: he would consider this. It was a stand-off, with both sides agreeing to take account of the others' points of view.

The discussions moved on to a long exposition of the ANC's political views, with the whites probing in detail to see how radical they really were. The suave Mbeki was not at any stage discouraged, even though he knew the movement was on trial for its moderation: the ANC believed in multi-party democracy; they were an organization of both black and white supporters; they would not give ground on the subject of nationalization – always a bugbear for white South Africa – but would take decisions on the subject democratically.

The white side listened, and was only partly satisfied. Esterhuyse and the others suggested the ANC should tone down the concept of 'one man, one vote, in a unitary state' – the core demand – as this would alarm the whites. If this infuriated the ANC delegates, they did not show it, staying silent. Somewhat patronizingly, the whites suggested the ANC should soften their stance on multi-party democracy.

* * *

After these somewhat strained exchanges, the discussion took a remarkable turn which had ANC members sitting on the edges of their seats: for the first time the whites quite openly began to discuss the nature of the relationship between the military and civil powers in South Africa. Esterhuyse quietly told them that he believed Botha would retire in about two years' time. This would create a major shift. The president had increasingly been governing through his state security council – a kitchen cabinet of top ministers and senior military, intelligence and police advisers – bypassing the constitutional organs of the state, the cabinet and parliament.

The military, as Young explained in his report of the meeting, 'believed that the politicians are not doing enough and must do more'. They wanted the politicians to do 80 per cent of the work, and themselves only 20 per cent. This was a consequence of the fact that the army, in the front line, had been relentlessly exposed to take the brunt of the government's enforcement of hardline policies. The military were holding their own, but only just, at a great cost in casualties. It was now the turn for a political solution. As Young reports, the Afrikaners considered that 'there is a body of opinion within the military which argued for the release of political prisoners, unbanning the ANC and others and ending the state of emergency'.

However, the army's views were not shared by the police – poorly educated, brutalized, patrolling the dangerous townships; the security police were only slightly more sensitive. The ANC – the Afrikaners' 'terrorist enemy' – were open-mouthed at this analysis of the divisions of their opponents. Once again, the ice had been broken, the suspicions receded.

The conversation moved relentlessly on to the subject of Botha's latest proposal for power-sharing, the National Statutory Body, which was regarded as a way of bringing blacks into the existing decision-making process involving coloureds and Indians: they had been excluded from the tricameral parliament, something Botha now regarded as a mistake. This gnawed at the very heart of black consciousness, but Mbeki was entirely smooth and unflappable in pointing out that it was unacceptable, as it left the government in voting control of the new body and thus determining the shape of South Africa's future constitution. Anyway, the 'body' would be required to report to parliament, from which the blacks were excluded.

The whites had no reply to this; and Young quickly moved the discussion on to a subject which encapsulated the genuine concerns of the whites, and in particular their personal security, as well as their language, culture and religion. One of those present eloquently outlined the fears of this defensive, stubborn people:

There are those who will not contemplate any change because by so doing they will be surrendering their privileges. The skilled and unskilled white work force will know that Africanization will mean job losses, not least in the overblown civil service. The whites generally look at the post-colonial experience of countries to their north and note that 'civilization' crumbles when Africans take over – roads deteriorate, electricity supplies become irregular and so forth. These the whites see as rights.

Further, many worry about their physical safety in the event of a black government. They fear that the blacks will retaliate and become violent once they have the upper hand. They know that a black administration will disturb the equilibrium in power terms between political, economic and military power.

They would tolerate a situation in which no group had complete control over the political, economic and military structure, but this would clearly fall short of what black people regard as implicit in the concept of majority rule. The propaganda of the right has worked to the extent that whites regard black government as meaning the establishment of a Marxist regime where conventional standards would fall, language and culture disappear, human rights be removed and a population explosion ensue which swamps the white minority.

Mbeki could have retorted, if he had been a lesser man, that those fears were only too justified after a century of oppression.

Instead, he listened closely and replied quietly that universal suffrage and multi-party democracy were fundamental to the ANC. He also expressed the view – misleadingly as it turned out, but he believed it at the time – that the ANC was not a party but an umbrella organization which would disintegrate into several different parties as soon as political freedom was established in South Africa. Mbeki accepted that the old apartheid system of homelands would have to go, but that provincial and regional governments would need to be established to protect local identity.

He tried to reassure the whites that any changes would be gradual, and that one of the ANC's priorities was a booming economy – which, he implied, could only be achieved through white cooperation and in the context of a mixed economy. He pointed out once again that white fears derived at least in part from the fact that the ANC could not beam its message into South Africa and reassure white people. He welcomed the BBC's decision to target South Africa with its news programme via satellite as a way of relieving white fears. He acknowledged that ANC spokesmen should be more moderate and temperate in their choice of words, but claimed that South African government propaganda distorted or even invented extracts from ANC officials.

This eloquent, measured response won the respect of all around the table. Young gently moved the two sides on to the issue of 'black-on-black' violence. There was complete agreement that this must come to an end, and the Afrikaners astonishingly and candidly acknowledged the role of the security police in encouraging violence and preventing mediation from outside.

Young then crisply summarized the three main conclusions of the meeting: that the ANC would go back and consider what concessions it could offer in exchange for the release of political prisoners; that the mechanics for a controlled and orderly release of political prisoners had been explored by both sides; and that they would meet again as soon as July, possibly, with a direct emissary of President Botha present.

It had been a marathon session, achieving far more than the terse conclusion suggested. For the first time the government had abandoned its precondition of an end to ANC violence for negotiating with the movement – although it would not announce this publicly. The ANC had hinted that violence would indeed diminish if political prisoners were released – although of course there was no formal link. And the ANC had also at last agreed to address the issue of 'white fears' – which was shorthand for white guarantees, a concept that diluted, if it did not contradict, the principle of pure majority rule. The Afrikaner side as good as accepted the ANC demand for a release of political prisoners – provided this was accompanied by a face-saver.

Thus the white side had made two concessions to the ANC's two. Mbeki had also gone a long way to erase the image of the ANC as viscerally committed to violence, or even as a particularly left-wing organization. The whites had been extraordinarily candid about the difficulties they faced from their hard-liners, as well as the divisions within the security forces.

The meeting was also for the first time characterized by intimate contacts distinct from the formal negotiations. Young had carefully set aside long periods for informal discussions. The most important channel was directly between Esterhuyse, reporting back to Barnard and Botha, and Mbeki, reporting back to Tambo. As Mbeki said, 'he [Esterhuyse] would come to me and say, "Look, these matters – this, that and the other – are of concern to the government. Can you get a sense from your people what their views are on these matters?" ... He squared with me right at the beginning. I knew all along that he was talking to Barnard and that Barnard was reporting to P. W. Botha.'

Mbeki would then seek specific information and authorization from his ANC colleagues in Lusaka, and convey the answers back to Esterhuyse at the next meeting. The negotiations could hardly have been more direct, although they were not labelled negotiations as such, and were secret. The process had begun.

* * *

The exchanges, while always polite, were not as free of clashes as the personalities involved suggest. Young had found himself wholly at ease with Pahad from the time of the Marlow meeting. At Eastwell Manor, the supremely self-confident Mbeki resisted Young's attempts to lead the discussions. The agenda for the meeting had been carefully prepared by Esterhuyse for the whites and Pahad for the blacks. More than once Mbeki interrupted Young as he sought to move the discussions on, 'You must realize this is not your agenda. This is our agenda.'

Young retorted cooly, 'I must ensure balance in the process. Do you understand that?' Mbeki would relent good-naturedly. Young comments that Mbeki, clad in his cardigan and puffing a pipe at Eastwell Manor, behaved 'like a prime minister in the first meeting he attended and like a monarch in the second [at Mells Park]'. This was unsurprising: with the support of the Soviet leader, Mikhail Gorbachev, Mbeki was almost *de facto* leader of the ANC as the authority of the ailing Tambo began to slip. When disagreeing with Esterhuyse, he would politely say, 'I've got a problem.' Nevertheless, after a number of fireside whisky drinks, he and Esterhuyse were by the end embracing.

Young, who was always critical of Mbeki's notorious lack of punctuality, insisted on not keeping 'African time', and was equally precise in trying to tie the two sides to specific conclusions so there could be no misunderstanding. 'Is this what we're saying?' became a constant refrain.

13
The Mandela Imperative

Parallel to the talks in Britain, without Young's knowledge, the secret conversations between Mandela and the negotiating group at Pollsmoor had at last begun. It is possible that none of the participants at Eastwell Manor knew of these exchanges. Yet word of them was soon to reach Tambo directly from Mandela via his lawyer, George Bizos – although not of course of their content. Mbeki was certainly to learn of their existence that summer. Esterhuyse, in close contact with Barnard, may also have learnt of them. Neither Young nor the others were to know until later.

But the only two men who were aware of the full content of both sets of negotiations were Barnard himself and the man he reported directly back to, P. W. Botha. The two, at the summit of the totalitarian structure of the South African state, had very precisely laid down the exact agenda for both sets of talks – which was exactly the same. Just as at Eastwell Manor the four principal elements addressed had been the cessation of violence, the ANC demand for majority rule, the fears about the ANC's reputation for radicalism and the addressing of white minority concerns for their own rights and cultures, so the themes addressed with Mandela were, in his words: 'the armed struggle, the ANC's alliance with the Communist party, the goal of majority rule, and the idea of racial reconciliation'.

The same man being briefed on the talks with the ANC by Esterhuyse, Neil Barnard, was one of the four men talking directly with Mandela across a table in prison. But the demands being put by Mandela's four interlocutors – Van der Merwe representing the civil service, Willemse representing the security forces, Coetsee representing the politicians, and Barnard the president himself – were significantly harsher than the conciliatory line adopted at Eastwell

Manor. The Mandela talks were almost brutally frank, with the government side, beneath a veneer of politeness, acting in the role of inquisitors, and the prisoner fighting back with all the imagination, strength of character and calmness the man possessed.

The government's strategy was clear: to compel Mandela to take a gradually more moderate negotiating stance than his colleagues in Britain, and then to confront the latter with a *fait accompli*: unless they made similar concessions, a separate deal would be announced with Mandela. There is no evidence that at this stage he had any idea that parallel talks were taking place between the government and the ANC in exile – or that he would have pursued his own private negotiations if he had known. He believed he was alone in initiating a dialogue – his was the only chance of reaching a peace in South Africa and avoiding racial war. He had been duped into believing so, and had thus fallen into the government's trap.

The government had been coldly cynical in misleading him to believe that no negotiations with the ANC – as distinct from Mandela – were possible without a prior cessation of violence, when in fact such negotiations were already under way in Britain, where the condition had privately been dropped! Mandela believed he was the only channel. Even more duplicitously, in fact, the very issue that dominated the first few months of the talks with Mandela was the cessation of violence as a precondition, permitting the government side to spin out the talks on a point which they had already privately conceded.

The first issue to arise was in many ways the most crucial, and that was the armed struggle. We spent a number of months discussing it. They insisted that the ANC must renounce violence and give up the armed struggle before the government would agree to negotiations – and before I could meet President Botha. Their contention was that violence was nothing more than criminal behaviour that could not be tolerated by the state.

I responded that the state was responsible for the violence and that it was always the oppressor, not the oppressed, who dictates the form of the struggle. If the oppressor uses violence, the oppressed have no alternative but to respond violently. In our case it was simply a legitimate form of self-defence. I ventured that if the state decided to use peaceful methods, the ANC would also use peaceful methods. 'It is up to you', he said, 'not us, to renounce violence.'

Coetsee and Barnard retorted that the government would lose credibility if it suddenly started negotiating with the ANC after so long refusing to do so unless it first renounced violence. Mandela rejoined evenly that this was a problem of the government's own making. 'It is not my job to resolve your dilemma for you.' In fact, the talks were already secretly under way. Coetsee and Barnard were clearly seeking a public declaration from Mandela that he would urge the ANC to renounce the armed struggle – with which they could then embarrass the ANC negotiators in Britain.

To his immense credit, Mandela would not be intimidated. But he had unwittingly been lured into a very dangerous game: playing chess blindfolded against four opponents – blindfolded, because all four had access to much greater information than he had in ignorance that a similar game was being played elsewhere. Moreover, he was under the psychological pressure of being a prisoner, in effect in solitary detention, in a damp and uncomfortable prison cell.

Although the venue itself was the relatively comfortable officers' club at Pollsmoor – presumably for the convenience of the whites rather than Mandela – the talks were disorientating and irregular, probably deliberately so, with the government calling the shots. 'I met them almost every week for a few months, and then the meetings occurred at irregular intervals, so sometimes not for a month, and then suddenly every week. The meetings were usually scheduled by the government, but sometimes I would request a session.'

The second issue addressed at Pollsmoor was the ANC's relationship with the Communist Party and its supposedly socialist views. The four men treated Mandela brusquely, in stark contrast to the polite tone adopted by Esterhuyse and his colleagues at Eastwell Manor and later Mells Park. They alleged that white and Indian Communists were the real power behind the ANC.

It is hard to judge whether the whites – and all four men were intelligent, even liberal members of the Afrikaner establishment – were just mouthing propaganda to spin out the talks in order to weary Mandela into submission, or whether they really believed this. Charitably, he thinks the latter: 'they were the victims of so much propaganda that it was necessary to straighten them out about certain facts. Even Barnard, who had made a study of the ANC, had received most of his information from police and intelligence files, which were in the main inaccurate, and sullied by the prejudices of the men who had gathered them. He could not help but be infected by the same biases.'

It is hard to believe this: even the South African security services had a less crude and paranoid concept of the ANC's make-up than that proffered by Barnard and Coetsee. While they may have believed that the Communist minority was sometimes capable of outwitting the more loosely defined mainstream of the movement – and there have been historical cases of a Communist minority seizing control of a larger guerrilla movement, for example in Cuba – the intelligence services must have known how small, albeit influential, a minority the Communists really were. If they were seeking a disavowal by Mandela, one of the most moderate of ANC leaders, of the Communist minority, they did not secure one. 'Which man of honour will ever desert a lifelong friend at the insistence of a common opponent and still maintain a measure of credibility among his people?'

Mandela insisted that 'no self-respecting freedom fighter would take orders from the government he is fighting against or jettison a longtime ally in the interest of pleasing an antagonist. I then explained at great length that the party and the ANC were separate but distinct organizations that shared the same short-term objectives, the overthrow of racial oppression and the birth of a non-racial South Africa, but that our long-term interests were not the same.'

After their talks about Communism, they pressed Mandela on the 'socialist' policies of his party, arguing that the ANC's freedom charter was a blueprint for a wholesale nationalization of the economy. Mandela replied that nationalization might occur for certain 'monopoly' industries, but that he had always considered it a blueprint for 'African-style capitalism'. In fact they were on firmer ground here: the Freedom Charter was a fairly collectivist document. But it also was old, and the attitudes of many of the ANC leaders had evolved after the failure of the socialist experiments elsewhere in Africa. It was the young militants that primarily adhered to it.

The third main topic of concern to the whites was the fear that the introduction of majority rule to South Africa would ride roughshod over their interests. Mandela responded with vague rhetoric, citing the preamble of his Freedom Charter. 'South Africa belongs to all who live in it, black and white.' The black majority would always respect the minority. 'We do not want to drive you into the sea.' It was a masterly performance by the old charmer. It gave away nothing.

Yet the pressure on him to cooperate remained relentless, if he was to secure any progress at all. The talks dragged on for months and remained primarily an exchange of hostile views. His initiative seemed in danger of petering out. He had no idea that the government was already negotiating with the ANC at Mells and no way of knowing that he might be used to undermine their negotiating position. The ANC outside had no way of knowing what was being said in the talks between Mandela and the government. The latter, it seemed, held all the cards.

* * *

Between the Eastwell Manor meeting in February and the next one at Mells Park in August 1988, an uneasy calm prevailed in South Africa – except for the behind-the-scenes violence in the townships between blacks and blacks and occasionally between the security forces and the blacks. There was also a wave of dignified protest against the proposed tightening of union legislation. At one stage no fewer than 3 million turned out to protest against the new act.

The government's two main initiatives were in areas outside the main liberation struggle. Botha's reform-minded finance minister, Barend du Plessis, at last managed to break the stranglehold of Afrikanerdom and the civil service over much of South Africa's private enterprise. The government announced a package of measures designed to encourage free enterprise and to move toward privatization of some major government holdings.

And following the South African defeat at Cuito Canavale, there was real progress towards a settlement in Namibia. In May and then again in July, with the United States acting as mediators and the Russians as observers, representatives of South Africa, Angola and Cuba held talks in a series of capitals, drawing up 14 'principles' to secure peace in the territory. South Africa agreed to implement Resolution 435 in return for a Cuban withdrawal from Angola over time. The South Africans had previously insisted that the Cubans withdraw first. All parties agreed not to allow their territory 'to be used for acts of war, aggression, or violence against other states'. The same month as the participants gathered in the genteel surroundings of Mells Park, South Africa, Angola and Cuba signed the Geneva Protocol which permitted a ceasefire in Namibia on 1 September.

That the Krugersdorp bomb – which had been sanctioned by Mbeki himself before the previous meeting at the Eastwell Manor Hotel, although he did not know the precise timing involved – did not derail the peace talks was remarkable. Botha himself was furious. However, the two sides were too committed to it, and had too much to lose by breaking off their single line of communication. Mbeki made it clear that the ANC national executive intended to press on. Esterhuyse confirmed that this was the case – giving precise reports of the executive's decision to Young; astonishingly, South African intelligence had been able to furnish this to him through an informer on the executive. However, the ANC decided not to take advantage of a South African government offer to set up a 'hotline' direct to the government in Pretoria – no doubt fearing that Mbeki might be tempted to go it alone in negotiations without awaiting the executive's authorization. The South Africans suggested that an intelligence officer might attend the next talks. But the Afrikaners changed their minds shortly afterwards, fearing this would give the talks too high a profile and might be leaked. In any event Esterhuyse provided all the information that Barnard needed.

* * *

Three other developments in the early summer of 1988 suddenly provided a deeply encouraging backdrop for the next meeting, scheduled for August at Mells Park, the secluded manor house owned by Consolidated Goldfields, which was now no longer afraid of being associated with the negotiations, as they had been approved at so high a level in Afrikanerdom. The first was the South African government's recognition of the key role to be played by Govan Mbeki, the crusty, elderly former Communist colleague of Mandela endowed with the necessary prestige and authority among ANC militants in South Africa to broker directly the detailed arrangements for his release.

This signalled that the government was indeed preparing to free the famous prisoner. Young, on a visit to South Africa in May, was promised that 'the decision to release has been taken in principle but the timing and the logistics need carefully to be worked out between the two sides'. The fact that the South Africans were prepared to use such a man as Govan Mbeki as a go-between – he had bitterly opposed negotiations with the government by Mandela or anyone else – simply because the ANC exiles in Lusaka had, through the Young negotiations, requested it, showed how serious they were. The more hard-line members of the ANC saw Govan Mbeki as a guarantee that no major concessions would be made in exchange for Mandela's release.

However the veteran leader, living in a form of house imprisonment in Port Elizabeth, now requested leave to visit his family in Lusaka. Barnard and the National Intelligence Agency were nervous. There would have to be authorization from the interior ministry, a hotbed of Afrikaner extremism; the news would almost certainly leak out.

This excuse was probably bogus: Barnard feared that Mbeki might refuse to return and set himself up as one of the ANC's leaders in exile – which indeed could have been his intention. Barnard suggested instead that the family secretly visit Mbeki in South Africa – which they, fearing arrest, were equally nervous about. The issue remained hanging for several weeks.

A second major factor that set the stage for progress, publicly, seemed to be a reassertion by Botha of his authority. The sense of drift the year before had been pervasive. The president seemed increasingly incapable of asserting his authority, to be merely reacting blindly to events, and to be in thrall to the hard-liners in the secret police. Now the National Intelligence Agency under Barnard and the senior army commanders seemed to be making their presence felt.

Botha was showing a new spring in his step; he was said to be leaning towards a long-term constitutional settlement and becoming more concerned with the fundamentals than bogged down in day-to-day events. Only a few months ago he had expressed interest in retiring within a year; now he was confident of carrying on. In order to achieve this he appeared to favour the appointment of a prime minister, a constitutional innovation, to take over many of the more immediate duties of government. This was seen as a positive development. At last the Old Crocodile was ready to move forward.

With elections looming and a major challenge to the National Party being mounted by the right-wing breakaway Conservative Party, any successor who lacked his authority would almost certainly have to come from, or at least pander to, the right. At the May 1987 general election, the National Party won an overwhelming majority; but the liberal Progressive Federal Party had been replaced as the main opposition party by the Conservative Party. The pressure was on the National Party from the right.

Voters had shifted to the Conservatives, which suggested the governing party was not being hard enough on the black opposition; and the Progressive Federal Party was losing support to the National Party as English-speaking white voters became alarmed by the growing violence and disorder in the country, and sought reassurance. Botha had the authority and right-wing credentials to perform a de Gaulle at last and act as South Africa's man of destiny – whatever his mistakes and irascibility in the past. He had, after all, initially been a reformist.

A third major factor favouring the next round of talks was a discernible lowering of the political temperature. With the United States Congress threatening to impose sanctions, the government was anxious to keep a low profile. Talks on Angola were also at a delicate stage. Black militancy and mobilization were undergoing a temporary lull. It was against such a favourable backdrop that participants gathered for the meeting held in the delightful and secluded surroundings of Mells Park, which lasted three days.

14
Hard Bargaining

Once again, the atmosphere was altogether different. To Young's satisfaction, this time, the two teams had been cut back to just three on each side: the time was over for cordial philosophical and intellectual probing. It was now down to hard bargaining. On the ANC side the three were Mbeki, Pahad and Trew; on the South African side Esterhuyse and Terreblanche, as before, as well as a newcomer, Willem (Wimpie) de Klerk, a man with a reformist background as a newspaper editor, but a friend of several ministers – and, above all, elder brother of the most conservative likely successor to Botha, Frederik W. de Klerk. Esterhuyse had been authorized by Barnard and Botha to make specific proposals to the ANC.

The first item on the agenda was political dynamite: the release of Nelson Mandela. The whites revealed that this was to happen after local government elections in October but before Christmas of 1988 – some 14 to 16 months before it actually happened. Botha, they said, had now decided to take the plunge. Even more strikingly, the government had dropped its public precondition for his release – that the ANC renounce violence. Instead a face-saving committee of enquiry would be set up to recommend that he be released on humanitarian grounds. In exchange, the government asked for only one thing: that the ANC control its supporters so that the release could take place without disorder – which would otherwise play into the hands of the Conservative Party.

Curiously Esterhuyse then asked Mbeki whether the ANC really wanted Mandela free (for him to have died in prison would have resulted in a massive surge of support for the ANC and in international condemnation of the government; Botha really believed that the exiled ANC wanted Mandela dead). Mbeki, astonished, replied in the affirmative.

The whites then proposed that Mbeki meet South African officials in secret to discuss the mechanics of the release. Mbeki was agreeably surprised. The fiction of no direct ANC–government contact was being dropped altogether. Mbeki made it clear, however, that Mandela would immediately re-engage in active politics and would not abide by any restrictions imposed by the government.

Again to his astonishment, this seemed to pose no problems for whites – if indeed they had realized its full implications: for he would immediately become the focus for the black opposition movement, and protest would mushroom as never before. Like a Lech Walesa he might launch a peaceful uprising that would paralyse the country.

These things were clear to the ANC but not, it seemed, in the higher reaches of the South African government. In Botha's mind there must have existed the hope that Mandela, having taken on the leadership of the black movement within the country, would seize the initiative from the exiled ANC leaders and the guerrillas, and be a man that the government could do a deal with. The divide-and-rule strategy against the ANC still seemed to dominate the president's thinking. Yet the consequences of releasing Mandela at this stage in South African politics, when political movements were still banned, were colossal, and could provoke an uncontrollable upheaval.

After this bombshell, the ANC gave its own concession: it put forward a set of constitutional guarantees dressed up as 'discussion document guidelines'. These suggested that the movement had evolved significantly, since the 1955 Freedom Charter, towards espousing a mixed economy. The new guidelines were seen by the whites as a major step toward easing fears of a socialized South Africa. Even so, they sought certain amendments and deletions, and stressed the need for lengthy transitional periods. These guidelines were to form the basis for the first public talks two years later between the ANC and the government. They reflected the priorities of Gorbachev in Moscow and the newly ascendant Mbeki.

The discussion now turned to much trickier ground: the subject of ANC violence. Here the three white delegates became grim and obdurate. They seized upon the Ellis Park and Hyde Park bombs. If this kind of indiscriminate violence against civilian targets continued, they said, even these secret talks would have to be broken off: the churches and other moderate groups were so appalled by the attacks that support was growing for hard-line solutions.

Thabo Mbeki was for the first time thrown on the defensive. Urbane, highly intelligent, an easy talker, this was the first time the whites had caught him on his most vulnerable point: the ANC's apparently wanton disregard for human life. He paused, and could have taken refuge in ritual condemnation of the same kind of callousness on the white side. He did not.

Instead he drew breath and gave a full explanation of the internal politics of the ANC command-and-control structure, which amounted to a repudiation of both explosions. He must have known this would provide invaluable intelligence for the South African security forces. Young, as chairman, was astonished; in his words:

> He reiterated ANC policy, which is that units should not bomb 'soft' targets and that military and economic targets were the only legitimate targets. He discussed the ANC command and control structure which he acknowledged sometimes behaved in a manner which did not please Lusaka. Only major explosions are planned by Lusaka, otherwise each unit leader is responsible for target selection within the guidelines set down for him by the executive in Lusaka. Training is sometimes poor and Mbeki gave an example of one mission in which three army trucks were to be destroyed, but because the unit's training had been conducted 'inside the country' (and was therefore inferior to that available outside the Republic), the angle of aim was not properly calculated. The attack resulted in many bystanders being killed and one truck only being partially disabled.
>
> He discussed too the tendency of units operating from townships to be subject to the emotions of the local community who do urge 'to get one in for us'. These elements do influence events but the ANC has been so disturbed by the mistakes made at Ellis Park that all unit commanders have been called to Lusaka where policy was re-explained.
>
> Mbeki told the meeting that cadres are supposed to be political animals before being military personnel and must be constantly alive to political effects ... During his wide-ranging explanation, Mbeki talked about remarks made by the ANC chief of staff in interviews with the *Times* of London and the *New York Times* concerning targets ... The impression he gave was that 'soft' targets were permissible. For the first time Oliver Tambo, the ANC president, rebuked the chief of staff in private and in public. The ANC believes that its command and control structure is fairly effective, and Mbeki re-emphasized that the military campaign could revert to purely political activity if Pretoria would allow the ANC to express itself inside the country.

Mbeki frankly promised to monitor operational units more effectively so that 'soft' targets would no longer be hit. The black delegation leader now dropped a bombshell concession: the armed struggle would be stopped if the ANC was allowed to operate as a political party within South Africa – in other words, was unbanned. As a further gesture, if the South Africans released the 54 political prisoners held within the country, the ANC would release the South Africans they held in their camps.

The concession had long been implicit in Mandela's parallel argument that South African violence against the ANC had to end before the movement would cease its own: but it had been vague, rhetorical, never spelt out and anyway derived from the mouth of the lone prisoner of Pollsmoor, not the high command in Lusaka. What did he mean by a cessation of state violence? The withdrawal of the police from the townships, merely, or a transition to majority rule?

Here was the ANC's first specific proposal, right from the top – from Mbeki, its operational leader behind the elderly and presidential Tambo. The guerrilla war in South Africa would cease if the ANC were legalized and permitted to act as a political party in South Africa. It was as simple as that. (There was an interesting contrast here with the IRA in Northern Ireland. There the political wing of the movement, Sinn Fein, which represented only around a tenth of the electorate, had already been allowed to operate freely as a political party decades before the ceasefire. The ANC were prepared to down arms in exchange simply for being allowed to seek power democratically and peacefully.) It was a demand of such direct reasonableness that Esterhuyse, Terreblanche and de Klerk could only collect their thoughts and promise to deliver it to Botha that very week.

That was not the end of the surprises. The white side now divulged that South Africa was on the brink of pulling out of the long war with Angola, viewed up to then as an unshakeable commitment on the part of Botha. In Young's laconic summary of the South African position:

As late as October last year the South African government had no intention of negotiating a settlement of the Angolan problem. The introduction of a new mine which can cripple South African armoured carriers, the heavy losses already incurred, together with growing worries about the financial implications of funding the operation, led Pretoria to think again. Since then a full South African division has been trapped by Cuban and Angolan troops, and given Angolan air superiority, the means of extricating this division does not exist short of a negotiated peace treaty. Thus P. W. Botha and the military urgently required an agreement as do the Russians, the Cubans, the Americans and the OAU. A negotiated settlement involving a Cuban and South African withdrawal will enhance South Africa's self-esteem in so far as she can regard herself to have negotiated a settlement to a problem which has been regarded as difficult.

The question of ANC bases inside Angola should not be allowed to prevent a settlement.

Mbeki promptly responded that his bases would be moved further north in order to facilitate a South African withdrawal. The Afrikaners now revealed that South Africa was also preparing to withdraw from Namibia, something beginning to appear inevitable, but none the less never directly confirmed, much less to the ANC. The main problem in Namibia was the presence of some 60,000 whites who would have to be resettled inside South Africa. The whole process would require American and Russian money.

The conference now reviewed developments inside South Africa with remarkable candour on the white side. The view of de Klerk in particular was that the National Party was drifting towards a split; some 40 per cent of the white electorate could be regarded as hard-line (three-fifths of them Afrikaners), while the moderate white electorate amounted to around 60 per cent. The real battle of the hour was being fought inside the National Party caucus, whose 'enlightened' members were rising to the top – a trait also evident in the Broederbond.

The Afrikaners as a volk were in fact moving out of their laager: Afrikaner unions wanted to join Cosatu, the black trade union federation. The South African rugby federation was seeking talks with ANC supporters in order to secure integration of the sport and hopefully end its isolation, which, contrary to views often expressed abroad, had had a major and damaging effect on white morale in South Africa. One factor contributing to the split inside Afrikanerdom was the growing economic crisis, as international investment declined, inflation accelerated and public spending was cut back so that poverty, both black and white, was on the increase. Poor whites were drifting towards the Conservative Party in protest.

By the time the delegations took their leave from Mells Park, they were elated and exhausted. Esterhuyse had in his suitcase the ANC's guarantee to cease violence if the movement was unbanned and an offer to exchange political prisoners and to rein back attacks on 'soft' targets, as well as a renunciation of the ANC's socialist goals. Mbeki had the white offer to release Mandela unconditionally – as well as a South African pledge to withdraw soon from Angola and Namibia. It was heady stuff. Unfortunately, the endgame was neither to be so simple nor so short.

* * *

The bright hopes raised by the August 1988 Mells meeting were not fulfilled. The 'Old Crocodile', it soon emerged, was still playing with his two interlocutors: Mbeki and the ANC leadership outside South Africa, and Mandela inside. The weary exchange of views between Mandela and his captors continued without any real results being reached. Botha was clearly hoping that delay would weaken the prisoner and force him into concessions, fearful of missing out on his place in history. This failed to happen.

Meanwhile Esterhuyse's promise of a direct meeting between Mbeki and the South African security services, as well as the proposal that a senior South African official attend the next set of talks, receded suddenly. The promised timetable for the release of Mandela did not materialize. Botha, newly confident, was newly obstructive. Instead of Mandela being freed, he developed tuberculosis, probably because his cell was so damp.

He was taken to Tygerberg Hospital in the campus of the University of Stellenbosch – ironically, the very bastion of white supremacy where Young had first made contact with the Afrikaners nearly three years before. The security forces were desperately nervous lest Mandela's presence become known and cause a revolt among the students, and cleared whole floors of the building before allowing him in. He spent six weeks there before being moved to a luxurious private clinic, Constantiaberg.

Even there he remained under a regime of nannying coercion. 'Because of my recent illness and my history of high blood pressure, I had been put on a strict low-cholesterol diet. That order had apparently not yet been conveyed to the clinic's kitchen, for the breakfast tray contained scrambled eggs, three rashers of bacon and several pieces of buttered toast. I could not remember the last time I had tasted bacon and eggs and was ravenous. Just as I was about to take a delicious forkful of egg, Major Marais [his jailer] said, "No, Mandela. That is against the orders of your physician", and he reached over to take the tray. I held it tightly, and said, "Major, I am sorry. If this breakfast will kill me, then today I am prepared to die."'

In December 1988 he was suddenly transferred to Victor Verster prison, 35 miles north-east of Cape Town. There he was taken to a remote wooded area, where a small one-storey cottage was set behind a concrete wall. The place was modest – a bedroom, a large drawing room and a kitchen. There was a swimming pool and small garden. It was both remote, keeping Mandela away from his potential supporters while permitting his lieutenants to visit him discreetly, and a major improvement on any prison he had been held in before – something halfway, in fact, between prison and freedom. Kobie Coetsee came the same day with a crate of Cape wine as a gift.

Mandela was given his own cook, Warrant Officer Swart, who became a firm friend. Mandela adored the place. 'The cottage did in fact give me the illusion of freedom. I could go to sleep and wake up as I pleased, swim whenever I wanted, eat when I was hungry – all were delicious sensations. Simply to be able to go outside during the day and take a walk when I desired was a moment of private glory. There were no bars on the windows, no jangling keys, no doors to lock or unlock. It was altogether pleasant, but I never forgot that it was a gilded cage.'

* * *

A few days after Mandela was given his first small taste of freedom, the six negotiators of the previous Mells talks gathered together at a new venue: Flitwick Park in Bedfordshire. The same friendliness between the participants was evident; but the mood was sombre. Mandela had not been released. Mbeki had not met an official of the South African government. No senior official had joined the talks. The suspicion existed on the black side that these men, while senior, were essentially dissidents within the South African establishment, unable to deliver. Botha, while monitoring the talks, was apparently pursuing his own agenda.

Esterhuyse opened with a frank but dispiriting analysis of the divisions afflicting Afrikanerdom. The hardliners within Botha's inner circle were still insisting that the ANC publicly renounce violence before the government could talk with it or unban it. They favoured restoration of the state of emergency and stricter control, and the preservation of the tricameral system of power-sharing with the blacks. The cabal of hardliners that had been formed within the president's inner cabinet was now getting its way.

Within the cabinet itself, the National Intelligence Agency and the Broederbond were doves who advocated the repeal of the group areas act and an end to the state of emergency, as well as direct talks with the ANC without preconditions (in ignorance that this was already happening). Esterhuyse's view of Botha had shifted sharply: as long as the president remained, he told the meeting grimly, the National Party would remain wedded to the old policies, under the illusion that it commanded the support of two-fifths of black people and followers.

Botha, moreover, enjoying a new lease of life, intended to remain for another two years before handing over to his current favourite, Barend du Plessis, the reformist finance minister. Chris Heunis, the most moderate possible successor, had lost support, his advisers even having had their security clearance withdrawn for his heretical views. Gerrit Viljoen, another candidate who favoured talks with the ANC, was keeping a low profile. Botha seemed set on the Indaba, his plan for a limited power-sharing arrangement with the blacks, and regarded the National Party triumph in the October elections – in which fewer than 2 per cent of blacks voted – as a ringing endorsement.

The only bright spot was the success of the Angolan negotiations, a personal triumph for foreign minister Pik Botha, who had forged an alliance between his ministry and the regular army which knew the true and drastic state of affairs in the field. This had secured South Africa a brief respite from the unrelenting hostility of the outside world, much to the president's gratification. In addition, the release of the Sharpeville Six had also improved South Africa's image.

De Klerk then proceeded to outline the idea of forming a 'new party', consisting of the rump of the Progressive Federal Party, the old English white party which had done dismally at the October elections; the Democratic Party, which was essentially a breakaway from the National Party on the left; and the reformist splinter party set up by the former South African ambassador in London, Denis Worrall. De Klerk was already far advanced towards forming the new party, to be launched in February, which was expected to secure the support of just under a third of the white electorate. The purpose of the party would be to create a national forum with the task of creating a new constitution for South Africans. The probable leader of the party would be the respected Zak de Beer, former director of the Anglo-American Corporation. One of its prime motives would be to root out corruption within the government machine.

Mbeki admired the frankness with which Esterhuyse and de Klerk analysed white South African politics. At the same time he could barely disguise his disappointment. The hopes held out that Botha was embarked on a reformist course the previous summer at Mells Park had entirely vanished.

The 'old crocodile' was behaving more like a water snake, manoeuvring first one way, then another in response to the pressure of events. Botha had decided to placate his conservatives. Now the Afrikaner moderates believed the only hope lay in splitting the National Party and forming a new organization in the hope that this would collect the support of a large minority of whites. Mbeki surprisingly accepted the idea of a national forum in which all groups could participate – provided this was intended to lay down the foundations for a black majority government.

The conversation turned to the question of Mandela's release which, like so much since the last talks, had failed to materialize. The new deadline was August or September 1989 – a year after the last. Botha had angrily vetoed the idea of a meeting between the National Intelligence Service and Mbeki to discuss the nuts and bolts of this, on the spurious grounds that it would be publicised by the ANC and used for short-term advantage. The government was worried about the strategy that would be pursued by Mandela once freed, and the possibility of violence on his release.

To this betrayal of previous promises Mbeki replied with commendable self-restraint, while calmly refuting the new South African position. The release needed to be orderly, have the support of all concerned, and once effected would permit the ANC to look at the question of a cessation of violence. Thus Mbeki, in a skilful inversion, had stood the white equation on its head. The release was to be a precondition for the cessation of violence, not the latter a precondition for the former; this was in fact a tacit concession by the ANC.

As to exchanging political prisoners as a conciliatory gesture, it was Mbeki's turn to be embarrassed. According to the National Intelligence Agency, none of its members were being held by the ANC in Zambia or anywhere in Africa. Only members of the reactionary Security Police – which the NIA despised – were held in Zimbabwe, and the agency was not pressing for their return with any urgency. However, the disappointment as the ANC delegation realized that the three white interlocutors did not really command a mandate from the government, and could not deliver, was acute; it was only modestly tempered by the realization that the whites present were wholly sincere. But to the black side, whose hopes had been dashed, raised and dashed again, a split in the National Party must have seemed a forlorn hope, and an eternity away.

Young tactfully moved the discussion onto the ANC's objectives. How had the new constitutional guidelines been received? Mbeki pointed out that the guidelines were not a take-it-or-leave-it document, but provided a basis for discussion with the other parties. The whites said that they were concerned by the implication that the powerful ANC state would administer a highly centralized system and a command economy.

De Klerk then went into a detailed critique of the proposals, suggesting that the guidelines implied the creation of a centralized one-party state, neglected the role of the judiciary as a check on the constitution, and favoured state economic planning in all sectors. He also questioned the ANC concept of state control as being close to communism.

The blacks replied that although they conceived of a unitary state – not one involving semi-independent homelands as under apartheid – they saw it as being a federal system under a central government. Mbeki suggested that a constitutional conference at the University of Zimbabwe would provide the forum for a more detailed exchange of views between white and black South Africans. Esterhuyse said he would look for friends in the academic community who might participate in such an exercise.

In the absence of further progress on domestic matters, the talks now shifted to Angola, where at last a settlement was close to being achieved. The main factors that had pushed the South Africans to the negotiating table were the drain on their finances and a shift in the military balance within the region, with the South Africans acknowledging that their aerial superiority no longer existed now that the Cuban forces were supplied with new Mig-23s – even though these operated at a shorter range than expected and their bases were therefore liable to attack.

The South Africans' response had been to convert their French Mirages into the new Cheetah aircraft – which inevitably was proving hugely expensive. Meanwhile the loss of life in Angola was also causing additional pressure on the South African government. As Angola had never been strategically essential to Pretoria – the objective there was to destabilize the region – and as the Americans were unwilling any longer to provide any legal and diplomatic cover for them (as the Cold War, of which Angola had been a little Third

World sideshow, was wound down), they had little alternative but to settle.

Yet Botha found the decision difficult: Jonas Savimbi, his ally in Angola as head of the UNITA guerrilla army, had been guest of honour at the South African president's inauguration, a black man that respected Botha's goals. Now he would be left twisting in the wind. One direct consequence for the ANC was that they would have to abandon their bases inside Angola as part of the agreement.

On Namibia, Esterhuyse said that a settlement based on UN Resolution 435 was closer. The ANC delegates expressed scepticism, believing that the South African government was content to continue to exploit tribal divisions in order to obstruct a settlement. To raised eyebrows from the black delegates, Esterhuyse explained that Pik Botha was pressing hard for a Namibian settlement because it would improve his chances of succeeding President Botha; one consideration was a growing outcry among Afrikaner mothers who resented their sons having to go and fight for the obscure issues at stake in Namibia. However, for President Botha himself, Namibia had long had the advantage of distracting attention from the issue of South Africa.

This rather desultory, if interesting, exchange seemed to mark the end of a conference which had achieved much less than the one before, beyond advancing mutual understanding. But there were two surprises in the closing stages: both sides urged Young to make a direct approach to the British prime minister, Margaret Thatcher, to act as an honest broker between the front-line states, western Europe, the United States and South Africa.

For the South Africans the motives were clear. After President Reagan's retirement, George Bush had shown himself much less favourably disposed towards Pretoria, while West Germany's Chancellor, Helmut Kohl, seemed more determined to press for harder sanctions to appease the Free Democrats in his coalition. Thatcher was the only friend of white South Africa in a hostile world.

The ANC, while clearly loathing her because of her role in obstructing effective sanctions, had nevertheless been put under direct pressure from one of their chief foreign backers and arms suppliers, Mikhail Gorbachev's Soviet Union – who himself had a warm relationship with Thatcher. The fact that the Russians were now acting as a major factor for restraint came as a surprise to the whites, and helped power the negotiations later on.

The disappointment that the talks were not attended by a senior official from the South African government was slightly assuaged by the sudden revelation that Neil Barnard, head of the National Intelligence Agency, had asked for his deputy to be allowed to attend the next round of discussions for at least part of the time. Young himself left with a new mission in his pocket: that of approaching 10 Downing Street to act as honest broker between the two sides.

If the hard results of this meeting were disappointing, Young was not exaggerating when he wrote afterwards that the 'depth of trust which has been established between the two sides is most gratifying and has provided a most frank exchange of views and concerns ... this exercise has now developed a momentum of its own.'

Wimpie de Klerk commented in his diary, in an indirect tribute to Young's chairmanship:

> For me personally [the talks] meant a great deal: the luxury trips and accommodation; the experience of sitting close to the fire and engaging in political breakthrough work to bring the National Prty and ANC to dialogue; the bonds of friendship that had developed between Thabo, Aziz, Jacob Zuma and myself; the access to direct confidential information; the position of intermediary, because from the beginning until now I have conveyed 'secret messages' from the ANC to FW and even the other way around, but FW was and is very cautious.
>
> Our agendas are very concrete and direct: on Mandela's release and ANC undertakings in that connection; on the armed struggle and a possible suspension of it by the ANC; on the various steps that must be taken before pre-negotiation talks with the government can take place; on constitutional issues such as a transitional government, minority safeguards, an economic system, etc.; on concrete stumbling blocks and the exploration of compromises to get out of deadlocks; on sanctions; on ANC thinking on all kinds of South African political issues and on government thinking on those self-same issues.
>
> I am convinced that the discussions have greatly increased mutual understanding; created a positive climate of expectations; brought a mutual moderation and realism to our politics; channelled important messages to Lusaka and Pretoria; and even included the germs of certain transactions. In general, therefore, a bridge-building exercise between NP Afrikaners and the ANC ...
>
> Our little group's unique contribution has been that we engaged

in extremely authentic private discussions that were taken seriously by both sides and that it exposed Thabo, Aziz, and Jacob to Afrikaners for the first time, and that they found an affinity with us and so with the group we represent.

15
Breakthrough

Few people believed that the year 1989 would do more than mark time in what was a relentless deterioration in the confrontation in South Africa. Negotiations with Mandela and at Mells Park seemed stalled. The pressures continued to intensify in the shape of sanctions, and in the alliance now formed between the UDF, the ANC's umbrella front organization within South Africa, and Cosatu, the main black trade union organization, to form the Mass Democratic Movement (MDM). This pledged to carry out a 'definitive campaign of civil disobedience'.

Yet that balmy but ominous mid-summer New Year's day in South Africa did, at last, mark the turning point. So often hope had been disappointed. The initial Botha reforms were succeeded by the dismal low point of the 1986 state of emergency, the slender hopes of 1987, and in 1988 by the let-down in the closing months of that year.

Mandela himself can have entertained few real hopes as he sat down to greet his former colleagues at Pollsmoor, in the comparative luxury of his new home, to discuss with them the terms of an 11–page memorandum he was preparing to send to President Botha. His talks with the secret negotiating committee had dragged on fruitlessly for months without the slightest progress; his request for a meeting with the President had been repeatedly shelved. Only the conditions in which he was held had improved. There are those who believe the memorandum explicitly offered a renunciation of violence in exchange for negotiations. Mandela vehemently denies this. But the issue was heatedly discussed among the jailed comrades, and in Lusaka.

The memorandum was a familiar, if eloquent, restatement of his own positions over the previous few months on the central issues.

Only at the end did it contain, cleverly concealed in the draft, a key concession. 'Two political issues will have to be addressed; firstly, the demand for majority rule in a unitary state; secondly, the concern of white South Africa over this demand as well as the insistence of whites on structural guarantees that majority rule will not mean domination of the white minority by blacks. The most crucial tasks which will face the government and the ANC will be to reconcile these two positions.'

Mandela was thus for the first time conceding a key white request: constitutional guarantees that would preserve their position. It was in fact a wholly reasonable demand, except in the context of historical vengeance by the blacks. But it did run counter to the concept of 'pure' black majority rule; and the ANC had never given any specific commitment before. On this, as before, Mandela had gone out on a limb: he was offering an olive branch on a subject that his own movement had opposed for many decades. Tambo and others, who were in ignorance of the memorandum at this stage, privately agreed that it would be impossible to get the ANC as a whole to be so sensitive to white susceptibilities.

When word of the memorandum reached Govan Mbeki, the peppery 80- year-old ex-Communist who was the father figure of the UDF, he sent out an irate edict instructing UDF members not to visit Mandela in prison. It seemed at last that the Old Crocodile's plan was bearing fruit: Mandela was beginning to move, making a key concession, while at Mells and English country hotels the South Africans had kept the exiled ANC leaders talking, but had actually agreed nothing.

The same month, though, Botha suffered a stroke which, while not putting him out of action, made him more difficult and bad-tempered than ever to deal with. In February Botha announced he was resigning as National Party leader, although retaining the presidency, in order to remain above party politics and address the long-term concerns of the nation. In fact, the reason may have been more down-to-earth: to lighten his workload, to concentrate his attention on the key issues and to distance himself from the continual pressures from his parliamentary colleagues who had become frustrated by their exclusion from his inner circle of military and intelligence chiefs – who were, in effect, staging a creeping coup.

The constitutional foundation of the Afrikaner community – something the black majority was loath to believe existed at all – was asserting itself against proto-dictatorial rule, the parliamentary basis of the South African system asserting itself against the presidential. Botha, by ruling through the state security council, was making himself more of a strongman than ever. But he neglected the point that under the South African tradition, as elsewhere in the West, power derived from his parliamentary base. He could ignore it, but without its assent had no majority in parliament. Almost certainly this arrangement was thrust upon him, and in his isolation and megalomania he accepted it.

His days were now numbered. The fight was on for the post of party leader – in effect, prime minister. It was between Chris Heunis, the reformist constitutional affairs minister, brave but isolated and now disowned by Botha; Pik Botha, the foreign minister who had achieved so much in mollifying South Africa's critics and extricating the country from Namibia and Angola, but who was widely regarded as an outsider, albeit an able and moderate one, with little real clout within the Afrikaner community; Barend du Plessis, Botha's favourite, the technocratic finance minister, who was extremely aware of the external pressures on South Africa, which tipped him into the reform camp, but who had much less political weight than the others; and F. W. de Klerk, the education minister, representative of the conservative bulk of the party and a former leader of the party in its most conservative state of the Transvaal.

To the disappointment of almost every overseas observer, de Klerk won by 8 votes out of the 130 National Party MPs. It was not understood at the time, but de Klerk's central appeal to other party members was that he was not, and could never be, a creature of Botha's. Alone of the candidates – the others had been elevated by Botha to their positions – he had an independent power base. 'I was not part of the inner circle dealing with security – in fact, I was never part of any inner circle of Mr P. W. Botha's,' he once remarked caustically. He loathed Botha, always had. He was calm, reflective, a listener rather than a talker, the polar opposite of the verbose, bullying, emotional and irascible Botha. He was a Transvaaler, a true voortrekker; Botha was Cape liberal. And Transvaal had changed. No critical observer at the time realized the significance of de Klerk's accession to the antechamber of the presidency – least of all Mandela.

* * *

Among the first to gain an insight into the dramatic changes about to hit South Africa were the participants in the fifth Mells Park conference, which was held between 21 and 24 April. With F. W. de Klerk as National Party leader and virtual prime minister, Willem de Klerk now effectively took over leadership of the white side from Esterhuyse. Although the two brothers had different political views, they were personally close and talked freely and openly to each other.

De Klerk, opening the discussion, said his brother saw the options before him as four:

1. F. W. can maintain the party's position in a structure based on racial principles. His personal instinct is to go for this option knowing that it won't rock the National Party boat.
2. He can move to the right, but recognizes this to be against the current trend and thus impractical.
3. He can move to the left in easy stages and in small ways. This is his expected course since, pragmatically, he senses its inevitability.
4. He can surprise everyone by moving sharply to the left and reject the racial model constitution which has long been the cornerstone of National Party policy. This course would be against his instincts and yet he is aware that the broad church of black African opinion would insist upon such a course.

Wimpie de Klerk went on to suggest that his brother had little patience with the 'securocrats' – the intelligence and military chiefs that Botha surrounded himself with, or the secret police that John Vorster, his predecessor, favoured. F. W. de Klerk had a civilian inner circle – and particularly close links with the Transvaal business community alienated by Botha. He enjoyed a personal reputation as 'Mr Clean' in a government tainted by corruption scandals.

His rise was viewed with suspicion by the military and security apparatus, as well as by the presidential household, which feared that a major purge could get under way should he become president. In particular, the reformist National Intelligence chief, Neil Barnard, was concerned that FW's accession would result in his quick dismissal. So much did the securocrats fear de Klerk that there was speculation about a military coup, possibly to retain Botha – talk which, however, was dismissed by de Klerk as extravagant.

The white delegation reckoned that the general election was likely to be held on 6 or 13 September, before the election for a constituent assembly in Namibia in November – for fear that the expected 60 per cent victory by SWAPO would alarm white South African voters. The white delegation was confident that the Conservative Party's support had by now peaked, and that white blue-collar workers were now reconciled to deal with the blacks.

In its place it was hoped that the newly formed Democratic Party would replace the Conservative Party as the official opposition following the election, winning 25 to 30 seats. That Party would campaign on a platform of opposition to the economic record and corruption of the National Party, as well as on a two- pronged approach of talking to the ANC and other representative groups in South Africa, coupled with the protection of minority religious and language rights – code for defending the interests of the white minority.

In this, the Democrats would be much more sympathetic to Afrikaner interests than the declining English-dominated Progressive Federal Party. They represented, in fact, the internal resistance within the National Party. It was recognized that continual sparring within the leadership – between Zak de Beer and Denis Worrall – would cause problems, but there was hope that this could be resolved. Both Wimpie de Klerk and Sampie Terreblanche were ardent supporters of the new party.

The latter argued that the emergence of the Democrats would be absolutely crucial in the events of the year. For the first time since 1948 the National Party was faced by the prospect of losing its absolute majority: a hung parliament could ensue, which would be a prescription for uncertainty and chaos. For if the National Party joined forces with the Conservatives, South Africa would lurch to the right and confrontation would be accelerated; if it made common cause with the Democratic party, it might split and disintegrate. This prospect, Terreblanche was later to argue, concentrated National Party minds into the fateful decision to oust Botha altogether, and to organize a 'dirty campaign' in which de Klerk was to give only the vaguest promises of reform, narrowly securing a fresh mandate in the shape of an absolute majority of some 20 seats. Willem de Klerk now brought the morning session to a halt with a bombshell. Saying he was asking a direct question on behalf of his brother, he asked the ANC whether it would be possible to start talks about talks. Mbeki was astonished by so decisive an approach. Would there be preconditions? None. What sort of agenda would be acceptable to the ANC?, de Klerk asked. The ANC leaders consulted each other. They must retire to discuss this.

The following morning they informed de Klerk that they were willing to go ahead. There would be no preconditions on their side and the talks could be as broad or narrow as FW wanted. Mbeki agreed, though, that such talks should focus on practical matters: who should attend? Where would they meet? The two sides agreed that pre-talks should remain confidential and that only subsequent formal negotiations should be open. The ANC suggested that the release of Nelson Mandela would establish the government's good faith for the talks, which could also focus on the problem of violence, who should participate in the negotiations, the ending of the state of emergency and the unbanning of the ANC.

*   *   *

This was the breakthrough. In effect the ANC was abandoning all its preconditions as a gesture to the new leadership of South Africa: they were linking a cessation of violence with Mandela's release and the unbanning of the organization. De Klerk was able to carry back this crucial linkage to his brother – who applied this knowledge with historic effect less than a year later. However, the ANC insisted that the 'pre-talks' take place at a junior level, to make secrecy easier to maintain.

What both Mbeki and Esterhuyse saw, and Willem de Klerk did not, was that the Mells talks were, in effect, such pre-talks themselves, as details of them were regularly relayed directly to President Botha's office and the ANC executive in Lusaka. It was necessary at this stage, however, to keep the elder de Klerk out of the Barnard–Botha loop, but it was equally necessary for the ANC to establish a direct link with the likely new president of South Africa. Incredibly, the ANC's chief fear at this stage was that the 'liberal' Botha would be replaced by the more 'hard-line' de Klerk; if the ANC had had any say, it would have plumped for Botha! Fortunately, the already circuitous Mells Park process had now established a new connection which enlightened them: not just with the current president but also the likely next president, through his older brother.

The whites now revealed that Botha's stroke had impaired the direct talks due to take place between the ANC and the National Intelligence Service. However, it was once again asserted that the decision to release Mandela had in principle been taken, that the release would be unconditional, and that he would be free to play a 'constructive' role in South Africa.

The timing of the release was still immensely controversial and linked to Botha's own fate. For the National Party it was clearly essential that Botha be removed before the September election. Although this was not discussed at Mells, Botha's stroke had in fact been very serious; a clot the size of the golf ball had been removed from his brain. Both his judgement and temperament had been affected. Not only was Botha likely to lose the National Party its absolute majority; it was clearly essential that de Klerk secure a mandate if he were to initiate any kind of reform at all.

It would clearly be best if de Klerk were to release Mandela as one of his first acts on taking office, as it would give his presidency enormous impetus and credibility within the black community. Botha, on the other hand, might want to release Mandela as his final act on giving up office or, failing that, to impose conditions on his release as an act of spite to bind his successor.

Mbeki and the ANC delegation then staggered the whites by arguing that it was better to delay Mandela's release until de Klerk took over – and the whites promised to relay this to their allies. In the event the fear that Botha was indeed about to release Mandela proved crucial to the timing of the parliamentary coup that deposed him.

A knotty problem remained. Before Mandela could be freed, the National Intelligence Service needed to talk with the ANC on the nuts-and-bolts of the release – in particular, the elaborate measures to prevent violence and rioting. This would require immense self-restraint by both the security forces and the ANC's followers.

But Botha's illness – the president was in semi-convalescence outside Cape Town, only occasionally sauntering in to deal with correspondence (indeed South Africa was effectively without a president at this crucial juncture) prevented him giving the necessary instructions to Barnard to start such negotiations. The intelligence chief feared to seek such authorization in case the erratic Botha should furiously veto it. Later that summer Barnard secured the necessary orders through the ingenious device of wafting them, couched in the vaguest possible terms, past de Klerk's desk during his first frantic week as president.

The ANC now made a further major concession. As a gesture, they had already withdrawn the bulk of their guerrilla army from inside South Africa – something which had been noted and appreciated by the South African government. Now they were prepared to impose a moratorium on violence as a prelude to negotiations – effectively conceding the cessation of violence in advance of the talks – albeit temporarily and predicated on their outcome. One by one the old stumbling blocks were being removed. The ANC had pledged quietly to suspend violence in advance of talks, while the whites no longer insisted that they publicly renounce it as a precondition.

The discussions then took up a theme raised at the previous

meeting. Young raised the issue of international mediation. Specifically he wondered aloud whether Britain's prime minister, Margaret Thatcher, was well placed to play the role of 'honest broker'. For the white South Africans, the choice was a natural one. She had immense credibility among them as the world leader who had done her best to resist the imposition of sanctions. There had been suggestions that at the Reykjavik summit, in which certain major countries had been assigned the role of seeking to end long-running Third World disputes, Thatcher had been given the job by both Reagan and Gorbachev of defusing the South African timebomb (whether this was true or not, it was certainly the perception of members of the white South African delegation at Mells Park).

Cautiously, Young sought the reaction of the black delegation to this suggestion. Mbeki had detested the British prime minister ever since she had denounced the ANC as a 'typical terrorist organization' at the October 1987 Commonwealth summit. She had acted as apartheid's apologist in the West, viewing the prospect of a 'communist-dominated' South Africa as more alarming than a white-dominated South Africa was morally reprehensible.

But Mbeki responded levelly. He appreciated that she had a central role to play because of her influence with the white administration; indeed, no other major government had any influence at all save for a negative one. But he pointed out that for such a mission to succeed, the ANC must have confidence in her ability to act as an 'honest broker'. Both the frontline states and the Soviet leadership would be heavily influenced by the ANC's judgement. Young came away from the exchange with the confidence he had a mandate to approach the Prime Minister directly, and that both sides in South Africa would welcome her intervention. It seemed, indeed, a remarkable opportunity.

The Mells meeting now moved on to the issues of Angola and Namibia. There was a discussion of the recent ferocious clashes between South African forces and Swapo which had resulted in 300 deaths. Swapo troops had crossed the ceasefire line unexpectedly and been ambushed by South Africans who knew of their offensive more than 24 hours in advance.

It seemed that Swapo's president, Sam Nujoma, had not expected the move by his men, which had been ordered by commanders on the ground. The carnage had threatened to wreck the agreement, but the ANC told the whites that Nujoma was still committed to peaceful elections. Esterhuyse for his part assured the ANC that the South Africans were still committed to leaving Namibia on time.

On Angola the ANC delegation revealed that several front-line states had resolved to find a solution that would allow Unita guerrillas to be dispersed from the country (a problem that has not been resolved to this day). On Mozambique all sides expressed their impotence to do much about Renamo, the once South African-backed liberation movement which the United States now regarded as '60 per cent bandits' and beyond all political control.

Esterhuyse revealed that some Portuguese in South Africa were still sending financial aid to Renamo, but that the government would do little about it because the Portuguese were placed in key marginal seats and the National Party could not afford to lose their votes. Esterhuyse also revealed that the South African business community regularly paid protection money to Renamo to safeguard their interests in Mozambique.

When the Mells Park meeting broke up on 24 April, Young had good reason to feel satisfied. From being a channel of communication between the president's office and the ANC, the talks had gone a notch higher, to becoming (through his elder brother) a channel between the ANC and the certain next president of South Africa. And Young himself had been charged with a potentially historic mission by both sides: that of approaching British Prime Minister Margaret Thatcher and asking her to mediate.

16
The Thatcher Opportunity

Britain's stance under Mrs Thatcher had been unambiguous. It was also one of the few areas where she was at odds with her foreign secretary, Sir Geoffrey Howe. Thatcher's approach was characteristically straight-forward. As she wrote in her autobiography:

Admitted that fundamental changes must be made in South Africa's system, the question was of how best to achieve them. It seemed to me that the worst approach was to isolate South Africa further. Indeed, the isolation had already gone too far, contributing to an inflexible siege mentality among the governing Afrikaner class. It was absurd to believe that they would be prepared to relinquish power suddenly or without acceptable safeguards. Indeed, had that occurred the result would have been anarchy in which black South Africans would have suffered most.

Nor, I knew, could the latter be considered a homogeneous group. Tribal loyalties were of great importance. For example, the Zulus are a proud and self-conscious nation with a distinct sense of identity. Any new political framework for South Africa had to take account of such differences. Not least because of these complexities, I did not believe that it was for outsiders to impose a particular solution. What I wanted to achieve was step-by-step reform – with more democracy, secure human rights, and a flourishing free enterprise economy able to generate the wealth to improve black living standards. I wanted to see a South Africa which was fully reintegrated into the international community. Nor did I ever feel, for all the sound and fury of the left, that this was anything other than a high ideal of which no one need be ashamed.

Ashamed, perhaps not. Yet in spite of the 'siege mentality', the whites did indeed end up relinquishing power suddenly and without acceptable visible safeguards. The Zulus were anything but homogenous in their political views, dividing bitterly between ANC and Inkatha supporters.

Thatcher had an instinctive and understandable bias towards South Africa's economic structure (although this was hardly a model of free enterprise), if not towards apartheid itself. 'South Africa was rich not just because of natural resources, but because its economy was at least mainly run on free enterprise lines. Other African countries, while endowed with natural resources, were still poor because their economies were socialist and centrally controlled. Consequently the blacks in South Africa had higher incomes and were generally better educated than elsewhere in Africa: that was why the South Africans erected security fences to keep intended immigrants out, unlike the Berlin Wall which kept those blessed with a socialist system in. The critics of South Africa never mentioned these inconvenient facts. But simply because I recognized them did not mean that I held any brief for apartheid. The colour of someone's skin should not determine his or her political rights.'

In June 1984, P. W. Botha met Thatcher at Chequers, where she did 'not particularly warm' to him, but pressed for the release of Nelson Mandela. Thatcher's straightforward view of the situation was aired at the October Commonwealth summit at Nassau, where she rejected a compromise proposal, insisting that the Commonwealth should include a call for an end to violence in South Africa as a condition. This, of course, was the South African government's official stance towards negotiations with the ANC. Thatcher made clear to Howe that she was 'firmly in charge of our approach to South Africa, making the main decisions directly from Number Ten'.

Having staved off demands for growing but modest sanctions, Thatcher now proceeded to do the same with the European Community, postponing any decisions until a visit by Howe. The British foreign secretary was by now seething. At Nassau in October 1985, he described his consternation: 'Before the world's television cameras, Margaret set out to present not the successful achievement of a concerted Commonwealth policy for change in South Africa, but only the triumphant insignificance of the concessions she had had to make to achieve it. With forefinger and thumb only a few millimetres apart and contemptuously presented to the cameras, Margaret proclaimed that she had moved only "a tiny little bit". With four little words she had at one and the same time humiliated three dozen other heads of government, devalued the policy on which they had just agreed – and demeaned herself. She had certainly ensured that things would be a good deal less easy at any future such meeting. Even I could scarcely believe my ears.'

Britain's position on sanctions was stated unequivocally in the Foreign Office submission to the Foreign Affairs Select Committee in December 1985. It could hardly have been in starker contrast to the views even of Afrikaners on the ground, and probably reflected Thatcher's, not Howe's, views.

> The government is firmly opposed to general economic and trade boycotts because we believe they would hold back, not advance, the achievement of the objectives set out above. We understand why many have called for such sanctions as a means to force the pace of change, particularly against a background of continuing violence. But we cannot agree with them:
> * Such sanctions would stiffen resistance to change. Market forces are already exerting telling pressure on South Africa. Unlike sanctions which are imposed from outside, these forces cannot be resisted by appeals to white solidarity against 'foreign bullying'.
> * They would hit the black population hardest, so worsening the cycle of frustration, violence and repression.
> * They would seriously weaken neighbouring African economies.
> * They would undermine the process of economic development which is increasingly showing apartheid to be unworkable as well as unjust.
> * They would damage UK interests in South Africa and increase unemployment in the UK.

Denis Worrall, South African ambassador in London, told me six months later that sanctions would have a major effect, and also issued a veiled threat of retaliation:

> First of all, the economic effect would be to add to unemployment very considerably. Secondly, it would mean that the eventual cake which has to be shared in South Africa would be smaller than it would otherwise be. Thirdly, there would clearly be an effect on our neighbours' economies. I do not have to tell a committee of this standing with its knowledge and experience of the economic interdependence of Southern Africa. Fourthly, it would very

considerably reduce the effect of what is a positive factor for change in the South African situation.

Page 44 of the paperback edition of the Eminent Persons' Group Report, which was intended for seven heads of government, contains a profound contradiction. The EPG says: 'Of course, big business has for some years favoured reform. Needing a more skilled and mobile labour force to service South African industry' – and here I come to the point – 'as the economy has moved away from a simple dependence on mining and agriculture, business has called for increased spending on education, better housing and the abolition of influx control.'

The point is that 'as the economy has moved away from a simple dependence on mining and agriculture' there has been economic development; it is growth which has contributed to these changes. This was true of the deep south of the United States of America. The speed with which the civil rights campaign took place and desegregation and integration occurred in the deep south was greatly assisted by an economic boom in the south. What one is saying here is that by cutting back on the economy you are heightening unemployment, generating grievances all round and creating a very difficult political situation in which the possibility of really serious violence is considerably increased.

'You are saying that sanctions would have a very major effect on the South African economy?' I pressed him. 'Absolutely.' 'A lot of people suggest they would not?' He replied with a veiled threat:

They are already having a serious impact, I do not play that down. Yes, you might get some import substitution going on, but the fact is that we do have a high degree of self-sufficiency and we are able to reciprocate with sanctions and cause chaos in Southern Africa – something which is not sufficiently recognized. I am not saying it would happen, but if there were sanctions on the scale indicated by the EPG, South Africa certainly would consider not repaying its international loans, which would be all Mexico and a few other countries would need as a precedent, and it would bring down the whole Western financial system. I am not saying this is a consideration at the moment; I must stress that. But if you put South Africa in an extreme situation that kind of thing might apply.

In July 1986, Howe, *pace* his leader's intransigence, bravely for the first time moved an historic step towards recognition of the ANC in response to a question of mine on the Foreign Affairs Committee:

I think there is an increasing recognition of the importance of the ANC as one of those bodies that are representative of a significant part of African opinion. And, granted the present circumstances and the need to try and promote a non-violent way forward, we have concluded that it is right to take the steps you have seen in recognition of further contact with the ANC among other representative bodies.

Howe was despatched on his reluctant and futile one-man mission in July 1986. Mandela, the ANC and Archbishop Tutu all refused to see him, so low had British stock sunk as a neutral in the dispute. Even Chief Buthelezi argued that the British government was mistaken in its attitude to South Africa. Howe was then humiliated by Botha. As he wrote in his autobiography:

P.W. Botha received me for two hours in 23 July and for as long again on the 29th, in a room that despite its size seemed curiously cramped and free of natural light. The setting and atmosphere immediately reminded me of the room in Warsaw where one year before I had been received by General Jaruzelski. The talks were tense, quite often heated. He was dismissive of my mission and 'would not have received you but for my regard for your prime minister'. He showed no willingness to comprehend, let alone accept, any view of the world but his own. He betrayed no understanding of the gap between such changes as he had [just] contemplated and what the world expected. He produced, rather angrily, a bizarre pie-chart to prove that Bishop Tutu's views were representative of almost nobody in South Africa. He gave every sign of believing this.

At our second meeting, P.W. was even more ill-tempered than at our first. Almost beside himself, he denounced 'damned interfering foreigners' and gave no ground at all. A sadly narrow shaft of light came at the very end of this last talk. P.W.B. did say that he accepted Britain's good faith but 'was more doubtful of that of some other European leaders'. In his press conference immediately afterwards, he described his own plea to me that South Africa should be left in peace and denounced my commons speech (of 16

July) as 'nothing but a threat against our country'. 'You won't,' he said, 'force South Africa to commit national suicide.' I still do not know which was the more testing experience: being harangued by President Kaunda in public or by President Botha in private.

At long last Britain joined its Commonwealth partners in imposing a package of sanctions in August 1986. As Howe put it, it was 'a pity that on the way so much effort had been expended and bad blood shed unnecessarily'. He added, 'the sadness is that Margaret Thatcher, right to the end, persisted in her often ill-concealed antipathy towards most of her Commonwealth partners as also towards the Foreign and Commonwealth Office and all its works – as though it had nothing to do with the devoted and detailed work that so many people put in on her behalf.'

Thatcher remained opposed to sanctions in principle:

> The worst aspect was that because of President Botha's obstinacy we did not have enough to show by way of progress since the Nassau [Commonwealth summit]. There had been some significant reforms and the partial state of emergency had been lifted in March. But a nationwide state of emergency had been imposed in June; Mr Mandela was still in prison, and the ANC and other similar organizations were still banned. With the fiasco of the Eminent Persons Group in addition, there was no prospect of a peaceful political dialogue between the South African government and representatives of the black population.
>
> The US Congress was exerting increasing pressure for tough ANC sanctions and later in the year forced a change in the Administration's policy by overruling President Reagan's veto on a new sanctions bill. It was clear that I would have to come up with some modest package of measures, though whether this would arrest the march towards full-scale economic sanctions was doubtful. In any case I had a little list. For use as a diplomatic weapon of a rather different kind I had another little list of Commonwealth countries which applied detention without trial and similar illiberal practices – just in case.

Thatcher's reaction to F. W. de Klerk's accession to the post of National Party leader was that 'it was surely right to give the new South African leader the opportunity to make his mark without hamfisted outside intervention'. The conclusion that Thatcher, while she was sincere, was also mistaken on this issue is hard to escape. Sanctions, and particularly financial pressure, had an immense impact in changing white opinion in South Africa, however defiant the regime might appear in public.

Every effort by the British prime minister to dilute the impact of sanctions reinforced the South African sense that their outside opponents were toothless. Sanctions certainly adversely affected the black community in South Africa, as Thatcher argued; but their leaders were prepared to pay that price for freedom. Where Harold Macmillan had been on history's side with his 'wind of change' speech in 1960, his successor had set her face against the gale two and a half decades later.

* * *

Against this unpromising backdrop, Young, a defrocked Conservative, dared to venture. He saw Chalker, who was sympathetic, consulted the British ambassador in Pretoria, Robin Renwick, and wrote to Thatcher. Renwick, a new type of ambassador who established contacts with the black opposition instead of with only white liberal critics, was deeply interested. Young was received courteously in 10 Downing Street by Charles Powell, her principal foreign affairs adviser. Powell made it clear that the prime minister regarded the ANC as an unreconstructed terrorist group, no different from the PLO or the IRA. Young pointed out that the ANC probably had the backing of a majority of the population. Powell politely shifted the ground, saying that neither side had asked for British involvement.

Young pointed out that he had been requested to seek this from both the ANC and white sides. Young's view was that 'Britain had an ideal opportunity to play a pivotal role at the request of all concerned. Britain could have been well placed to help in the establishment of peace and building the future of South Africa. Mrs Thatcher missed a major opportunity to help negotiate peace.'

Powell then wrote to Young politely rejecting his approach. F. W. de Klerk's offer of talks about talks 'would certainly be a step in the right direction, and one which we have consistently urged on the South African government. But the Prime Minister remains convinced that there is no role for us as an honest broker. As I explained to you when we met, we are maintaining, indeed increasing, contacts with all parties within South Africa itself and encouraging them to work for and prepare for negotiations. But we continue to feel that any attempt to play a direct role from outside would be unwelcome and that it is for

the various parties in South Africa themselves to sort out these problems. Of course we will give help and encouragement along the lines
which I explained to you. But we do not want to intervene directly.'

On the face of it, this was indeed a missed opportunity by the
British prime minister. For both sides at the highest levels to be ready
to use Britain as a mediator – in particular for the ANC, which had
good reason deeply to distrust Thatcher – was astonishing. It offered a
major opportunity and potential triumph for British diplomacy to
broker the first public negotiations between the two sides – which
certainly was not beyond the wit of its diplomats. It would also have
re-established Britain's centrality to South African affairs. Moreover,
de Klerk, by signalling his readiness to seek overseas mediation, was
breaking with the old white South African objection to outsiders
meddling in the country's affairs.

One highly authoritative observer, who by no means always agreed
with Thatcher's position, nevertheless thus defends the British decision not to intervene: 'I was totally against a high-profile invitation
[for Britain to mediate]. This was already being done privately – a
British open initiative would have sunk it. It was part of the psyche of
the country that change must come from within. Rhodesia had been
a colony in legal terms, South Africa was not. Whites were hypersen-
sitive on this score.'

While these were all valid points, de Klerk had himself signalled that
the whites would have accepted mediation from Thatcher – presumably because of her standing among the white community. Certainly
de Klerk initially sought it, because it would have let him off the hook
of proposing the changes himself. Thatcher's refusal meant he had to
take the plunge himself. But the British government had taken a
colossal gamble which it may even have been unaware of: for if de
Klerk had failed to rise to the occasion, it would have passed up the
chance to defuse a massive and bloody potential civil war.

Did the British have any reason to be confident about de Klerk's
reformist tendencies? The signals are mixed. Renwick, the British
ambassador, had dinner with the Transvaal boss a long time before his
accession as party leader, and was deeply impressed. 'He made it clear
that he was not part of the security apparatus, that he was against the
death squads and Renamo in Mozambique, and that he was much
closer to the Johannesburg business community which had been
alienated by Botha.'

When Botha visited Chequers on that celebrated occasion in June,
it was impressed on him that 'if you do these things then there will be

a response'. That was how the private pressure was being applied, and it could have been derailed by Young's public initiative. In the event, de Klerk exceeded all expectations and the story ended happily. But if things had turned out differently, rejecting the Young initiative would have been a catastrophic mistake on the part of the British government.

The British government had in fact become a very indirect conduit between the two sides. In spite of Thatcher's 'hang-up' about the ANC, Renwick had frequent meetings with the organization, and she raised no objection; he was also in touch with Tambo. Renwick also saw de Klerk every couple of weeks, and was to see Mandela frequently after his release. Mandela believed Renwick had influence, and he later accepted that Thatcher had played an important role. Thatcher herself, in spite of her public stance, was a sincere opponent of apartheid, believing as she did in meritocracy. This did not obviate the fact that at Mells such major issues as Mandela's release were being considered, that both sides wanted British intervention, and that, as Young puts it, 'we missed a vast trick'. Thatcher's minimalism also influenced the Reagan White House: Young had an unsatisfactory meeting shortly afterwards with White House officials, although the State Department South Africa Bureau chief was more sympathetic.

Initially Renwick, like Thatcher, was sympathetic to Buthelezi's Inkatha Party, which had long been promoted by prominent Anglo South Africans like Sir Laurens van der Post. Much later Renwick came round to agreeing with Young that the ANC were the major players. The ANC, in his view 'had support across the country. Inkatha had no support outside Kwazulu. Buthelezi was a difficult man.' In spite of Renwick's own role, he acknowledges that Mells Park was 'important and influential' in the process, although 'it was not a negotiation'.

17
The Fall of Botha

Botha was still in charge of the state; but his country was moving away from him. This included the majority of members in his inner circle, headed by Barnard. At last the intelligence chief decided to act without the approval of his boss, knowing full well that a coup against him was in the making, and that he would not remain in place much longer. Barnard, who for so long had played the double game of talking to Mandela and the exiled ANC through the Mells talks simultaneously, who had never been prepared to step forward and take action without Botha's explicit authorization, had decided that the time had come to initiate direct contacts between the South African government and external ANC forces in the spring of 1988. But why, as Barnard already knew the external ANC's position through the Mells talks, was such a direct contact viewed as necessary?

There were two reasons: first, the ANC had grown tired of being stalled and was pressing for a sign that the government was sincere in its dialogue. For two and a half years now they had been talking at arm's length: the Mells Park talks could be disowned at any time by the South African government as being between dissident members of the Afrikaner establishment and the ANC.

Second and more important, Barnard wanted to short-circuit the negotiating process with Mandela. He had come to understand that Botha's tactic of detaching Mandela from his colleagues was a dead end. Any separate deal concluded with Mandela would be disowned by the external ANC and the UDF. Mandela could not deliver peace.

Worse, if a separate peace were to be concluded, Mandela, whatever his personal prestige, would be excoriated by his own movement and eventually marginalized; and the single figure most likely to exercise a moderating influence on the ANC would be lost. Mandela was too precious a commodity to be thrown away thus in a cynical piece of political manoeuvring by Botha. The time for deceit, for double-games, for divide and rule, for the perpetuation of apartheid by other means, was over.

If white South Africa wanted peace, it would have to talk not just to its illustrious prisoner, but to the men who commanded the fighters in the field. If it came to conflict, white South Africa would inevitably lose after a long war involving thousands of lives. Barnard concluded this, and did not inform Mandela of what he was about to do: to implement the pledge at Mells Park of the previous August and initiate direct contacts between the ANC and the South African security establishment. He soothed Botha by insisting that a meeting between intelligence officials and the ANC could be dismissed as a fact-finding exercise should it ever leak out. Mandela, engaged on his personal mission, would have been furious if he had known what was going on – which he did months later.

In June 1989, Esterhuyse flew to London to meet someone who had by now become an old friend: Thabo Mbeki, second-in-command of the ANC. They met in a pub to avoid surveillance or bugging. They made the arrangements for Mbeki to meet the senior South African official. 'I gave Thabo a personal assurance that if I picked up anything that indicated to me that it was a trap, or that something could go wrong, I would alert him.' The ANC and the South Africans were still at war: it would not be surprising if the security services were carefully luring Mbeki into their hands, either to capture or eliminate the second-ranking official in the ANC.

The agent Barnard had charged with the mission was his chief director of operations, Maritz Spaarwater, a veteran of the service who had risen to become an acquaintance and to spy personally upon Zambia's President Kaunda and even Namibia's Sam Nujoma. The meeting, which was set up in secret through phone calls between Lusaka and Pretoria, with Spaarwater calling himself John Campbell and Mbeki John Simelane, took three months to prepare.

Botha, now facing the biggest crisis of his presidency, was only dimly aware of what was going on and, when presidential authority was at last requested, it was in the vaguest possible terms: 'It is necessary that more information should be obtained and processed concerning the ANC, and the aims, alliances and potential approachability of its different leaders and groupings. To enable this to be done, special additional direct action will be necessary, particularly with the help of National Intelligence Service functionaries.'

But the man who authorized this directive was not Botha. It was F. W. de Klerk, in his first week as head of state, presiding over the State Security Council after the coup by the National Party caucus that finally toppled Botha.

* * *

Botha's downfall was in fact a textbook example of political assassination at the top. As the Mells meetings had revealed, for two years now senior South Africans had been grumbling that the old man was past it, that he was an obstacle in the way of new thinking, that his temper and indecisiveness were a liability. Yet there existed no easy way under South Africa's constitutional system to depose a president (a new post), who had the authority of a head of state and the power of a prime minister.

Ultimately, Botha's overthrow was the result of an elementary political mistake: he forgot to nurture his own power base, the parliamentary party and the cabinet, preferring to rule through the State Security Council and a coterie of advisers, many from the security services. He believed he could rule alone, without the consent of his peers. But under the old British-style constitution, even as amended, his power derived ultimately from parliament, a point he neglected. Parliament had power, but no influence; his inner circle had influence but no power. When the parliamentary party and its representatives in the cabinet chose to act, they did so with deadly effect.

Ironically, Botha sealed his downfall through the very act that he had so long hesitated to perform – arguably the most enlightened of his rule, but one which derived from cynical political motives and left him starkly exposed to his enemies. He saw Nelson Mandela at last.

On 5 July 1989, at 5.30 on an early winter morning, Major Marais, commandant of Victor Verster prison, called at Mandela's bungalow to inspect him in a new suit and shirt issued the day before. Marais undid the tie Mandela had partly done up, and reknotted it. They drove in a five-car convoy – two police cars ahead, two behind, telling the security guards at the gate of the prime minister's residence in Pretoria that an African politician was visiting by night – in case the hardliners in the security forces got to hear of the meeting – and parked in an underground garage.

They went upstairs in a lift to the floor where Botha had his office in the attractive nineteenth-century Dutch building, the Tuynhuys, where men like Verwoerd and Vorster had presided over the grimmest impositions of apartheid. Kobie Coetsee and Neil Barnard were there to meet him. Barnard got down on his knees to tie the prisoner's shoelaces properly. Mandela, even more nervous than the two whites, who had long been pressing for this meeting and had at last secured it, takes up the story:

> From the opposite side of his grand office, P. W. Botha walked towards me. He had planned his march perfectly, for we met exactly half way. He had his hand out and was smiling broadly, and in fact, from that very first moment, he completely disarmed me. He was unfailingly courteous, deferential and friendly ... From the first, it was not as though we were engaged in tense political arguments but a lively and interesting tutorial. We did not discuss substantive issues so much as history and South African culture.
>
> I mentioned that I had recently read an article in an Afrikaans magazine about the 1914 Afrikaner rebellion, and I mentioned how they had occupied towns in the Free State. I said I saw our struggle as parallel to this famous rebellion, and we discussed this historical episode for quite a while. South African history, of course, looks very different to the black man and the white man. Their view was that the rebellion had been a quarrel between brothers, whereas my struggle was a revolutionary one. I said that it could also be seen as a struggle between brothers who happen to be of different colours.

The only sticky moment came at the end, when Mandela called for the release of all political prisoners, in particular Walter Sisulu. Botha told him that he could not do so. After just half an hour Botha 'rose and shook my hand, saying what a pleasure it had been. Indeed, it had been. I thanked him, and left the way I had come.'

> While the meeting was not a breakthrough in terms of negotiations, it was one in another sense. Mr Botha had long talked about the need to cross the Rubicon, but he never did it himself until that morning at Tuynhuys. Now, I felt, there was no turning back.

Mandela's elation was unbounded, after so many years of seeking such a meeting; he felt he had made a personal breakthrough and been received – after decades as the lowest of the low, a political prisoner – by the state president as the leader of South Africa's blacks. In fact, while the symbolic significance of the meeting could not be denied, it was the climax of a squalid personal manoeuvre designed to try and preserve Botha in office – but which went disastrously wrong, precipitating his downfall.

Botha had prevaricated about meeting Mandela for nearly two years, sometimes blowing hot, sometimes cool. Almost certainly he had initially had no intention of doing so unless Mandela could be induced to conclude a separate deal from the ANC in Lusaka. But Mandela had not done so, except in his 11-page memorandum, when he went further than the ANC had in offering implicitly to renounce violence and to guarantee white minority rights in the constitution.

Although this was a significant step forward, it hardly provided Botha with the propaganda coup he sought. However, after his sudden replacement as party leader, he became increasingly desperate to regain the initiative from the disgruntled cabinet and parliamentary party which had chosen the man most inimical to him, de Klerk. The other three contenders, even though reformist, had been elevated by him to office, and owed him a good deal.

De Klerk was the only outsider, a provincial boss who had made his own way up the party through a coalition of local interests, notably in the Transvaal. Botha could see the writing on the wall. De Klerk, however, had one disadvantage: he was known to be an uncompromising conservative. Alarmed by the possibility that he might be ousted, Botha reckoned that by seeing Mandela at last, he might suddenly seize the mantle of being the man of the future in South Africa after all.

By seeing Mandela for just half an hour, and apparently discussing nothing at all, Botha hoped to get the best of both worlds: to demonstrate he was not the unbending conservative portrayed in the media, while reassuring the Afrikaner community that he was doing his best to secure the agreement of the black Africans to his own constitutional settlement. Indeed, the very fact that Mandela chose to meet him suggested approval of his new constitutional plan – a system by which blacks would be elected by the homelands and townships for their own separate chamber in parliament.

This was the reverse of the truth, of course; but Botha could put it that way; and it is hard to see what advantage Mandela had obtained from the meeting, other than to suggest that the state president was treating him, an ANC leader, as worthy of a perfunctory chat. Certainly to no outsider would it look as though Mandela, a prisoner patronized by the government leader, had finally pushed Botha to negotiate. One very well-informed diplomatic observer is blunt:

'Botha never had any intention of releasing Mandela. The meeting was a gimmick. He knew he was on the skids.' Others suggest the meeting in fact put the seal on Mandela's agreement with the government. A tape-recording of the meeting made on Botha's instructions was later destroyed by Barnard – possibly in order to cover this up.

News of the meeting quickly leaked out, to Botha's ostensible fury. On the contrary, he thought he had seized the political initiative and trumped his opponents, and may even have been responsible for the leak. He had shown he was not inflexible after all; he was prepared to talk to a famous black political prisoner – on his terms, of course, and about nothing of substance. In fact, Botha's hardline supporters were infuriated, while the whites who long felt he had to go were not impressed – indeed ,regarded the gesture as a sign of Botha's instability and inability to make up his mind about what he really wanted, an act of desperation.

* * *

Events moved on with the inevitability of a Greek tragedy. Two events, in particular, were to hasten Botha's demise. The first was a sudden panic in the National Party that it might for the first time be deprived of its absolute majority in the election scheduled for September. If some opinion polls were to be believed, the Democratic Party stood to gain so much support that it and the Conservative Party might between them create a hung parliament, forcing the ruling party to choose between retrenchment – an alliance with the Conservatives – or a deal with the Democratic Party. It would probably have had no choice but the latter: an alliance with Treurnicht against the tide of history would have led to disaster.

Among National Party leaders, the talk was of little else – how to force Botha out before the impending electoral disaster and save the government's freedom for manoeuvre. In the event the Democratic Party won a record 24 seats and, after a bitterly fought election campaign, replete with intimidation and dirty tricks, the National Party retained its majority only through the poor performance of the Conservatives – a sign of the changing tide of white opinion. The atmosphere at the heart of the National Party at the time, says one prominent Afrikaner observer, was 'one of hysteria'.

The second event was the reawakening of black protest from the comparative lull of the previous year. Already the ANC had declared 1989 a 'year of mass action'. A massive hunger strike had forced the

Botha government to start the process of releasing political detainees. Cosatu launched a series of protests against the Labour Relations Act.

On 2 August, the Mass Democratic Movement, a kind of reincarnated UDF after its banning, held a series of rallies against the segregation of hospitals, beaches and public transport, as well as a massive strike of some 3 million in protest against the 6 September election. The demonstrations were once again met with savage repression.

The new campaign, which had huge support and was peaceful except where it was repressed, raised the spectre of a repeat of the years of protest of 1985 and 1986. Once this was allowed to get out of control, the government would be forced into a familiar cycle of escalating protest followed by crack-down. Botha had effectively wasted nearly two years since the 1985–6 protests had died down. De Klerk would have to move fast before black protest got out of control and inspired a white backlash. The speed of his subsequent actions owed as much to this consideration as to anything else. But first he had to get rid of Botha.

What happened next was, in the words of a prominent Afrikaner, 'a brave, clinical coup'. Within a month, on the cold mid-winter day of 14 August, Botha summoned his cabinet to express his indignation that de Klerk, the effective prime minister, was to meet Zambia's President Kaunda later in the month without seeking his (Botha's) authorization. Botha had been preparing to give them all a furious lecture, to show them who was boss. Instead, one by one, they told him he had been a great leader of South Africa but the time had come for him to take a rest and appoint an acting president – for the good of his health. Even Botha's loyal defence minister, General Magnus Malan – no doubt partly influenced by news of the Botha–Mandela meeting ('he really has gone over the top this time') – concurred.

By all accounts, Botha lost his temper, accusing de Klerk, the leader of the conspirators, of acting 'with a smile on your face and a dagger in your hand'. When de Klerk told Botha that he was concerned for his health, the reply was 'I am fit. Is any one of you in possession of a medical certificate that proclaims you to be healthy? Let me hear, how many of you are sitting here with pills in your pockets while you drag my health into this matter? Oh, so that's going to be your new tack, your new propaganda: he's not *compos mentis*.' He refused to appoint an acting president, and resigned his office later the same day in an angry, blustering broadcast on television.

It seemed, once again, that white South Africa had turned on a leader who had dared to negotiate with the regime's principal opponent. The truth was very different. Botha had wasted the opportunity to make white South Africans comprehend the reality of their predicament, whereas de Klerk, although no sentimentalist, was nothing if not a realist.

* * *

The dramatic fall of Botha was followed by five rapid-fire events: a new outbreak of mass black protest (which had already started on 2 August); the Harare Declaration of 21 August by the ANC; South Africa's general election on 6 September; the first direct meeting between South African officials and the ANC on 12 September; and the resumption of the Mells Park talks on 19 September.

The Harare Declaration was a document adopted by the Organization of African Unity which committed the ANC to intensifying the guerrilla struggle but which also for the first time outlined peace terms explicitly – and committed the movement as a whole to them. It was secured only after intense internal wrangling, and paved the way for the direct negotiations between the ANC and the National Intelligence Agency that followed. Specifically, the Declaration set out five preconditions for suspending the armed struggle and starting formal negotiations: lifting the state of emergency, ending restrictions on political activity, unbanning the parties, releasing all political prisoners and ending all executions.

It declared that 'a conjuncture of circumstances exists which, if there is a demonstrable readiness on the part of the Pretoria regime to engage in negotiations genuinely and seriously, could create the possibility to end apartheid through negotiations'. The declaration also set out the guiding principles of the new constitution: the formation of a united, democratic and non-racial state; common and equal citizenship and nationality for all South Africans; the right of participation in the government and administration of the country on the basis of universal suffrage exercised through one person, one vote; the right of everyone to form or join any political party (provided that the party concerned does not try to further racism); an entrenched bill of rights; a legal system guaranteeing equality before the law; an economic order promoting the well-being of all South Africans; and a democratic South Africa respecting the rights, sovereignty and territorial integrity of all countries. The declaration was in fact the direct result of the Mells Park negotiations so far, and was beautifully timed to permit the new South Africa to respond.

The election resulted in a respectable victory for the National Party under its new, more level-headed but apparently conservative leader. Conservative Party support had clearly peaked, and the ruling party was still seen to be the best guarantor of the whites' interests through the stormy years ahead.

The meeting between the National Intelligence Agency and the ANC was scheduled to be held in Switzerland, the one country in Europe which did not require South Africans to have visas. The five-man South African delegation consisted of Spaarwater, Barnard's deputy Mike Louw, and three field agents. They checked into the Palace Hotel at Lucerne. The three supporting agents were then sent to Geneva to watch Mbeki and Jacob Zuma and to tail them, in case the ANC men had set a trap (the converse was much more likely). Instead, they had only a driver – a local-based ANC supporter.

They reached the hotel to meet the intelligence agency officials. Louw takes up the story: 'I remember we said, "How can we expect these guys to trust us?" I mean, we might have been sitting there with guns and the moment they opened the door just blown them away. So we opened the door so that they could see in, and we stood there in full view.

'We could hear them coming, talking, and then they came around the corner and they could see us standing there. Thabo walked in and said, "Well here we are, bloody terrorists and for all you know fucking Communists as well." That broke the ice, and we all laughed, and I must say that from that moment on there was no tension.'

The two delegations went over the familiar ground already trodden by the Mells meetings: but this time the whites had a decisive mandate from the president. When they returned home, De Klerk, who had not taken in the true nature of the mission, was at first extremely angry, but then realized he had indeed authorized it during his first week as president, and was fascinated by the ANC's willingness to negotiate – something Botha had long known about, and long suppressed.

18
Face to Face

The Mells Park talks, having achieved the astonishing Lucerne face-to-face ANC–South Africa talks, now became nothing less than direct negotiations on an agenda dictated both by the president's office and the ANC executive. This September meeting was the decisive session at which the new government and Mbeki agreed how to cross the Rubicon.

The meeting was modestly complicated by the fact that the secret of the talks had at last been exposed in the press, after so long. They were reported as taking place, but not where or who was backing them, to Agnew's and Young's intense relief – although by this stage they had so much support from the South African government that there could not have been a backlash against Consolidated Goldfields.

On the white side, three more took part: the Reverend Ernst Lombard, Cape moderator of the Dutch Reformed Church, the first senior cleric prepared to attach his name to direct talks with the ANC; Louis Kriel, a prominent member of the business community and managing director of the Fruit Industry Board; and Ebbe Domisse, editor designate of the Afrikaner newspaper *Die Burger*.

With the election of his brother as president, Wimpie de Klerk in effect took charge of the South African side from Esterhuyse. The two sides met as old friends, in ebullient mood after the astonishing events of the previous two months. Wimpie de Klerk opened the proceedings by telling them that he spoke with authority after having consulted both his brother and other members of the president's office. He expressed a little disappointment that the Democratic Party had not secured more votes in the election of 6 September, but warm satisfaction that the Conservative Party had not done better.

He was guardedly optimistic about what would now happen within the National Party, saying his brother had to act as he chose. In Wimpie's view, the perception of De Klerk as 'the new man, the open man, with credible contacts overseas' had enormously benefited the National Party in the election, effacing the bitter circumstances of Botha's deposition. The outcome of the election would enable intensive negotiations to begin with all parties in an attempt to devise a new constitution based upon group structures.

This was a new concept, and one which immediately aroused ANC suspicions: it seemed to many like yet another form of disguised apartheid. De Klerk replied that the concept was entirely different: the idea was a bill of rights to protect the language, culture and religion of the whites, presumably under black majority rule, although de Klerk did not spell this out. He went on to assert that reform would be swift because it was urgent.

De Klerk believed his brother had a clear mandate for reform. If he failed to move, the strength of the Democratic Party would increase and Afrikanerdom would split. In practice an alliance between the Democratic Party and the National Party was still the only conceivable option if the latter's support continued to fall: it could not go into alliance with the Conservative Party. However, if the country was allowed to drift into chaos, Conservative Party support would increase.

De Klerk now spelt out how his brother saw the process of transition. First, an agreement would be forged through negotiations between the government and the ANC over three years; then the transition to majority rule would be carried out over the following five years. This timetable was a colossal concession: the first complete acceptance that majority rule was inevitable. While Wimpie de Klerk was not his brother, if he spoke with his authority, it was an astonishing step forward.

The ANC representatives replied with smiles: the process would certainly have to be shortened considerably. De Klerk said nothing, but acknowledged that the first step would have to take place with exceptional speed: specifically, his brother had just 8 months to move before being forced back into confrontation and isolation. The election had given him the initiative, and he knew he must not drop the ball. Specifically, any decision to release Mandela would presuppose the unbanning of the ANC – because he would immediately return to his old political activities and could not be reimprisoned.

Mbeki interrupted forcibly to argue that the unbanning of the ANC was not a matter for negotiation, but a precondition for any serious discussion with the ANC. De Klerk promptly laid down a series of detailed questions. First, what would the ANC's stance be on violence if negotiations did start? The ANC's reply was equally specific: violence would cease during the negotiating period although the ANC's guerrilla army would not be disbanded until a treaty was signed. This at last spelt out the terms for a ceasefire implicit in the Harare Declaration.

De Klerk then raised an old chestnut – what were the links between the ANC and the Communist Party? Once again, the ANC delegation made clear that some members of their central committee also belonged to the Communist Party, but this should not obstruct the need for talks. De Klerk asked point blank whether the ANC would take part in a power-sharing arrangement – and Mbeki surprised him by not giving a flat no: power-sharing would be acceptable during a transitional period.

Would the ANC accept other black representatives around the negotiating table? Mbeki's generous response surprised de Klerk. Inkatha, the homeland leaders and the PAC – in fact any genuinely representative black leaders – would be acceptable. The ANC was not claiming a monopoly of black support and was prepared to enter a dialogue even with those black movements that were its bitter rivals. De Klerk then raised a novel point: he wondered whether the ANC would seek a UN role in any South African settlement, such as that applying to nearby Namibia. The ANC replied – to white satisfaction – that it did not envisage a role for the UN or any outsider.

Mbeki in turn now put three points to the whites. The release of Mandela and the unbanning of the parties must take priority: he accepted that the government only had 8 months to act – which was as good as saying that the ANC would back off aggravating the internal situation in South Africa during the period. However, he wanted the whites to spell out what they meant by 'group status' and by the protection of minority rights – always the key to the whole negotiating process as far as the moderate whites were concerned.

Mbeki and Zuma then went on to elaborate on the Harare Declaration. They insisted that the document, although formulated under international auspices, was not an OAU declaration and could be amended without reference to the member states. It was intended to show the way forward politically rather than through armed struggle. A member of the white side expressed the fear that the UN security council might adopt a resolution based on the Declaration – which would enrage the right as an example of external interference in South Africa's affairs. Mbeki reckoned that this was highly unlikely, and would be resisted by the ANC, as it would be 'too limiting on all concerned'.

In a long exchange, Mbeki was asked bluntly when the armed struggle would be suspended, and when he would negotiate. He replied that the armed struggle would end – as opposed to being suspended – when the final treaty was signed. He said that sanctions would be lifted as soon as the ANC was satisfied that the negotiating process could not be reversed. When the constitution was agreed, violence would end. In concluding this part of the discussion, the ANC raised the question, for onward transmission to Pretoria, of who would monitor the agreement.

The whole exchange had been remarkable and historic, marking a great step towards closing the divide between the two sides, with the ANC spelling out in precise, measured and agreed language the exact terms on which it would cease fire. For his part de Klerk had offered an astonishing preview of his brother's impending revolution of February 1990. At Mells Park, Mbeki had provided the assurances the new government needed to take the plunge.

The issue of why and when his brother F. W., generally viewed as one of the most conservative National Party leaders, had undergone his Damascene conversion was to exercise many minds over the coming years. Leon Wessels, the first cabinet minister publicly to repudiate apartheid, for example, dates de Klerk's conversion to the time when, in 1986, the National Party had accepted the principle of 'a single South Africa' as opposed to one founded on tribal homelands. De Klerk remarks of the occasion, 'once we had gone through the process of reassessment I took a leap in my own mind, more decisively than many other National Party politicians, that power-sharing with the blacks was the right course for a new political dispensation.'

Allister Sparks remarks that 'from that moment on, there occurred what Wimpie calls "an evolutionary conversion". Others agree. None among his closest friends and colleagues was aware of any blinding moment of change, yet imperceptibly, incrementally, de Klerk shifted one hundred and eighty degrees.' De Klerk's law partner, Ignatius Vorster, adds, 'my guess is that at some stage – I don't know when – he realized that if you go on like this you are going to lose the game, the cup, the league, everything.'

Sparks subscribes to a dramatic version of events: 'The climactic event in de Klerk's evolutionary conversion was undoubtedly his inauguration as president on September 20, 1989. Despite his denial of any

Damascus road experience, friends and relatives say de Klerk talked of being seized by a powerful sense of religious "calling" on that day, which his favourite pastor, the Reverend Pieter Bingle, reinforced in a sermon at the inauguration service in Pretoria.'

Wimpie de Klerk takes up the story. 'He was literally in tears after the service. In tears he told us we should pray for him – that God was calling him to save all the people of South Africa, that he knew he was going to be rejected by his own people but that he had to walk this road and that we must all help him. He grew very emotional, confessing his belief that God had called upon him and that he couldn't ignore the call. I remember, too, that he said, "I am not a fundamentalist, I don't think I am important in God's eyes, but I believe in God and I believe I am being called upon to perform a specific task at this time in this new situation."'

Yet Wimpie de Klerk's own summation at Mells Park months before suggests that the process was much less a sudden spiritual one than that of a canny politician, who, on taking office, had immediately understood the practical realities he faced – and the reality was that white South Africa was totally boxed in. Moreover, he believed he had only one chance to act: within 8 months the honeymoon would be over.

Although his ideas were light years ahead of those of most of his fellow Afrikaner politicians, he was still impaled on a fundamentally anti-democratic concept – that of power-sharing as opposed to majority rule – and he really believed that once the negotiating process had started, the transition could be spread over 8 years. In practice the ANC was much more far-sighted about this: it believed that once Mandela was released and the organization was unbanned, the pressures for reform would spin out of the government's control.

It was this insight that made Mbeki and his team so unbending about the need for their unbanning, yet so flexible and vague about the shape of the negotiations themselves. For once the political process became unstoppable, once the blacks of South Africa were mobilized behind them, the ANC leaders knew they would be able to direct the pace and terms of the negotiation. This fact was not appreciated by the white side, which still thought it could set the timetable for change. But F. W. de Klerk, by the time of the Mells Park conference, had clearly made up his mind to do what Botha had only toyed with: release Mandela and unban the ANC unconditionally.

* * *

The Mells discussions now reached a much more delicate subject: the extent to which the ANC in fact controlled the internal resistance: in particular, what was the purpose of a conference that had been called by Cosatu, the UDF and the Churches? The ANC side told the whites the conference would discuss three issues: negotiations; the role of the international community; and a programme of action. Some 2,500 delegates would attend, from any political party which subscribed to at least four common principles: non-racialism; lifting the state of emergency; unbanning the parties; and the release of political prisoners. The ANC was in full support of the conference and hoped for the widest possible attendance.

Esterhuyse then asked a deeply loaded question, one that South African intelligence had long sought a specific answer to: what was the status of Mandela? Mbeki replied that his position before his arrest was president of the Transvaal section of the ANC; that Tambo was senior to him, and Walter Sisulu senior to both. Tambo was likely to remain ANC president when Mandela was released. Thus Mbeki was quietly telling the South Africans that even if they secured a deal with Mandela, he could not deliver: they would not be securing agreement even with the leaders of the ANC, let alone the movement as a whole.

The discussion shifted to the apparent reluctance of the ANC to meet with Chief Buthelezi to discuss how black-on-black violence could be reduced in Natal. The Zulu leader, according to the ANC, had behaved impossibly, demanding that the talks be held in London, seeking equal representation for Inkatha with the ANC, Cosatu and the UDF together, on the grounds that they were the same organization, and insisting on a personal invitation from Tambo. The ANC reluctantly gave way on two out of the three demands, but was finding him troublesome to deal with.

Mbeki moved from the defensive onto the offensive, raising the issue of group rights, which deeply concerned him. If this concept was based on racial differences, it would be unacceptable. If however it was defined in terms of a bill of rights to guarantee legitimate cultural and religious rights, it was acceptable. The ANC turned to the constitutional settlement within Namibia. In spite of the agreement, and what the whites present acknowledged seemed an imminent election victory for Swapo of around two-thirds of the votes, there was considerable fear on the part of Namibia's blacks that the whites would re-intervene.

Specifically, the South African defence force still had around 1,500 soldiers and a further 1,000 back-up troops, and a skeleton officer corps in Namibia ready to lead the country's demobilized troops. Further, the South West Africa Territorial Force continued to report to its old commanders. The fear was that they would engineer disorder after a Swapo victory, providing the pretext for a return by the South African army to restore law and order. (The fact that this did not happen was later crucial in reassuring the blacks that peaceful evolution was also possible within South Africa itself.) Willem de Klerk was asked to convey their fears to his brother to ensure that Namibian peace was not sabotaged by rogue elements within the South African security forces.

Michael Young then led a discussion on the international context. He   explained that George Bush in America would be much more reluctant to veto the imposition of sanctions by Congress than Ronald Reagan had been; moreover the black caucus in Congress was more militant on the issue than ever before. The administration, which had other important matters on its agenda, was unwilling to fight Congress over sanctions. The South African government accepted that Thatcher would require some sign of flexibility on their part if she was to fend off yet another concerted drive for sanctions at the forthcoming Commonwealth summit in October.

In addition, because the Russians were seeking negotiations between the parties in South Africa – rather than inciting the ANC to continue the armed struggle – the Americans were taking a much more relaxed view of the conflict, no longer viewing the South Africans as part of the wider struggle against Communism. In fact this was of monumental importance, and provided perhaps the decisive push for both sides towards a settlement. The ANC was no longer assured of unlimited support from its principal sponsor, which now sought peace; and the whites could no longer count on tacit sympathy from the Americans.

Young suggested that the Cold War had ended in South Africa; both sides were pushed together by those that had previously sought to divide them, the two superpowers. More than any other factor, this helped to give the peace process impetus at this stage. For the whites to admit this openly caused Mbeki to draw breath. The participants at this Mells Park meeting did not behave just like old friends. They felt the process had undertaken a quantum leap. They were now talking about nuts and bolts, not just abstract concepts. Yet the parties had nearly been to the top of the hill before, only to discover another ridge just ahead. A year before, heady optimism about the imminent release of Mandela had been dashed by Botha; now the hopes that Wimpie de

Klerk offered could prove just as evanescent. His brother had just a few months before his country would be plunged back into confrontation once again. Was he a big enough man to seize the initiative? His elder brother believed so, but remained committed to forming the Democratic Party, along with Sampie Terreblanche, as a kind of insurance policy if F. W. failed (although Wimpie was soon to resign in deference to his brother's family susceptibilities). On the roller coaster offered by the Mells talks, the participants were once again riding high – and might soon come crashing down again.

19
The De Klerk Revolution

The first concrete sign of white South Africa's transformation took place a week before de Klerk's inauguration, when protesters led by Archbishop Tutu decided to stage a march in Cape Town after a number of demonstrators had been killed by the police. Usually the protest would have been banned, gone ahead anyway, and a confrontation with police would have ensued. This time de Klerk permitted the demonstration after its leaders had promised it would be peaceful. Some 30,000 marched without incident.

At the inauguration itself, the Reverend Pieter Bingle (in a sermon almost certainly cleared in advance, if not coordinated with the new president – and therefore highly unlikely to have caused his conversion) intoned prophetically, 'He who stands in God's council chamber will be aggressive enough to tackle problems and challenges fearlessly. New ways will have to be found where roads enter cul-de-sacs, or are worn out or cannot carry the heavy traffic. Excess baggage will be cast aside. Certain things will stay and others will have to be discarded. Those stuck in the grooves of the past will find that besides the spelling, death is the only difference between a groove and a grave.' What the sermon lacked in feel for words, it made up for in its underlying message.

After the Mells Park meeting, events moved with a suddenness that stunned even Young and Agnew. In the early hours of 15 October, Walter Sisulu and six other key ANC prisoners, including Ray Mhlaba, Andrew Mlangeni and Ahmed Kathrada (the four closest Robben Island colleagues of Mandela) were released and permitted to engage in political activity. The release generated an intensely emotional reaction, and not just from Albertina Sisulu, who sobbed, 'I don't know how I'm going to cope with having him around the whole time'. Tens of thousands took to the streets across South Africa bearing ANC banners – which were still officially banned.

In Soweto, huge crowds surged around the Holy Cross Church, where Sisulu, the 77-year-old former political prisoner and highest-ranking ANC member, intoned with statesmanlike calm, 'We believe that in our lifetime there will be a government that includes black people. We are not seeking a black government as such. We are seeking a democratic system in which a black man can be president and a white man can be president. There is no question of judging people on the basis of colour.'

It was the first concrete result of Mandela's pleading for Sisulu's release, although its timing had been determined by the whites for maximum effect to assist Thatcher in her efforts at the Commonwealth summit. Still, it marked a great leap forward – and was not accompanied by the rioting that Afrikaners had feared. It was also a useful test for de Klerk of what might happen if he actually released Mandela.

At about that time, the exiled ANC's suspicion that Mandela would be tempted to do a deal with the whites began to diminish. In a sense, that had already happened. It was Mandela who, in his memorandum of the previous January, had first concluded that the whites had special interests which would have to be protected. With deep reluctance, because it smacked of apartheid under a different guise – preferential treatment for the whites ran against the spirit of 'pure' majority rule – the ANC had been forced to enshrine the protection of minority white interests in the Harare Declaration. Mandela had already conceded the point.

But at Mells Park they had sought to insist that this should amount to no more than protection under the constitution in a bill of rights. Now they had to get that message through to Mandela before he gave away anything more. Fortunately, for the first time, a direct channel of communication had been opened up between Mandela and the ANC in Lusaka.

Mac Maharaj, a thin, cerebral, taciturn Indian-descended member of the ANC executive who had served a 12-year sentence on Robben Island, infiltrated South Africa from Lusaka in 1988 by crossing the border in disguise, then set himself up with a small computer equipped with a modem, transmitting messages from public telephone boxes to London and Australia which were then retransmitted through to Lusaka. This elaborate system was necessary to by-pass the monitored telephone link between South Africa and Lusaka.

Maharaj then set up a system to smuggle messages in and out to Mandela in his bungalow at Victor Verster. Maharaj made use of the continual flow of visitors that Mandela was permitted to receive. 'I would print out a message in a small typeface on a thin strip of paper that could be folded in such a way that you could pass it to him while you were shaking hands. It was a trick we had learned on Robben Island ... I offered Mandela other techniques, such as invisible pens. I even told him that if he could describe some article, a wallet or item in the house, I could have an exact replica made, and then just swap them and exchange the messages in that way. That would give him more time to prepare his replies. But he rejected these as too complicated. I think he was also nervous that there might be hidden video cameras in the house.'

Once the contact was established, Tambo was delighted and sent Mandela his most urgent message: 'Look, there is only one problem: don't manoeuvre yourself into a situation where we have to abandon sanctions. That's the key problem. We are very concerned that we should not get stripped of our weapons of struggle, and the most important of these is sanctions. That is the trump card with which we can mobilize international opinion and pull governments over to our side.'

Tambo had heard rumours that Mandela was contemplating urging Western countries to call off sanctions in exchange for his release and the unbanning of the ANC. Mandela's reply is not recorded. However, news of his memorandum to Botha reached UDF members as well as ANC members in Lusaka. Govan Mbeki angrily instructed UDF officials not to visit Mandela any more. In Lusaka, Tambo was mortified by initial reports of the memorandum and resolved that he would not tell fellow ANC members the contents of his communications with Mandela; they would have been incensed. When, however, the contents of the full memorandum were passed on through Maharaj's channels, the fear that Mandela was selling out was assuaged.

Tambo, who had so assiduously tried to keep the show together for two decades, had a major stroke in August 1989, almost certainly brought on by the exertion of a long trip selling the Harare Declaration to African leaders. Leadership of the ANC-in-exile effectively passed to Thabo Mbeki. Thus when South Africa's two top intelligence officers, under the president's direct control, met Mbeki, they were effectively meeting the leader of the ANC.

The anger of his UDF and ANC colleagues, fanned by the South African Communist Party and transmitted by Maharaj, shook

Mandela, and he considered his position. His meeting with Botha, his willingness to agree that white rights should be enshrined in the new constitution, and now the fear that he would begin advocating that sanctions be lifted had left the ANC in Lusaka deeply apprehensive.

* * *

De Klerk now gave a remarkable, if guarded, imprimatur to the Mells Park process. On one of his visits to South Africa to broker the Mells talks, Michael Young was pointedly invited to attend the budget address as a guest in the presidential box. He watched Barend du Plessis, the finance minister, deliver his speech, with the new prime minister sitting beside him: both looked up at Young. After exchanging notes, de Klerk came to the head of the stairs and shook hands with Young, exchanging an intense glance; du Plessis followed. 'It was as though they didn't want to be seen with me,' recalls Young. 'But it did take place' – an official endorsement of the Mells process from the very top.

Meanwhile de Klerk ushered in a series of moderate reforms. South African beaches were opened to people of all colours. The Reservation of Separate Amenities Act was to be repealed: this provided for segregation of public facilities such as restaurants, buses, parks and public lavatories. The National Security Management System, a parallel military structure to coordinate anti-guerrilla activities, was dissolved.

On 4 December he subjected his whole cabinet, along with senior officials, to a private brain-storming session at a remote retreat called D'Naba in North West Transvaal. There de Klerk presented them with the *fait accompli* that Mandela would be released and the ANC unbanned. The sticking point was legalization of the Communist Party.

Magnus Malan argued grimly against this, but common sense prevailed among the majority. If the Communist Party remained proscribed the other parties would mount a massive campaign for its legalization until the government was forced to give way. De Klerk must have been surprised by the ease with which he convinced his colleagues. Yet all but the most die-hard whites realized there was no other way out.

The stage was now set for the president's first meeting with Mandela on 12 December. By this time, the prisoner at last had a clear line of communication with the ANC in Lusaka through Maharaj. He reckoned he could give no more hostages to fortune. Equally de Klerk was serious in talking, not seeking to bully him. This was no mere political stratagem, such as Botha's had been, into which Mandela had unwittingly fallen. De Klerk listened to what the prisoner had to say even though he knew most of what Mandela had to tell him.

Mandela talked tough. In particular he sought to repair the damage with his followers that had resulted from his concession on the issue of 'substantial guarantees' for the whites. He took an even stronger stand against the concept of 'group rights' than Mbeki had at Mells Park the previous summer.

> One of the issues I emphasized that day was the National Party's recently introduced five-year plan, which contained the concept of 'group rights'. The idea of 'group rights' was that no racial or ethnic group could take precedence over any other. Although they defined 'group rights' as a way of protecting the freedom of minorities in a new South Africa, in fact their proposal was a means of preserving white domination. I told Mr de Klerk this was unacceptable to the ANC.
>
> I added that it was not in his interest to retain this concept, for it gave the impression that he wanted to modernize apartheid without abandoning it; this was damaging his image and that of the National Party in the eyes of the progressive forces in this country and around the world. An oppressive system cannot be reformed, I said; it must be entirely cast aside. I mentioned an editorial that I had recently read in *Die Burger*, the mouthpiece of the National Party in the Cape, implying that the group rights concept was an attempt to bring back apartheid through the back door. I told Mr de Klerk that if that was how his paper perceived group rights, how did he think we regarded it? I added that the ANC had not struggled against apartheid for 75 years only to yield to a disguised form of it, and that if it was his true intention to preserve apartheid through the Trojan horse of group rights, then he did not truly believe in ending apartheid.

De Klerk listened carefully and was non-committal. Mandela was impressed by the man.

> From the first I noticed that Mr de Klerk listened to what I had to say. This was a novel experience. National Party leaders generally heard what they wanted to hear in discussions with black leaders, but Mr de Klerk seemed to be making a real attempt to listen and

understand . . . I was able to write to our people in Lusaka that Mr de Klerk seemed to represent a true departure from the National Party politicians of the past. Mr de Klerk, I said, echoing Mrs Thatcher's famous description of Mr Gorbachev, was a man we could do business with.

De Klerk soon afterwards went on holiday, where he remained in seclusion for a long time, writing the speech that was to revolutionize South Africa. He finished the speech just 12 hours before it was delivered.

Mof Terreblanche (Sampie's brother), one of de Klerk's closest businessman friends, gives this view of the origins of the speech. 'The Friday before, I was with de Klerk, playing golf, before a birthday barbecue in the evening. I got into the golf cart with him that took us to the restaurant. He took out the draft speech ready for the opening of parliament, and showed it to me, asking for my reaction. When I had read it through, I was attracted by its reforming tone . . . He slapped me on the leg. "Don't worry, we're moving into a new world," he told me. The birthday party was enjoyable, but FW had to leave early, he said, "to finalise one paragraph".' That was the paragraph delivering the big concessions; even at that late stage he had not made up his mind – and he would not show the rest even to his closest associates. The most difficult decision of all was that to legalize the Communist Party, over which Malan had nearly resigned (but the defence minister was ultimately a functionary, a loyal supporter of Botha, not a military strongman).

Mof Terreblanche believes that the two main factors that motivated de Klerk were the state of the economy and external pressure – as well as a stubborn streak of courage. In taking the world by surprise on 9 February, 'we decided the pace at the end'. One key consideration, in the view of two intimate observers of the process, had been a long interview de Klerk had with British prime minister Margaret Thatcher in June 1989, which went way beyond its scheduled time. Thatcher was deeply admired by the Afrikaners for her stand against sanctions. But she warned de Klerk that she could no longer sustain her position in the face of foreign pressure. In her opinion, de Klerk had to move fast.

Mof Terreblanche, who was invited to dinner at Downing Street at the time as an intimate of de Klerk's, was impressed at how Thatcher took him to one side for a private chat and made the same point to him afterwards. Three months later, during the South African cabinet meeting in which the decision was made to release the Sisulu Seven, in September 1989, de Klerk left the room to telephone Thatcher to announce the news. As one observer wryly put it, 'that seemed a strange priority. After all, we are no longer a British colony.'

* * *

On 2 February, 1990, at 11.15 a.m., F. W. de Klerk addressed his first parliamentary session as president. His first line – 'the general election on September 6, 1989, placed the country irrevocably on the road to dramatic change' – made his listeners start. They knew he intended to introduce some reforms, but not how far they would go.

With dizzying speed, he proposed the legalization of the ANC, the Pan-Africanist Congress, Umkhonto we Sizwe, the ANC's guerrilla wing, and the South African Communist Party, as well as 30 other illegal organizations. All political prisoners not specifically jailed for acts of violence were to be released. The newspapers were henceforth free to publish what they liked about these organizations.

De Klerk declared himself willing to negotiate with all the new parties to evolve a new national constitution. He did not, however, completely end the state of emergency or promise to bring the troops out of the townships. But it was startling enough, the culmination of everything that had been worked towards in three years of talks at Mells Park and with Mandela.

Allister Sparks recalls his own 'astonishment as I flipped through the pages' of the speech. 'My God, he's done it all.' However, de Klerk reiterated his commitment to power-sharing with the blacks rather than majority rule. Only those who had attended the Mells meetings knew that the white South Africans accepted that this would have to be for a transitional period only. It was a breath-taking move, the real crossing of the Rubicon for white South Africa.

The speech was followed breathlessly by the second of the clandestine meetings between the deputy head and head of operations of South African intelligence, Louw and Spaarwater, and the ANC's effective leader, Mbeki. The purpose of this meeting, even more than the first, was to iron out the operational nuts and bolts of permitting a banned and armed paramilitary organization to re-enter South Africa, and of its forces ultimately being disbanded and absorbed into the defence forces.

The first priority was to get ANC leaders back into South Africa safely, past the security force hard-liners who still regarded them as murderous terrorists. Secondly, the two sides needed to find common ground on who exactly counted as a political prisoner. Third, they had to decide the form of the 'pre-negotiations'.

Louw took a tough line: 'We told them that the state president had taken an enormous risk, and if they did not respond positively the whole mood of the country would swing decisively to the right. An eventual destructive war between ourselves, themselves and the right wing would then be the only result.'

They haggled long into the night on the exact mechanism of Mandela's release, as well as of the other prisoners, the beginning of negotiations and the need for contacts between the South African intelligence services and the ANC. However, the meeting broke up hurriedly when it became obvious they were being watched. As the two South Africans had travelled under false names and passports, they could have been arrested by the Swiss, and they fled.

South Africa itself was flooded with speculation about the imminent release of Mandela. On 9 February the prisoner was again summoned to the president's residence at Tuynhuys. There he was greeted by a smiling de Klerk who, as they shook hands, told him he would be freed the following day. Mandela, on his account, was astonished. In turn he surprised de Klerk by insisting he needed a week's notice of the release so that his family and supporters could prepare for it. 'After waiting 27 years, I could certainly wait another seven days.' Moreover Mandela wanted to be released from Victor Verster outside Cape Town, not Johannesburg, where the government intended to free him.

In fact, Mandela's account is misleading. His condition for his own release was the freeing of other political prisoners. It was an audacious response. De Klerk, blinking at the reluctance of his prisoner to embrace freedom, eventually agreed to let him out at Victor Verster, but insisted on sticking to his timetable, as the foreign press had already been informed. Other releases were promised later. Mandela eventually agreed to the compromise, and they drank Glenfiddich whisky in celebration.

* * *

Mandela's liberation was watched by hundreds of millions on television round the world. One of the greatest events of media history of the twentieth century, it was not a little staged. Mandela, who was driven from his beloved cottage, had been asked to get out of the car a few hundred yards from the gates so that he could be filmed walking towards freedom.

When just 150 yards from the gate, Mandela saw the throng of television cameras, journalists, and thousands of supporters, 'I was astounded and a little bit alarmed. I had truly not expected such a scene; at most I imagined that there would be several dozen people, mainly the warders and their families. But this proved to be only the beginning; I realized that we had not thoroughly prepared for all that was about to happen.'

Engulfed by the crowd, Mandela raised his right fist in a salute of liberation; then he and Winnie jumped back into the car; on the way they saw people waiting to catch glimpses of the motorcade, some of them, to his astonishment, young whites. On reaching Cape Town itself, Mandela's driver plunged into the thick of the crowd waiting to greet him in the Grand Parade.

Mandela's next experience was as shaking as anything he had experienced during his long and suffering life: he was very nearly killed by the enthusiasm of his own people. 'Immediately the crowd surged forward and enveloped the car. We inched forward for a minute or two but were then forced to stop by the sheer press of bodies. People began knocking on the windows, and then on the boot and the bonnet. Inside, it sounded like a massive hailstorm. Then people began to jump on the car in their excitement. Others began to shake it and at that moment I began to worry. I felt as though the crowd might very well kill us with their love ... We sat inside – it would have been futile even to attempt to open the door, so many people were pressing on it – for more than an hour, imprisoned by thousands of our own supporters.'

The time for the scheduled beginning of the speech had long passed. Mandela had narrowly escaped with his life at his own moment of triumph. The terrified driver eventually turned the car in the opposite direction and by a circuitous route delivered Mandela to the back of the podium hours later. When he arrived, there was pandemonium at the Grand Parade. He had left his own spectacles behind, and was forced to borrow Winnie's, which kept slipping down his nose.

His speech, crafted in just a few hours with the help of colleagues, started on a rhetorical and moving note. 'Friends, comrades and fellow South Africans. I greet you all in the name of peace, democracy and freedom for all! I stand here before you not as a prophet but as a humble servant of you, the people. Your tireless and heroic sacrifices have made it possible for me to be here today. I therefore place the remaining years of my life in your hands ...'

Even on such an occasion, his words were those of a calculating politician. Mandela was deeply anxious to dispel the rumours that he had been negotiating a separate deal with the Afrikaners. He insisted, 'I wish to stress that I myself have at no time entered into negotiations about the future of our country except to insist on a meeting between the ANC and the government' – which was not strictly true. He went on to assert that he hoped that the climate which would lead to a negotiated settlement could soon be achieved and the armed struggle be called off. He endorsed the ANC's Harare Declaration, and called for an end to the state of emergency and the release of all political prisoners. He even paid tribute to de Klerk as 'a man of integrity'.

For a population radiant with excitement, it could hardly have been a more measured speech, carefully aimed at his ANC critics. But to the joyous tens of thousands before him, he could have read the telephone book and been greeted with rapture. He was later hugely amused to receive a letter from a white Cape Town housewife that said, 'I am very glad that you are free, and that you are back among your friends and family, but your speech yesterday was very boring'.

For the multitude, this was Mandela, the legend who had emerged unscathed from 27 years in prison. Afterwards he was put up at Archbishop Desmond Tutu's house. There Oliver Tambo rang him from his hospital bed in Sweden, where he was recovering from his stroke. Next day Mandela addressed his first press conference, laying special emphasis on his subordination to the ANC.

> I was mindful of the fact that most senior ANC people would be watching my release from abroad, and attempting to gauge my fidelity from a distance. I was aware that they had heard rumours that I had strayed from the organization, that I was compromised, so at every turn I sought to reassure them. When asked what role I would play in the organization, I told the press that I would play whatever role the ANC ordered.
>
> By now even the ANC's radical leader, Chris Hani, who had urged an intensified armed struggle, had begun to moderate his line. I told the reporters that there was no contradiction between my continuing support for the armed struggle and my advocating negotiations. It was the reality of the threat of the armed struggle that had brought the government to the verge of negotiations. I added that when the state stopped inflicting violence on the ANC,

the ANC would reciprocate with peace. Asked about sanctions, I said that the ANC could not yet call for the relaxation of sanctions, because the situation that caused sanctions in the first place – the absence of political rights for blacks – was still the status quo. I might be out of jail, I said, but I was not yet free.

Mandela went on to pay special attention to the fears of the whites. 'Whites are fellow South Africans,' he told the open-mouthed journalists present, 'and we want them to feel safe and to know that we appreciate the contribution that they have made towards the development of this country.'

In all, it was a remarkable performance. A man given a platform to arouse his people, to transfigure his own years of pain and suffering into a call of moral righteousness that could have evoked a great cry of rage from the heart of an oppressed nation, chose instead to preach reconciliation with the oppressors and the need for negotiations, and to mend his fences with his suspicious comrades. It was Lincoln rather than Martin Luther King – although a trifle less eloquent than Gettysburg.

It was clear that Mandela was determined to fulfil the pledges he and Mbeki had made – to keep a firm hand on a potentially explosive situation following his release. Also, he was shrewdly pitching for the leadership of the ANC now that Tambo was incapacitated; no doubt de Klerk's timing in releasing him was heavily influenced by this. It was essential that an authoritative and moderate leader should take the reins of the ANC as soon as possible after Tambo's departure. Otherwise anything could happen.

Mandela played the game with all the skill of a professional politician, as though his experience in his cell had refined in him the art of statesmanship, rather than endowing him with the defensiveness of an incarcerated man. A fortnight after his release he flew to Lusaka where he explained himself before the sceptical but respectful national executive of the ANC. He was appointed deputy president of the ANC, with Alfred Nzo as acting president while Tambo was incapacitated.

A few weeks later Mandela was in Cairo, where he told his audience that the ANC was prepared 'to consider a cessation of hostilities'. He then flew to Stockholm to visit the moribund Tambo. There the enfeebled old warrior begged him to become president of the ANC, but Mandela insisted on going through the proprieties of being elected.

20
The White Collapse

The meeting at Mells Park on the weekend of 13 February, 1990 proved the most dramatic of all the discussions. Just the week before, de Klerk had electrified the world with his speech of 2 February. There were several new faces on the Afrikaner side. Among them was Mof Terreblanche, one of de Klerk's closest associates and the brother of Sampie; he was a large man with an infectious sense of fun and the quick-thinking casualness of a prominent businessman.

Mof vividly recalls the 'unreal' experience of his first conversation with the ANC.

To me Mbeki was just another ANC person. I thought of the ANC as tough people. But he impressed me from the first day. It was strange to meet him at an English-type dinner, with silver, the real stuff. As South Africans we were keen to get a solution. It was important because we had to see what these people really wanted. The meeting ended with us all drinking whisky around a fireplace at 4 o'clock the next morning. We got really acquainted with one another in a personal capacity. The masks came off.

After the meeting, though, I felt there was something wrong: hell, the ANC couldn't be this positive. They must be bull-shitting. So when I flew back to the next meeting I said to my colleagues, this time we won't be taken in. We must be tough. I guess they felt the same. So for the first half an hour we were tough with each other. Then we realized that the dispute between us was not that big. As with a lot of things, common sense is the most wonderful thing to reach understanding. Previously there had been no common sense at all.

Another first timer at Mells was Attie du Plessis, a serious, straight-talking Afrikaner business leader, the younger brother of Barend, who remembers being invited to the talks the day after de Klerk's historic speech. He was astonished. 'I told my wife I would have to go to London to talk to the ANC the following week. She asked how I could talk to the ANC. I replied that until yesterday they were an enemy. Now they were an opponent. With one's opponents one must talk.' Du Plessis recalls that what most struck him in his discussions about economics with the ANC was that 'many had been exposed to the eastern bloc way of thinking'.

Ebbe Domisse, editor of the Afrikaans newspaper *Die Burger*, one of whose predecessors, Daniel Malan, had been the father of apartheid and the first Afrikaner prime minister after the war, attended the February meeting to talk to the representatives of the party that was soon to replace three centuries of white rule. 'There was a feeling that apartheid was collapsing, and of the need for talks. It was important that there were direct face-to-face negotiations, not through so-called "facilitators". I was an observer, a *verkenner* – a reconnaissance scout, out in front of the lines to see what was going on. There was no doubt that the ANC was very important. The ANC would not have embarked on negotiations if communication had not been established. It was a crucial moment.' Another prominent Afrikaner observer present was the charming and influential businessman Willem Pretorius.

The atmosphere of the 13 February meeting, on the ANC side, was one of quiet confidence. On the Afrikaner side there was apprehension mixed with genuine camaraderie towards the ANC adversary, but the backdrop could not have been more dramatic. At the meeting, Willie Esterhuyse, who was in the know, had heard that de Klerk was preparing to release Nelson Mandela the following day. But Mandela refused to be released. According to Esterhuyse, this was because he insisted that de Klerk should privately promise to release all ANC political prisoners before he would agree to be set free. It was a remarkable piece of cheek on Mandela's part – to refuse his own release as a bargaining chip for the freeing of his colleagues. De Klerk gave way only 24 hours before Mandela was scheduled to be set free.

Mbeki himself, the ANC's number three at Mells Park, only learnt of the imminence of Mandela's release an hour before, when Esterhuyse informed him. 'A lot of champagne was consumed,' one of those present recalls. Soon the BBC was on the line, seeking an interview with Esterhuyse, who was known to be in England. The BBC also wanted to establish the whereabouts of Mbeki. Esterhuyse informed them that 'Thabo was in London – but not where – he was in fact sitting just next to me! In order to keep the discussions secret, we put Thabo on the train, and then I allowed myself to be picked up from Mells Park in a BBC car; then we met again across the table in the studio as if for the first time.'

Pretorius nevertheless recalls tough exchanges on the subjects both of the economy – dear to the hearts of Mof Terreblanche and du Plessis – and law and order. Pretorius recalls that the two sides agreed to differ on the former. 'We were not trying to impose our positions. We would discuss an issue and see the differences. On poverty Thabo was very emphatic. We accepted that the poverty of the blacks was to some extent a product of the system.'

On law and order 'there was great mistrust. The ANC knew that certain things were going on that we didn't know [the 'third force' assistance by the white security forces towards Inkatha]. We checked on the information the ANC gave us afterwards in South Africa [with the security services], and it was confirmed. We weren't pleased. Mandela was later to attack de Klerk about it because he said the president must have known about it and was in a position to stop it. De Klerk knew, but I thought he could only change so far. He considered the forces of law and order could not change overnight.'

* * *

Pretorius, a descendant of the great voortrekker leader, was a gentle, amiable, reflective man enjoying the autumn of his life in a leafy Stellenbosch villa with a garden magnificently tended by his delightful wife. His own intellectual evolution was typical of that of many thoughtful Afrikaners of his generation.

A close friend, even mentor, of Esterhuyse, their families would go hiking and climbing together, holding barbecues around campfires, drinking beers and talking until two or three in the morning, 'debating politics, religion and sex' before turning in, then rising at six. It was all an unconscious evocation of voortrekker life, as aspired to by many urban Afrikaners today: a people drawn to the outback and the vast panoramas of the South African interior, displaying the ruggedness of Australians or the Americans of the Old West.

Pretorius recalls that in those campfire talks he had concluded as far back as 1972 that 'in 15 years there must be majority rule. Dr Verwoerd was very fond of mathematical models. As an accountant, so am I. I calculated that in 50 years some 98 per cent of blacks would be highly educated and well-trained, and would then be pressing for revolutionary changes to be made. So the sooner changes were made the better. There is no point in defying the inevitable when it is inevitable. In fact majority rule occurred in 1992. I was only five years out.'

In 1979 Esterhuyse himself published a far-sighted book, *Apartheid Must Go!*, in Afrikaans. He was allowed to state his views and remain within the Broederbond – a sign of how even the inner councils of Afrikanerdom had evolved – although not to relay the split in tribal ranks to the world outside. Pretorius, like others, applauded P. W. Botha for initiating the process of change. 'He got people to think and make concessions. Not major concessions, but they were regarded as such by the Afrikaners.'

Like others, Pretorius believes Botha would 'not have been the one to preside over the transition to majority rule – although he may have accepted that it was inevitable. Nor would Botha ever have negotiated with the Communists, as de Klerk did. He was violently anti-Communist. De Klerk was much younger, more pragmatic, with no fear of the Communist Party. The National Party was the only party that could make the change – unlike the English liberals.'

Like many other Afrikaners, Pretorius, however moderate in his approach, does not condemn apartheid as morally evil, but merely as a product of its time, closely related to colonialism. 'We made the mistake of introducing institutional apartheid. You have social apartheid in the ghettos of America and in the big cities of Britain.'

Pretorius, Mof Terreblanche and Ebbe Domisse all concur that white South Africa could have held out much longer – but at the end there would have been only revolution, scorched earth. Even so prominent an opponent of apartheid as Archbishop Desmond Tutu indirectly confirms this when he admits he never expected majority rule so soon. 'I have to keep pinching myself that it is all for real.' The whites astonished and disarmed their opponents by throwing in the towel before the real struggle began.

* * *

Cyril Ramaphosa, in conversation with the author, says that it was 'difficult to point to a single cause of the white collapse. It was a combination'. There was the 'bigotry, greed and selfishness of the whites, seeing everything in the short term; foreign pressure; the fact that sanctions were biting; the fact that the black areas had become ungovernable; the erosion of the whites' "moral" position; the internal dissension among them; the resolution of the Namibia/Zimbabwe problem, which meant that independent countries were being created all around them; the fact that they could no longer keep Mandela in prison; and the internal resistance had reached a point where they had to give in – they wanted to do it in an honourable way. The catastrophe was coming.'

Reformist Afrikaners, as well as the best informed diplomatic observers, believe that the whites could have held out another 15 years. Ramaphosa strongly disagrees. 'They could have held out three to four years – not past another white election. The situation had reached boiling point.'

Domisse says that 'Botha would have been much tougher with the ANC than de Klerk was – he was a Bismarckian figure. He could have stuck it out. He wanted to release Mandela, but on his own terms.' Mof Terreblanche, de Klerk's confidant, insists, 'we dictated the pace at the end. To influence the process forward, we had to be tough in the mid-1980s.' There seems to have been a general recognition among senior Afrikaners that the right moment had not arrived in the mid-1980s, when the blacks had first scented victory and believed the white regime's overthrow was imminent. If they had grabbed for power then, matters would have got out of hand.

The extent to which moderate ANC leaders like Tambo, Mandela and Sisulu themselves dampened down expectations at the time must be a matter of conjecture. Mandela, who still has occasional lunches with ex-president Botha, seems to bear him no grudge. The spectre of uncontrollable revolution had raised its head in 1985–7, and both black and white elders seemed to have conspired to damp it down and await a more auspicious time for an orderly transfer of power – although the whites undoubtedly believed they could still control the process.

The Afrikaner participants at the key February meeting point to the same common factors as influencing de Klerk and at last tipping the balance of opinion in Afrikanerdom toward the inevitability of majority rule. One was the crucial year just ended, 1989, with the collapse of Communism and the fall of the Berlin Wall. 'De Klerk had no alternative after the collapse of Communism,' says Domisse. 'The spectacle of the people in revolt against the autocrats of eastern Europe might have prompted South Africa's masses to do the same. Moreover, the Russian Communist leaders now put pressure on their South African comrades to negotiate; and with the end of the global Communist threat, South Africa could hardly credibly claim that it was the target of an international Communist conspiracy.'

Sampie Terreblanche also sees 1989 as a year of global history, akin to 1848 – and as an academic was disappointed that de Klerk's February 1990 speech was not made a few months earlier, to round off the historical parallel. All the Afrikaner participants at Mells saw the economy as the second crucial factor in the timing of the white government's demise. According to Sampie Terreblanche, this was 'desperate ... Sanctions did some harm, but not much ... the outflow of capital was the important thing.' He believed that 'outside pressures and the economy were the decisive factors in the regime's change of heart'.

Attie du Plessis is much more emphatic. 'Up to February 1990, South Africa was at economic war with the world. It is a miracle that this country survived during the late 1980s. After Botha's Rubicon speech there was a withdrawal of the country's credit facilities. We had to repay – like a couple building a house which is still half finished when the mortgage is suddenly withdrawn. It was a miracle that there was no raging hyper-inflation.' At least one prominent observer remains flatly of the opinion that disinvestment was disastrous for South Africa. Of the 200 or so American companies that left South Africa, only around a quarter had come back two years after the handover to majority rule.

Du Plessis points to two further turns of the economic screw: the huge cost of the war in Angola and of the security apparatus in terms of the national budget, and the impact of sanctions. 'We had to manufacture our own sophisticated weapons, to develop our own helicopters, our electronics industry, even manufacture our own boots. There were no sophisticated computers – all had to be smuggled in. The cost was enormous.'

Willem Pretorius says baldly, 'Sanctions attained their objectives in South Africa. When Mr Reagan and Mrs Thatcher backed down in their opposition to sanctions it was the final straw.' For Pretorius there was an additional psychological impact. Not only were those inside South Africa cut off from foreign opinion, but those who did travel suffered. 'We weren't proud of being South Africans. We didn't try to defend South Africa. Now at last we are proud again.' He cites an experience of when he was ostracized at a conference in Scotland. 'We admired the Scots as one of the toughest people in the world – it really was something being despised by them.'

A third consideration was the drift of the war in Angola. 'We didn't know what was going on in Angola. The authorities denied we were there all the time. In fact South Africa withdrew when we believed we had a major military victory on the cards.' This, to say the least, was debatable. The withdrawal was almost certainly prompted by the fear of over-extension. If the South Africans had thrown in substantial forces and ended up propping up a Unita–FNLA government in Luanda, large numbers of South African troops would have been tied down there; moreover, international condemnation would have become a clamour.

Even the Americans, chafing for the Cubans to get out, could not defend a South African occupation of Luanda. Instead, a settlement was reached involving a mutual South African and Cuban withdrawal, which was also made possible by the decision of Soviet president Mikhail Gorbachev to end the costly and futile support of their allies in this surrogate anti-imperialist war. Michael Young claims that the army in 1989 offered Botha a stark choice: they could either continue the war and patrol the borders of South Africa, or police the townships, but not both. In practice the townships were largely unpoliced, except by the security forces *en masse*, which were deeply incompetent.

This then was the combination of events that, by the time of the Mells meeting of February 1990, brought about such a staggering rethink in South Africa's governing party: a growing consensus within Afrikanerdom that majority rule was inevitable; the collapse of Communism in eastern Europe; the mounting economic and sanctions pressure on South Africa; and the realization that the armed forces could not fight on all fronts at the same time. A push from South Africa's best friends, America (now run by the less conservative President Bush) and Britain's Margaret Thatcher, was all that was needed.

Could all this have happened much sooner? Leaving aside the impossible riddle of what would have happened if the National Party had not come to power in 1948 and apartheid never been installed, the later years of Botha stand out as ones of extraordinarily missed opportunities. Only far-sighted men like Esterhuyse, Terreblanche, Pretorius and Willem de Klerk believed apartheid to be doomed and majority rule inevitable as far back as the late 1970s – although F. W. de Klerk had probably come to the same conclusion by 1985.

When revolution and insurrection raised their heads in the wake of Botha's modest reforms in the early 1980s, most liberal Afrikaners, and even the moderate ANC leaders, seemed surprisingly agreed that this was the wrong moment to give way. The terrible years of 1985 and 1986 may have been necessary to knock sense into both sides. However, Botha, having missed one opportunity, missed a further chance in 1987–8, when the government had decisively restored its authority and he could have changed policy from a position of strength. Instead he prevaricated – and was overthrown by a man who moved with lightning speed politically, before South Africa had passed the point of no return towards racial war.

Those who suggested that Botha's tough approach would have secured a better deal were wrong: by refusing to make concessions when he was not under pressure, and only doing so in the teeth of a black uprising, he encouraged black movements to believe that their only course was that of militancy and radicalism. This was the backdrop against which an ANC delegation, led by the man who would soon be vice-president of South Africa, had toasted Mandela's release with half a dozen senior members of the dissident Afrikaner establishment, including the new president's elder brother and two of the country's most prominent business leaders.

* * *

Meanwhile the secret talks about the practical means of ending the armed struggle were carrying on between the National Intelligence Agency and Mbeki's delegation. This time they took place a week after the Mandela release, in the old-world luxury of the Bellevue Palace Hotel in Berne. For the first time Barnard himself was present, along with Fanie van der Merwe. Mbeki and Pahad were accompanied by a prominent guerrilla commander, Joseph Nhlaphla.

Discussions ranged not just over possible provisional arrangements for a ceasefire, but over the security measures concerning the return of the exiles, and the first meeting between the government and the ANC executive. Barnard immediately told Mbeki that it was impossible for Joe Slovo, head of the South African Communist Party and a member of the ANC executive, to attend the talks.

Mbeki retorted it was not for the whites to determine the composition of the ANC delegation. De Klerk, whom Barnard telephoned on the subject, was equally adamant; but in the face of the ANC's threat to boycott the talks, the government had to give way, extracting only the debating point that they could nominate whomever they wanted to their own delegation, even the hardest of hard-liners – which of course would not be in their interest.

Barnard was relieved when the meeting was at an end without any apparent signs of surveillance. 'We can laugh about it today, but for us to go and see the ANC in Europe then was a hell of a thing. We had to prevent the KGB and CIA and other intelligence services from finding out. It was a very sensitive operation.' Two weeks later the two sides finalized arrangements for the return of the exiles and for the next government–ANC meeting in Geneva.

21
The Unravelling

The release of Mandela seemed at first more like an opening of Pandora's box than a cutting of the Gordian knot. In spite of the heroic efforts of moderate ANC leaders, the unbanning of the movement's energies was received with bitter reservations by Chief Buthelezi's Inkatha Freedom Party. Its bluff had been called, and it would not now be the chief political interlocutor with the government; the far more broadly-based ANC would. This dispute threatened to engulf the country in 'black-on-black' violence. Meanwhile the 'homelands' descended into chaos. All this had been predicted and feared by the Afrikaners, and it lent furious urgency to the quest of the Mells Park interlocutors to seek open face-to-face negotiations between the government and the ANC. Neither side could afford the luxury of dragging its feet.

The Transvaal townships erupted into violence, with 700 being killed in the first two-thirds of the year. Kwazulu-Natal became a battleground, and de Klerk was forced to deploy thousands of troops there. The worst blow-up took place in Pietermaritzburg on 25 March 1990, as ANC activists attacked a Zulu rally.

It later emerged that the white security police had been providing financial support to the IFP for such rallies, and that Buthelezi, according to documents, 'was very emotional and expressed extreme gratitude' for one donation of around $50,000 organized by foreign minister Pik Botha. Later there were allegations that Buthelezi's own chief aide had had contacts with right-wing elements determined to disrupt the ANC, and that the Zulu leader had himself at one stage opposed the release of Mandela.

The fault was by no means entirely on one side. The ANC in Kwazulu-Natal was determined to launch an offensive to dislodge

Inkatha from its traditional control of the province. Both sides were guilty of atrocities and both of struggling for control of the territory. Simultaneous to this threat of incipient civil war, a coup took place in Transkei, the first 'independent homeland'. Its new military chief pledged his support for the ANC, asserting that the homeland experiment had failed. A coup followed in Ciskei and in March South African troops had to be sent into Bophuthatswana to put down unrest against the homeland government there, which still continued to assert its 'independence'. The homelands declared their support for the ANC – with the exception of Bophuthatswana, Kwazulu-Natal and Qwaqwa.

In this fast-deteriorating situation, de Klerk and Mandela reached agreement in March to start the first 'talks about talks' on 11 April. Mandela, who had just been formally appointed ANC deputy president to the ailing Tambo, had just affirmed his commitment to negotiations.

At the end of the month, however, inexperienced policemen opened fire on an ANC demonstration at the township of Sebokong near Vereeniging. Eight people were killed, and nearly 350 injured. Furiously, Mandela called off his meeting with de Klerk, and only after a judicial inquiry was promised by de Klerk – which later blamed the police – did Mandela agree to meet on 2 May 1990.

After the surrogate Mells Park talks, with Wimpie de Klerk, Mof Terreblanche and Willy Esterhuyse representing F.W. de Klerk, and Mbeki representing Tambo and Mandela, it was the real thing at last. The two sides met across a 30-seat dining-room table in the prime minister's Groote Schuur residence.

Three of the most prominent conciliators on the white side flanked de Klerk: they were foreign minister Pik Botha, Gerrit Viljoen, the first reforming head of the Broederbond and now minister of constitutional affairs in charge of the negotiating process, and Kobie Coetsee, the justice minister who had chaperoned Mandela to his position as South Africa's unofficial opposition leader.

Mandela was flanked by Mbeki, Walter Sisulu, now internal leader of the ANC, Alfred Nzo, the organization's secretary general, representing the exiles in Lusaka and, in a deliberate provocation to the whites which de Klerk took in his stride, the amiable, shambling, but sharp-witted figure of Joe Slovo, white secretary of the South African Communist Party and allegedly a colonel in the KGB. The first hours of talks and discussions were largely ceremonial, a reiteration of previous positions already covered by the Mells Park discussions, while agreement had already been reached on the major issues of dealing with political prisoners and the returning exiles.

De Klerk still argued that it was necessary for all violence to come to an end, but the ANC reaffirmed its right to continue the armed struggle and press for the maintenance of sanctions, while the government stood by its security legislation (in particular the power to impose a state of emergency and the intervention of troops in the townships) for the time being. Mandela said afterwards, 'at the end not only are we – the ANC and the government – closer together, but we are victors – South Africa is the victor'.

After this breakthrough, both de Klerk and Mandela felt buoyed up enough to depart on world tours. De Klerk visited 9 countries, citing the change in South Africa as 'irreversible' and receiving favourable treatment from his hosts. Mandela toured 13 countries, and was greeted by huge, enthusiastic crowds; he urged governments not to let up the pressure on South Africa. His ticker-tape reception in New York was attended by 1 million people, and he reached agreement with President Bush on 'almost all issues'; he was accorded a standing ovation when he attended a joint session of Congress. Both de Klerk and Mandela had cause for satisfaction.

Mandela then went on to meet Thatcher for the first time. The meeting was surprisingly cordial, although with the inimitable touches of the British prime minister. Mandela recalls

On the day I was to see Mrs Thatcher it was wintry and raining and, as we were leaving, Winnie told me I must take a raincoat. We were already in the lobby of the hotel, and if I went back for my coat we would be late. I am a stickler about punctuality, not only because I think it is a sign of respect to the person you are meeting but in order to combat the Western stereotype of Africans as being notoriously tardy. I told Winnie we did not have time, and instead I stood out in the rain signing autographs for some children. By the time I got to Mrs Thatcher I was feeling poorly, and was later diagnosed as having a mild case of pneumonia.

But it did not interfere with our meeting, except that she chided me like a schoolmarm for not taking her advice and cutting down on my schedule. Even though Mrs Thatcher was on the opposite side of the ANC on many issues such as sanctions, she was always a forthright and solicitous lady. In our meeting that day, though, I could not make the slightest bit of headway with her on the question of sanctions.

Mandela at least did not share Mbeki's visceral dislike of her. In fact both Mandela and de Klerk had reason to feel satisfied by their trips. European community leaders, meeting in Dublin in June, applauded the 'important changes' in South Africa. The cultural, sporting and academic boycotts were dropped. Thatcher proclaimed at the summit: 'Trade is increasing, investment is increasing, and I believe restrictions on South Africa will continue to be eased.' However, both the Americans and the Europeans decided not to lift economic sanctions immediately, but re-examine them, while other countries decided not to abandon sanctions until 'significant progress had been made in negotiations'.

* * *

Mandela's initial warm regard for de Klerk was now changing into a wary suspicion.

The government was in no great rush to begin negotiations; they were counting on the euphoria that greeted my release to die down. They wanted to allow time for me to fall on my face and show that the former prisoner hailed as a saviour was a highly fallible man who had lost touch with the present situation.

Despite his seemingly progressive actions, Mr de Klerk was by no means the great emancipator. He was a gradualist, a careful pragmatist. He did not make any of his reforms with the intention of putting himself out of power. He made them for precisely the opposite reason: to ensure power for the Afrikaner in a new dispensation. He was not prepared to negotiate the end of white rule.

His goal was to create a system of power-sharing based on group rights, which would preserve a modified form of minority rule in South Africa. He was decidedly opposed to majority rule or 'simple majoritarianism', as he sometimes called it, because that would end white domination in a single stroke. We knew early on that the government was fiercely opposed to a winner-take-all parliamentary system, and advocated instead a system of proportional representation with built-in structural guarantees for the white minority. Although he was prepared to allow the black majority to vote and create legislation, he wanted to retain a minority veto. From the start I would have no truck with this plan. I described it as apartheid in disguise, a 'loser-take-all' system.

Mandela's thesis, that de Klerk was simply a reinvented version of Botha determined to ensure continued Afrikaner rule, does not bear examination – although it was a convenient stick with which to beat the National Party leader, and also – even more helpfully – to push the view that the ANC wrested power in a terrible struggle with the Afrikaners. In fact, the evidence shows that de Klerk was more than aware that the unbanning of the ANC and the release of Mandela could result in black majority rule.

For Mandela to suggest that de Klerk had 'no intention of putting himself out of power' and 'wanted to ensure power for the Afrikaner in the new dispensation', and to blur this with the attempt to 'create structural guarantees for the white minority', is a piece of intellectual sleight-of-hand. For de Klerk to retain power, of course, would have been completely different from attempting to create structural guarantees for the white minority through proportional representation: the one was a continuation of autocratic, racist apartheid, the other an attempt to salvage whatever protection he could for the whites after the collapse of minority rule.

It was perfectly fair for Mandela to object that the whites deserved no such protection; but that is entirely different from arguing that de Klerk was seeking to retain white domination. As intelligent a man as Mandela certainly appreciated the difference. In fact, while de Klerk conducted a rearguard action in defence of white interests, at no stage was there any sign that he was seeking to block the prospect of black rule itself – merely to defend the interests of the whites against the possible excesses of the new black majority.

Where Botha could not conceive of allowing black majority rule, de Klerk could and did – and handed power to the blacks far more rapidly than most thought possible. Certainly Mandela and his associates wrested a better deal than expected, partly through their political and negotiating brilliance, and partly under the sheer pressure of events. But the decision in principle to surrender power was taken by de Klerk and the whites, for the reasons suggested earlier – principally that if they had resisted, they could have held out, but South Africa would have become a wasteland.

The extraordinary leniency and lack of revanchism shown by the blacks after they took power owes a great deal to this: most expected to win power after a long struggle, not to have it handed to them by the whites. It does not detract from the staggering achievement of Mandela and the blacks that the whites threw in the towel before the heavy-weight contest really got under way, understanding that however much damage they inflicted in the first 14 rounds they would be knocked out in the last. Indeed, the greatest victories are those won without recourse to war. But by claiming that de Klerk was indistinguishable from Botha in seeking to retain Afrikaner domination, Mandela appeared to be seeking to set up a myth every bit as misleading as the old Afrikaner historical fables.

* * *

The ANC and the government were poles apart in their approach to constitutional negotiations. The ANC favoured setting up an interim government to oversee the transition to elections for a constituent assembly; the government wanted the existing system adapted to allow for black majority rule while retaining a white veto over legislation. In June 1990, however, a giant step towards reconciliation was made with the lifting of the state of emergency everywhere except in Natal.

It was under these circumstances that the Mells Park participants met again for what was to be their final gathering: gone was the pretence that this was an exchange between disinterested individuals; this was negotiation by another name, aimed at advancing the formal processes already begun. Attending for the first time was a senior minister, Dawie de Villiers, as well as Esterhuyse, de Klerk, du Plessis, Pretorius, Mof Terreblanche, Marinus Weickers (South Africa's leading constitutional expert, seeking to unblock the constitutional impasse) and Dr Fanie Cloete.

The Afrikaners opened the innings with a business-like, even aggressive approach. Wimpie de Klerk claimed that, contrary to Mandela, it was the ANC that was seeking to delay proceedings. He asserted that Mandela had departed for overseas leaving the peace process in abeyance. A new working group was needed, with access to de Klerk and Mandela, to monitor day-to-day developments. Wimpie de Klerk further argued that a joint security secretariat was necessary to resist the escalating violence, and to help the ANC control Natal.

The government supported ANC participation in a transitional government with the National Party – a clear step towards the opposition demand for a joint government to oversee elections. De Klerk also suggested that the ANC was reluctant to confront its youth and left wings, and insisted on the need for cooperation with the whites. They, after all, had their own problems on the right. The key message from the older de Klerk was that the ANC should now draw up its 'bottom line' negotiating position and get down to serious talks. De Klerk said Mandela's bitter complaint that the whites were dragging their feet looked rather ridiculous. In fact, his reluctance to talk stemmed from a bitter power struggle within the ANC to restrain the hot-heads advocating an immediate overthrow of the South African state. By the standards of the polite atmosphere at past Mells Park meetings, this was strong stuff, reflecting Mof Terreblanche's desire for tough talking. Mbeki took it all in his urbane stride, making light of the lack of progress, insisting that President de Klerk had himself wanted to wait until Mandela returned before resuming talks. Mbeki said the ANC leaders would have to convince their supporters of the need for compromise, but that they did not doubt the government's integrity in trying to find an agreement (in marked contrast to what Mandela later claimed).

Mandela was taking risks for peace, having been booed and hissed by ANC supporters when he spoke of the need to find peace in Kwazulu-Natal and to share a platform with chief Buthelezi. 'Like the government, the ANC urged the need for speed in the peace process since black expectations are high and slowness breeds nervousness and instability.' Aziz Pahad claimed that the ANC was addressing the issue of violence, and secured agreement with the far left groups, the PAC and AZAPO, to end it. But he pointed out that many younger ANC members had not been to school since 1976. He urged a joint approach on violence, with the idea of setting up a monitoring group, and insisted that neither side gained from delays.

Mbeki said the main stumbling block to formal negotiations was agreement on who was to sit at the table. He pointed out that, in an important symbolic move, the ANC leadership – but not yet its followers – already called de Klerk president – a major step forward for an organization that previously had considered his power illegitimate and undemocratic. The ANC was thus prepared to recognize the continuity of the South African state, even after nearly half a century under the hated oppressor.

Mbeki continued, however, to reiterate his objection to the concept of 'group rights' – code in the ANC's view for apartheid, albeit of a defensive, laager kind, rather than domination and oppression. The violence, he went on to suggest, was not general but very specific – in fact caused by the apparent pursuit by Inkatha of an alliance with the whites against the ANC. Mbeki specifically demanded that the police chief in Natal be dismissed, that two of the police forces there be removed and reorganized, and that the federal police be sent to Kwazulu-Natal. He also wanted a large press and public relations offensive to counter violence. The discussion now turned to the second major issue of white concern – the economy. De Villiers, the economy minister, tactfully began this by asserting that the government had put past priorities on the back burner. Instead the priorities were growth, new jobs, and the economic disparities between blacks and whites. South Africa's record, he said, was one of profound neglect of the private sector. He wanted to reduce controls in the market-place. He set out the government's intention to break the transport sector down into different units – airways, railways, pipelines and so on – in order to measure their productivity and efficiency. But neither the railways nor Escom could be privatized for the moment.

Having outlined the government's own plans, de Villiers now touched gently on the ANC's views on socialism and nationalization. The Afrikaners also pressed their adversaries to support the removal of sanctions to help de Klerk move forward, while acknowledging that the government must make concessions in return. He was puzzled: the ANC had revised its commitment to nationalizing key industries after the Harare Declaration. Yet only in May Mandela had insisted, in an address to 300 business leaders, that there had to be some state intervention: fewer than 10 companies, he claimed, controlled nine-tenths of the Johannesburg stock exchange. De Villiers reiterated that nationalization would mean lower profits and fewer jobs.

Mbeki was distinctly conciliatory in his reply. The ANC was pledged to a mixed economy, he said. The issue was what sort of mix. The ANC's prime interest was the survival of the South African economy: if the economic question were not resolved, no political settlement would work. On the stock exchange issue, Mbeki said the ANC was looking at a British-style monopolies and mergers commission, to curb unfair competition. Even Cosatu economists had moved a long way from earlier socialist logic. 'Participation' and 'planning' were now the vogue demands.

The ANC had a problem on its flank, said Mbeki with remarkable frankness, in that the South African Communist Party was slowly beginning to assert itself and could win support from socialist parties on the left (although Mbeki did not refer to Moscow's attempts, under Gorbachev, to convince the party that old-style Communism had no future). The economy, said Mbeki, required capital and education as well as 'black empowerment' to reduce the 226,000 shortfall in middle management. Technical shortages should also be addressed.

He was confident sanctions would soon be lifted in order to encourage international investment, which the ANC was continually urging in its discussions across the world. This was the first admission by a senior ANC leader that the sanctions campaign would soon be ended. The issue would be addressed by Mandela on his return to South Africa on 18 July. The problem was to ease the organization off the political hook on which it was impaled, with their supporters insisting that sanctions should not yet be lifted; they would need the government's help to escape. Mbeki was, in effect, with typically charming *sang froid* asking for a major government concession in return. Sanctions could then be lifted, possibly as early as this year. The extraordinarily conciliatory tone of the ANC leaders' remarks deeply impressed the businessmen.

Mbeki now moved onto constitutional issues. He claimed the government had rejected the proposal for a transitional government; instead he pressed for a constituent assembly: the new constitution could self-evidently not be drawn up and ratified by the white government alone. The Afrikaner side replied that they did not like the idea of a constituent assembly as, unlike Namibia, South Africa was an independent country with a long-standing constitution. In Namibia third countries had been involved in drafting the constitution. The South African government would regard a constituent assembly as an affront to its sovereignty. There was some truth, and much posturing in these arguments.

The ANC then put its view that a council of state should be set up to share power with the main opposition parties, which could include Inkatha and the PAC, but not too many more 'leaders' claiming spurious followings, who would otherwise swamp it. The ANC's concern that elections and a new constitution be supervised by something manifestly more impartial than the existing government was entirely reasonable.

Marinus Weickers, who had drafted the Namibian constitution, now gave his view of the prime elements of a constitutional settlement: a bill of rights; the main organs of the state defined through a separation of powers; the establishment of local authorities and subordinate interests; and the transitional arrangements for a new constitution. In the discussion that followed, three further key components were identified: affirmative action in favour of blacks, particularly over property rights; the authority of the courts; and measures to protect the white minority.

Both sides immediately took up the need for a bill of rights – both to prevent a repetition of past injustice and to protect the interests of the white minority. On the judiciary, the ANC pressed for constitutional courts to reflect 'social justice'. Black judges must be appointed. The new parliament would be a two-chamber one with constitutional checks to represent minority groups. Proportional representation was the favoured electoral system and there should be provision for referenda.

A new subject surfaced over lunch. Already the ANC had pressed for reorganization of the South African Broadcasting Corporation – under Piet Meyer. All now agreed that Radio Truth, beamed into Zimbabwe from South Africa by certain elements of the defence forces, should be wound up.

Finally on Sunday, 1 July, the chairman raised the subject of the future of the Mells Park meetings themselves. Consolidated Gold Fields, having fended off a bitterly fought take-over battle by Minorco (with the ANC, astonishingly, lending its support to Consgold), had finally succumbed to take-over by the Hanson Group in August 1989. The last two conferences had been funded by Hanson, and this would be the last they would support. Patrick Gillam, chairman of Standard Chartered Bank, had also helped to raise funds, notably from Colin Marshall of British Airways, who provided airline tickets. The purpose of the meetings had been to bring together reform-minded Afrikaners and the ANC, and this had now been achieved. All parties agreed that without the meetings the progress thus far could not have been achieved.

Young was asked to convey the warmest thanks of the participants to Rudolph Agnew and Lord Hanson. It was resolved that South African businesses should finance further such meetings to be held in South Africa every three months. In practice, as Young must have half expected, this was not to happen: the process of negotiation had begun too much in earnest to require a parallel track. Mells was over.

* * *

What, after all, had been the historical significance of this marathon of 8 meetings lasting 24 days spread over 3 years? The participants today are extremely guarded for clear political reasons. Michael Young leaves it to historians to determine their true significance. Thabo Mbeki, now President of South Africa, who regularly presided over an annual reunion of the participants, held a dinner in August 1991 in which he warmly commended Esterhuyse and Terreblanche for their role in the talks, which he labelled 'a negotiation within a negotiation'.

Esterhuyse himself says coyly that the talks helped 'to create the conditions for negotiations ... They helped us to understand the views of senior participants – the things that were discussed at Mells all surfaced in the real negotiations. They also helped to create confidence and trust.' He saw them as a kind of dress rehearsal for the peace talks. Mof Terreblanche considered them 'important because we learnt what these people really wanted ... Young played an important role as chairman, balancing between both sides. He was very professional.'

For du Plessis, 'they were not a peace process. We had no mandate on either side. But it was important for us to get to know our future governors.' To both whites and blacks the talks were something of an embarrassment even then, and certainly are so today: they showed that the two sides were sounding each other out in considerable depth, on the terms for peace, and on all the major issues, economic, constitutional and military, that were to be the subject of direct negotiations after 1990, fully three years in advance – when both sides were ostensibly at war and refusing to speak to each other.

Progress was thus made much easier in the talks after the secret negotiations conducted by Mandela with his gaolers at Pollsmoor; both sides knew the questions each would ask, and both had formulated their answer. In this the talks were of immense historical significance, justifying the time spent by the operational leader of the ANC-in-exile – Mbeki, and his senior aides, Pahad, Zuma, Trew and others.

As the only point of contact between ANC leaders and the Afrikaners apart from the Mandela discussions, they established that when talks started, there would be much to talk about and that compromise was possible. Without this preparation, the 1990 talks, even if they had begun, might well have ended in mutual incomprehension and disaster from the beginning.

Yet the inner significance of the talks went much further than that. Esterhuyse today talks vaguely and disingenuously of them as 'one of many initiatives designed to discover the bottom lines of the various parties ... they were one element in a whole variety of processes.' This does not stand up to examination. True, there had been contacts between the two sides before Mells Park; yet these were getting-to-know-you encounters with no follow through or substantive agenda. One such had taken place at the end of 1984, when the head of the

Broederbond, de Lange, along with Esterhuyse and Sampie Terreblanche, met Mbeki in Harare. Following the meeting the whites were summoned by President Botha to his Cape Town residence, where he told them bluntly they should not speak to 'murderers'. They agreed not to do so again, on pain of losing their passports and being ostracized by the Afrikaner community. In 1986, de Lange met Mbeki by accident in New York – where Sampie Terreblanche also saw him. In October 1988, after the Mells talks had begun, Terreblanche did the great unpardonable and met Joe Slovo, head of the South African Communist Party, as well as Mbeki, Pahad and Trew at a conference with Russian academics. The Progressive Federal Party leader, Van Zyl Slabbert, had also blotted his copybook by meeting ANC leaders in Lusaka.

But these were no more than one-off affairs, never protracted sessions which were followed up. There were no other direct contacts between the Afrikaners and the ANC high command throughout those three years except for the meetings between Mbeki's teams and the National Intelligence Agency in Switzerland arranged by Esterhuyse as a direct result of the Mells Park talks. The only other continuing conversation was that between Mandela and the secret government negotiating committee.

To suggest that the Mells Park talks were principally 'getting-to-know-you' affairs might also be misleading. This was true of the individuals like du Plessis who attended only one or two sessions. But for the constant attenders – Esterhuyse and Terreblanche initially, then Esterhuyse and de Klerk, and Mbeki, Pahad, Zuma and Trew on the ANC side – there was clearly a pressing agenda for each set of talks. The high command of the ANC was hardly likely to waste its time on 8 successive three-day meetings in getting-to-know-you discussions with the same whites.

Most significant of all, the wider discussions also served as a useful cover for the private conversations between, in particular, Esterhuyse and Mbeki. What were these secret discussions about, and what, in particular, was the crucial relationship between them and the prolonged talks taking place between Mandela and the government? Neither Esterhuyse nor Mbeki will divulge the substance. But Esterhuyse offered a vital clue. 'There was feedback in both directions,' he says, 'from Mbeki to Mandela and to Pretoria and back again. The Mandela talks in Pollsmoor were absolutely decisive,' he says emphatically.

What seems to have happened was that in 1987 there was a major rift within the 'Higher Organ' of the ANC in Lusaka as to whether there should be dialogue with the government – with many advocating the immediate overthrow of the government, shown to have been caught off guard by the unrest. Mbeki was instrumental in advocating and seeking a dialogue, and had secured the blessing of Oliver Tambo, the ANC president. Through the Mells Park talks, Mbeki was able to get the message across to Esterhuyse that Mandela should be informed he had the approval of the ANC pragmatists in Lusaka to start his dialogue with the government.

Thus Esterhuyse acted as a channel of communication for Mbeki and Tambo, via Neil Barnard, head of the National Intelligence Service, to Mandela in prison. Similarly, messages from Mandela, and the substance of the private negotiations, were conveyed through Barnard and Esterhuyse through to Mbeki and Tambo at Mells Park. An astonishing secret conduit had been set up between the ANC's principal external and internal leaders via South Africa's senior intelligence service and the presidential office of the enemy (although it is not known how closely Botha himself was involved).

The advantage of this conduit was not just that Mandela had no means of smuggling messages to Tambo in Lusaka and vice versa until Maharaj began to act as a secret messenger in 1989. It was that it bypassed the ANC as a whole, much of which was deeply suspicious of – indeed opposed to – talks with the government, and permitted Mandela to talk to Mbeki, and hence Tambo, on an indirect 'hot' line; they could coordinate their positions. The South Africans, who had once crudely tried to divide Mandela from the external movement (and Botha may still have wished to do this), now realized the advantage in getting both Tambo and Mandela to agree on a common negotiating strategy; otherwise any deal reached with Mandela might be disowned by the external movement, and the strife would continue.

It is possible that Barnard was masterminding this strategy without the full knowledge of his boss, Botha. Moreover, the ANC itself had been heavily infiltrated by the South African security services, which would otherwise have learnt details of the discussions between the government and Mandela and, along with ANC militants, might have sought to disrupt them. Finally, the hard-line security services in South Africa were eager to learn details of any indirect discussions such as those at Mells Park between the government and the ANC in order to sabotage them.

The key to both the Mandela talks at Pollsmoor with the secret government negotiating committee and the Mells Park talks was absolute secrecy, in particular from observation by the security services on either side – except for Barnard's tightly-woven intelligence high command, which was pushing hard for a peaceful settlement. Through the Esterhuyse–Mbeki link, Mandela was able to coordinate his message – and sometimes differ – with the ANC high command in Lusaka, by-passing the hard-liners on all sides. It was an extraordinary channel – through the office of Mandela's and Mbeki's chief enemy.

'The Mandela talks were absolutely decisive.' Indeed they were: although they originated as an attempt by Botha to separate Mandela from his colleagues in Lusaka – something about which that confident old prisoner was not concerned, so certain was he of his own strength. Far from being the sterile exchange of fixed positions which he misleadingly describes in his autobiography, they ended up as decisive and substantive negotiations covering virtually every aspect of the peace process that unravelled over the following years. They were coordinated with Mbeki and the ANC external high command through the Mells Park secret talks.

There were a staggering 48 meetings in all – something which Mandela does not reveal in his book. For Barnard, the great manipulator, it was vital no longer to split Mandela from Tambo and the exiles, but to coordinate their positions so that any agreement reached with Mandela would not immediately be disowned by the ANC. The Mells Park link between Esterhuyse, reporting directly to Barnard, who in turn was reporting to Mandela, and Mbeki reporting to Tambo, did just that, and permitted a resolution when Mbeki did differ from Mandela. Thus Mells Park played an absolutely key role in the prison-cell deal which resolved the conflict and altered South Africa's destiny irretrievably.

The destruction of the tape of Mandela's only meeting with Botha was also considered of crucial significance by those close to the Pollsmoor talks: the meeting was clearly much more than the 'history lesson' that Mandela makes it out to be. It set the seal on the deal worked out between Mandela and the whites during the 48 meetings, which had been coordinated with Mbeki, and through him, Tambo, at Mells Park.

Botha, who was deeply reluctant to meet Mandela, only chose to do so in desperation as his own political demise grew near (he was deposed by de Klerk the following week). No record of the meeting was allowed to remain because it would have compromised both

Mandela and Botha (who still occasionally lunch together in the new South Africa, a sign that Mandela recognizes the 'Old Crocodile's' grudging contribution). The president met Mandela to set his seal of approval on the deal.

22
Endgame

Events in South Africa after the final Mells Park conference moved relatively speedily, if erratically, towards their historic climax. On 20 July, as predicted by Mbeki at Mells Park, Mandela, on his return from abroad, had a surprise meeting with de Klerk to resume the peace process: new talks were set for 6 August. But events turned against both parties over the next few days. A series of vicious attacks by armed gangs, believed to be Zulus, on trains left dozens injured or killed; between 1990 and 1994 some 600 died and 1,400 were injured in such attacks.

Just a week after the surprise Mandela–de Klerk meeting, the new South African Communist Party held its inaugural rally of 50,000 supporters outside Johannesburg. Mandela himself addressed the rally, describing it as 'an important day in the history of our country ... which should give hope to everyone who calls himself a democrat'. The appearance of Slovo, the party's secretary- general, who said he was committed to peaceful negotiations, sent shivers through many white South Africans.

The same month, 40 ANC activists were arrested, including executive member Mac Maharaj. Several arms caches were seized, in what police described as a Communist plot to overthrow the government by force, code-named Operation Vula. This was apparently intended to set up ANC enclaves throughout the country in the event of negotiations failing: the arrests provoked financial tremors.

The National Party threatened to boycott the August talks if Slovo attended, but after a three-hour meeting between Mandela and de Klerk on 1 August, they went ahead as planned. They resulted in a formal suspension of the ANC's armed struggle – a major step towards reassuring the whites. In fact the courtship between Mandela and de

Klerk now settled into a curious pattern: when an outrage was committed by one side, the other threatened a boycott, and had to be drawn back to the table with the offer of a generous concession by the offending party. This time it was the whites' turn to benefit.

Murderous violence now broke out in the townships – brutal and apparently motiveless killings by a 'third force' – which later was alleged to be associated with the Civil Command Cooperation Branch of the South African Defence Forces. The allegations were never proven, however. But Mandela, for one, was in no doubt of their provenance.

> Over the next few months I visited townships all across the violence-racked Vaal Triangle south of Johannesburg, comforting wounded people and grieving families. Over and over again, I heard the same story: the police and defence force were destabilizing the area. I was told of the police confiscating weapons one day in one area, and then Inkatha forces attacking our people with those stolen weapons the next day. We heard stories of the police escorting Inkatha members to meetings and on their attacks.
>
> In September I gave a speech in which I said there was a hidden hand behind the violence and suggested that there was a mysterious 'third force', which consisted of renegade men from the security forces who were attempting to disrupt the negotiations. I could not say who the members of the third force were, for I did not know myself, but I was certain that they existed and that they were murderously effective in their targeting of the ANC and the liberation struggle ... Those opposed to negotiations benefited from the violence, which always seemed to flare up when the government and the ANC were moving towards an agreement. These forces sought to ignite a war between the ANC and Inkatha, and I believe many members of Inkatha connived at this as well. Many in the government, including Mr de Klerk, chose to look the other way or ignore what they knew was going on under their noses. We had no doubts that men at the highest levels in the police and the security forces were aiding the third force.

In fact, although there certainly was collaboration of elements of the security forces in the township violence, de Klerk could almost certainly not have stopped it. But the violence added to the growing disillusion of young ANC activists towards their leadership. In December 1990, the ailing Tambo returned to the ANC's consultative conference in Johannesburg. There he ignited a storm of controversy by urging that the movement abandon its support for sanctions. Younger members were furious, and attacked the leadership for 'tactical errors' and refusing to 'dirty their shoes' in the townships. Mbeki was whistled at by younger delegates. Mandela, in his closing address, acknowledged that mistakes had been made, but insisted,

> Our organization has in the past dealt with a variety of weaknesses and mistakes on the part of our membership as well: factions and cliques, men and women who used the platforms of the organization for unprincipled discussions, who played to the gallery, whose aims in meetings of this nature are to prove how revolutionary they are – who have no idea whatsoever of working in a mass movement, who are totally incapable of putting forward constructive ideas and who are quick to pull down what others have built ... the overwhelming majority of our people generally and the delegates here in particular support negotiation between the ANC and the government.

Behind the velvet glove, there was an iron fist. The ANC's internal troubles slowed down the pace of preparing for negotiations; but the climate of violence, which escalated dramatically in 1991, provided a new urgency. In spite of meetings between Mandela and Buthelezi, deaths from political violence rose from 2,700 in 1991 to 3,400 in 1992 and 3,700 in 1993.

* * *

De Klerk was increasingly under fire from his own extreme right. Eugene Terreblanche was head of the Afrikaner Resistance Movement (AWB), the most prominent of some 80 splinter groups sporting some 150,000 weapons between them, many trained as paramilitaries. In August 1991, de Klerk decided to fight back and addressed a rally in Ventersdorp, Terreblanche's home town. Some 2,000 AWB marchers besieged the hall in which de Klerk was speaking, attacking police and blacks indiscriminately.

Mandela, meanwhile, had regained control over his militants with his election as ANC president in place of the dying Tambo in July. Cyril Ramaphosa, the fast-talking young mine-workers leader, was elected as its secretary-general. Tambo died in 1993. Young attended Tambo's funeral along with Trevor Huddleston – two lone white faces in a group which included Nelson Mandela, Aziz Pahad and the American civil rights leader Jesse Jackson. The crowd was enormous. At the graveside Winnie Mandela, 'an extraordinary woman with penetrating eyes', kept working the crowd. After the old warrior had been laid to rest in the dusty soil, the crowd erupted with chants of 'viva! viva! viva!' 'It was intensely moving, and not a little frightening,' says Young.

* * *

At last, in December 1991, after more than a year and a half of talks about talks and nearly 18 months after the last Mells meeting, the government and other parties signed a declaration of intent about the new South Africa which promised to 'bring about an undivided South Africa with one nation sharing a common citizenship, patriotism and loyalty, pursuing amidst our diversity freedom, equality and security for all, irrespective of race, colour, sex or creed; a country free from apartheid or any other form of discrimination or domination'. Thus was Codesa, the Council for a Democratic South Africa born, boycotted among major Parties only by the Communist Party and the Pan-African Congress.

The negotiations proper were now set to begin at the World Trade Centre at Johannesburg airport. Buthelezi stayed away on the grounds that the Zulu government and the Zulu king were not permitted to bring their own separate delegations. Mandela demanded that democratic elections should be held in 1992. Yet even the first day was marred by an unseemly squabble with de Klerk, who asked whether the ANC was united enough to abide by its agreements. Mandela retorted that de Klerk was the 'leader of an illegitimate, discredited, minority regime'. It was clear that de Klerk, worried about Conservative inroads into National Party support, was playing electoral politics.

In February the Conservative Party won a stunning by-election, and de Klerk suddenly decided to gamble everything by holding a referendum on his reforms the following month. If it had gone wrong, all the progress so far would have been lost, and South Africa would have been plunged into a civil war between black and white. Perhaps that fear was what persuaded the white electorate. About 80 per cent of white voters turned out, and a staggering 69 per cent voted in favour of de Klerk.

The president now felt strengthened to proceed with negotiations, but also to behave more obdurately when the parties to the negotiations met once again in May 1992 for the second plenary session, Codesa Two. The groundwork had been prepared by five discussion groups, and Mandela and de Klerk met the day before the negotiations opened.

Ramaphosa, the masterly leader of the black negotiating team, told the author that from the outset of the talks 'we were all convinced it would end in majority rule. The problem was how to attain it. As the threat of the [white] right wing became real, we had to reach an accommodation. The coalition [with the whites] worked well. It was symbolic – of no real value. De Klerk played an important role.'

The two sides had more or less agreed on a two-stage move towards majority rule. First, a transitional electoral council would be appointed from the Codesa delegations to supervise the move towards elections and establish an interim constitution; then elections would be held for a constituent assembly, which would also make laws. All parties with more than 5 per cent of the vote would participate in the cabinet.

However, two huge disagreements remained: the government wanted an interim constitution drafted before the provisional government took office; and also demanded a senate of regional representatives with a blocking veto for the whites. The first requirement seemed to the ANC to be no more than a delaying tactic, although the whites believed it would establish a limited framework for the interim government to act within. The second was much more fundamental for both sides. As the negotiations got under way the blacks became more suspicious. De Klerk seemed in effect to be demanding a white veto over provisions in the new constitution, as well as extensive regional powers and, in effect, an interim constitution that would become a permanent constitution. It seemed that de Klerk, buoyed by the referendum result, now felt that he was negotiating from a position of strength.

* * *

Codesa Two broke up without agreement, and the blacks decided to increase their bargaining power by staging a new campaign of 'rolling mass action' to show the government that the country was ungovernable without black consensus. The campaign was scheduled to start on 16 June 1992, the 16th anniversary of Soweto.

The day after it began, surely not by coincidence, a force of Inkatha members raided the township of Boipatong, killing 46, mostly women and children – the fourth and worst such attack that week. It was a particularly gruesome massacre. One survivor, Simon Mdloi, described it:

> I went to the door to see what could be going on. I saw two men chopping my neighbour with axes ... I and my wife decided to run and hide in a swamp. I never had a chance to get dressed, so I fled with my underpants ... We had to go through a barbed wire fence to reach the swamp. I tried to lift the fence so that my wife could creep under it, but because of her pregnancy, she could not.
>
> The attackers were hot on our heels. My wife pleaded with me not to leave her behind. With bullets ricocheting in the ground past me, I had no choice but to run away, hoping that they were looking for me and would not hurt a pregnant woman. I spent the night in the cold swamp. In the morning ... I found [my wife] still lying under the fence but covered with a blanket. I lifted the blanket and saw it was her. She had been shot and hacked. That is how I lost my pregnant wife.

The killings reverberated across the nation. Some ANC members angrily insisted that negotiations be suspended and the armed struggle be resumed. Mandela, visiting the scene of the massacre, declared: 'I am convinced we are not dealing with human beings but animals. We will not forget what Mr de Klerk, the National Party and the Inkatha Freedom Party have done to our people. I have never seen such cruelty ...'

At a rally three days later, 20,000 ANC supporters heard him announce that the talks were suspended; he compared the situation to that at Sharpeville, and the National Party to the Nazis in Germany. If the government now sought to impose restrictions on freedom of expression, the ANC would launch a campaign of national defiance.

In fact Mandela's reaction was well over the top. Blame for the Inkatha campaign, even though abetted by hard-line members of the security forces, could in no sense be laid at de Klerk's door. The whites did not control Inkatha; and de Klerk did not control the rogue elements in the security forces. He may be criticized for failing to do so – but he was under immense pressure within the white community to abandon even the concessions he had already made. It was no easy matter to institute a purge through the ranks of his most entrenched opponents. He was more culpable for failing to launch a proper investigation. Even so, he could hardly be compared to Vorster or the Nazis. If de Klerk had sought to blame Mandela for the outrages of his extremist ANC supporters, uproar would have ensued. De Klerk sought a meeting with Mandela, but was turned down. The ANC was intent on a show of mass strength, rather like the mock charge of a king of the jungle, before negotiations resumed. In so doing, the organization was about to make its own disastrous mistake. The mass rolling action campaign of strikes, demonstrations and boycotts climaxed with a general strike on 3 and 4 August affecting 4m workers – the biggest in South African history. Some 100,000 protesters marched to the Union Building in Pretoria. It was a crushingly impressive display of non-violent strength.

De Klerk's response was to say that if the country became ungovernable, he would take drastic action. In fact the campaign had involved a substantial loss of earnings by black workers, and could not be sustained much longer. De Klerk was seeking to call Mandela's bluff. The ANC was determined not to return to the negotiating table with the terms unchanged since the Inkatha massacres – and as long as the impasse continued, foreign investment in South Africa remained blocked and sanctions remained in place.

Unexpected tragedy then sliced through this pre-battle parade of positions and egos. On 7 September the ANC, confident of its control of the streets, decided to march into the Ciskei homeland of the Eastern Cape, run by a military council headed by Brigadier Oupa Gqozo. It was an incredibly irresponsible decision, believed to have been opposed by Mandela. The Ciskei troops were young, inexperienced and jittery, out of the control not just of the white government but of their own black commanders.

Some 70,000 took part in the march, and when a group of them broke through a barbed wire fence off the main road into the Bisho stadium, the soldiers opened fire, straight into their ranks, killing 29 and leaving 200 injured. The ANC had marched straight into the jaws of a cowed and dangerous animal, and been mauled. It was not hard to see where the real responsibility lay.

Sobered, the ANC began to review the path they were going down, leading to confrontation with Inkatha and massive bloodshed among their own people. They had the numbers; the government and its allies still had the guns. Equally, de Klerk was alarmed that the country was now heading back towards confrontation and isolation. He offered another summit, and this time Mandela accepted. 'The dark hour is before dawn', was Mandela's epitaph on the narrowly avoided confrontation.

At the meeting on 26 September they agreed at last to set up a mechanism for dealing with such bloodshed: an independent body would review police actions, the hostels would be fenced in, and 'tribal weapons' – assegais and knobkerries – would be banned at rallies. De Klerk and Mandela also decided how to resolve the deadlock on transitional arrangements. Elections would take place for a single assembly which would draft a new constitution and act as a temporary parliament. This record of understanding had been reached after nearly three weeks of frantic behind-the-scenes negotiation between Ramaphosa and de Klerk's mild-mannered protégé, Roelf Meyer.

The deal between the two main parties was furiously denounced by all the outsiders, including Inkatha, the homeland leaders, and the Conservative Party, which set up Cosag – the Concerned South African Group. A secret part of the agreement, probably already in principle agreed during the Pollsmoor and Mells Park negotiations, provided for ANC acceptance of the 'power-sharing' which they had bitterly opposed for so long.

Slovo, with his impeccable radical credentials as leader of South Africa's Communist Party, was wheeled in to suggest a 'sunset clause' of power-sharing, providing for the gradual retirement of civil servants (rather than their immediate replacement by the ANC, as had happened when the National Party took power in 1948), a National Party presence in government and, most crucially, an amnesty for security officers – an absolutely bottom-line demand by the whites, desperate to avoid a witch hunt and 'war crimes tribunal' after losing power. It was, understandably, a bitterly controversial move.

Between December and February the final parts of the agreement were hammered out, allowing for a five-year 'government of national unity' and the creation of a transitional executive committed to overseeing elections, which were scheduled for the end of 1993. After a promising start in December 1992, a year and countless lives had been lost. But the peace process was on track again.

* * *

A few hiccups were still to mar the last full year before South Africa's astonishing transition from white racist-led autocracy to majority rule. The ANC accused the National Party of dragging its feet in setting an election date. A succession of atrocities in Kwazulu-Natal underlined the need for urgency.

Then on 10 April Chris Hani, the 51-year-old former leader of the ANC's military wing, and now general secretary of the Communist Party in succession to Slovo, was assassinated by a Polish immigrant with links to the white far right, provoking a spree of violence and strikes. If the intention was to derail Codesa, it failed; all parties continued to draft the new constitution. Crucially, the ANC had given way to white and Inkatha demands for a second chamber representing the regional governments to be set up.

Two months later, the far right staged its most spectacular, yet ultimately impotent, coup by driving an armoured car through the plate-glass windows of the World Trade Centre. Delegates fled as Eugene Terreblanche and his AWB thugs rampaged through the negotiating chamber, smashing computers and daubing slogans on the walls. Outside, they lit fires and cooked barbecues, as Terreblanche told the assembled crowd of some 2,000, 'this is the beginning of protest. We don't want war, but we don't want peace under the heel of Communism.' The far right had fired its last shot.

Its mainstream now decided to unite under the Afrikaner Volksfront, headed by General Constand Viljoen, a former head of the armed forces, championing the establishment of a volkstaat, a white-only homeland, a pathetic rump of white-dominated South Africa, begging for the same miserable fate to which apartheid had tried to consign the black peoples of the country. It was the last gasp of the creed.

A month later the interim constitution was published, which the far right denounced as 'the completion of the Communist revolution'. In September parliament approved the establishment of the Transitional Executive Council, a kind of cabinet to oversee the government's impartiality in the run-up to elections, and passed bills ensuring the independence of the media. Buthelezi and the Conservative Party walked out of the agreement. A month earlier, a date for the general election had been set at last: 24 April, 1994.

In mid-October the world's seal of approval was finally granted. After massive runs on the rand and renewed sanctions jitters following the Boipatong massacre and Hani's assassination, the UN lifted non-mandatory sanctions on 8 October while the Americans lifted sanctions in November. The UN ban on oil exports to South Africa was dropped in December. The economy at last registered a period of small growth, while the gold price rose to around $400 an ounce. The establishment of the National Economic Forum of business, labour and government, as well as the ANC's plan for a Reconstruction and

Development programme, also held out the prospect of recovery. In October, Mandela and de Klerk were jointly awarded the Nobel Peace Prize.

* * *

November 1993 was another landmark date in the reconciliation process. The Pan-Africanist Congress, the most extreme of the major black organizations, at last accepted a 'moratorium' on violence that month. On 18 November, an interim constitution was agreed to, after yet another emergency session between Mandela and de Klerk. The deal was hailed by the conference chairman, Ismael Mohammed: 'This is the breaking of the dawn for a nation wrestling with its soul. No force can stop or delay our emancipation from our shameful racist past, blighted by the ravages of apartheid. This is the last mile to freedom.'

The main provisions were the setting up of a Transitional Executive Council, which effectively supervised the government between December and April; a multi-party coalition lasting 5 years for all parties polling more than 5 per cent of the vote; a 400-member national assembly; 9 regional legislatures, each with a premier – a bow in the direction of devolution, as demanded by both the whites and Inkatha; a senate with 10 per cent representation for each province – again a concession by the ANC; an independent judiciary; a black bill of rights; representation for tribal leaders – a further concession to the whites and Inkatha; a single defence and police force – a major victory for the ANC; 11 official languages; and an independent commission charged with overseeing the elections. In November the short-lived, ill-fated, tricameral parliament met for almost the last time (it would sit again for just one day before the election).

When Mandela and de Klerk went to collect their Nobel Prizes, the former paid surprisingly generous tribute to the latter, after the rancour of the past three years. 'He had the courage to admit that a terrible wrong had been done to our country and people through the imposition of the system of apartheid. He had the foresight to understand and accept that all the people of South Africa must, through negotiations and as equal participants in the process, together determine what they want to make of their future.'

It was quite an accolade from a man who had earlier written, 'I told the people that de Klerk had gone further than any other Nationalist leader to normalize the situation and then, in words that came back to haunt me, I called Mr de Klerk "a man of integrity". These words were flung back at me many times when Mr de Klerk seemed not to live up to them.'

The election campaign got under way in February 1994, with the ANC staging 'people's forums' and the National Party a more traditional kind of campaign. The ANC's slogan was 'a better life for all'. The party promised to build 1 million new homes with electricity and lavatories; to end poverty; to provide 10 years' free education; to redistribute land; and to end VAT on food.

The endgame was now in sight, with only one further drama to come: the collapse of the 'independent homelands'. All their residents had been given South African citizenship on 1 January. Both Buthelezi and the government of Bophuthatswana had refused to register for the elections (as had the Conservative Party and the Afrikaner Volksfront). Mandela met Buthelezi in an effort to persuade him to register on 1 March, and the Zulu chief at last relented, as did Viljoen, whose party was now renamed the Freedom Front.

Lucas Mangope continued to rule in Bophuthatswana, but thousands of ANC supporters in the homeland took to the streets. After attempting to call in supporters from the far right, the government finally collapsed in March, precipitating three days of looting and killing which left 70 dead and 300 wounded – alarming South Africans as to what might follow the fall of their own white regime. Brigadier Gqozo of Ciskei wisely asked South Africa to take over his country before such a point was reached. But the real confrontation was in Kwazulu-Natal. Already Buthelezi had declared that he would resist any attempt 'to wipe us off the face of the earth as Zulus'. He refused to have the hostels fenced in, or to order his men to give up their traditional arms. On the 100th anniversary of the Battle of Blood River in December, King Goodwill Zwelithini, Buthelezi's nephew, called on his people to defend Kwazulu 'with their lives'.

In February he demanded independence, a call repeated by Buthelezi the following month. Late in March, ANC demonstrations led to the deaths of 16 people in Natal. On 28 March the Zulus, equipped with weapons, marched through Johannesburg and, after being fired upon by ANC defenders of their party's headquarters, went on the rampage: 53 people were killed. It seemed as if one of the worst predictions of apartheid racists was being fulfilled: South Africa was degenerating into tribal warfare.

To de Klerk's credit, he made no attempt to exploit the situation, and joined with Mandela in furious attempts at a settlement. At last, just a week before the elections, Buthelezi agreed to take part. In spite of right-wing bombings, South Africans turned out in their millions on polling day on 26 April.

It was a vast exercise in which some 20 million people voted for the first time, with huge queues, allegations of fraud, unscheduled extensions of voting and delays in counting. But the results were accepted by all major parties. The ANC won 62.7 per cent, giving it a thumping 252 seats in the 400-member parliament – but not the two-thirds majority needed to write the constitution on its own. The National Party won 20.5 per cent (82 seats) and was the majority party in the Western Cape. The IFP won 10.5 per cent (43 seats), and a majority in Kwazulu-Natal. The far right Freedom Front won just 2.2 per cent (9 seats). The Democratic Party, which had played so decisive a role in 1989, won only 1.7 per cent (7 seats) and the PAC just 1.3 per cent (4 seats). On the evening of 2 May, de Klerk conceded defeat, and the 44-year-old rule of the Afrikaner Volk was over, as was 300 years of white rule.

* * *

On 9 May, 1994, Nelson Mandela, sworn in as the first black president of his country on a bullet-proof stage before huge crowds on the lawns of Pretoria's Union Building, declared, 'We have triumphed in our effort to implant hope in the breasts of millions of our people. We enter into a covenant that we shall build a society in which all South Africans, both black and white, will be able to walk tall ... a rainbow nation at peace with itself and the world.'

Michael Young, sitting near to the leaders of government on a seat reserved for Mandela's guests, next to Joe Slovo, Aziz Pahad and Mac Maharaj, sets the scene:

> Pretoria had put on her best dress for the day. The capital city of South Africa had never looked or felt so good. The sun was hot and high against a clear blue sky so typical of a winter's day in the Transvaal. The stately and yet sombre Union Building was bedecked as never before to greet the new black President of the Republic of South Africa.
>
> What really made the difference this May 10, 1994, was the complete absence of the awesome and traditional feeling of repression which one felt in South Africa prior to the country's first full and free election. The tension between black and white had gone and the nation as a whole was preparing to celebrate the inaugura-

tion of President Nelson Mandela before a large and cosmopolitan gathering of the leaders of the world.

Pretoria was not used to receiving such international political luminaries encompassing the full international political spectrum. The pariah state was never able to attract many to its capital and yet the world had come to pay tribute to the culmination of the ultimate peaceful revolution. Yasser Arafat of the PLO rubbed shoulders in the crowded amphitheatre with Prince Philip of the United Kingdom, Al Gore of the USA pushed against Mario Soares of Portugal, Benazir Bhutto of Pakistan sat relatively close to the Indian delegation. East met West and South hosted North ...

Sitting as I was, among the new political elite, the ceremony came to its finale as the dull thud of helicopter blades could be heard approaching the auditorium. The noise grew louder until almost instantly three army helicopters appeared directly over the presidential stand, heading straight towards the assembled guests. The clatter of blades and the roar of engines caused many around to duck. Watching this scene and hearing cries of encouragement, 'It's one of ours', guests once more stood tall. This reminded me how men and women who were formerly harassed by these machines, now recognized their harmlessness and indeed their collective ownership of the military might of the nation – the people and the state were at one.

To have made a major contribution to the achievement of that day was the reward of a lifetime for Young. It had been a long road from those timid first steps at Stellenbosch 7 years before. It had been a much longer road for Mandela from his birthplace at Mvezo on the banks of the Mbashe River more than 75 years before, to becoming the father of his nation.

For de Klerk, sworn in as one of his two vice-presidents (Thabo Mbeki, the chief protagonist of Mells Park, was the other), it had been an even tougher journey. He represented in all its poignancy the latest twist in the unending trek of the Afrikaner nation, subject first to Dutch colonial rule, then British administration, escaping to the High Veld and the Low Veld, forging two independent states only to be annexed twice by the British, the second time after a bitter and cruel war, then seeking the domination of all of South Africa, an achievement secured in 1948.

The Afrikaners had ruled with triumphalism as a chosen, exclusive, superior people, their hauteur springing from their previous sense of inferiority. Now, after an epic struggle, they had been forced to surrender to long-term inevitability. Their trek, which had seemed over at last, seemed set to start again. The descendants of the trekboers, the voortrekkers, the Boer commandos, the Broeders and the ox-wagon trekkers had lost their land again after nearly half a century. Like the Jews fleeing Egypt in search of the Promised Land, the history of the Afrikaners has been one of persecution and self-sufficiency in the face of overwhelming and hostile forces. The Afrikaner volk had taken their revenge against the Zulus at the Battle of Blood River in 1838; they had gathered at Wonderfontein in 1879; they had won their republic back at Paardekraal; they had accepted their bitter defeat at Veerininging in 1902; they had gathered at Monument Kopple in 1938 after the Oxwagon trek; they had seized absolute power after the 1948 election and had had it confirmed in the 1960 republican referendum; they had gathered to celebrate their triumph at Bonsraad at Tweefontein in 1963; and now it seemed they had lost everything again. It had been a long journey.

The unending trek of the lost tribe of Africa appeared set to resume. Or did it? In the maturity displayed by men like F. W. de Klerk, Willie Esterhuyse and Sampie Terreblanche, it seemed that at last the wanderlust of the Afrikaner was being laid to rest. These men envisaged the Afrikaner not as a people set against a hostile world, but as part of a wider South African community.

Ramaphosa speaks movingly of his children bringing back white playmates to his house. 'Children are completely colourblind. There is a silent revolution going on – the deracialization of South Africa is beginning to take place.' If the Afrikaner has truly accepted that he must live with the other peoples of South Africa – and they with the Afrikaner – the need to run away, or to dissimulate, will be at an end. Then at last the world, so long rightly accustomed to condemnation of the sufferings inflicted by the Afrikaner against their fellow South Africans, might also recognize the immense contribution the white tribe has nevertheless made to the country's history and progress. Perhaps the long trek is over at last.

Select Bibliography

Adam, Heribert and Kogila Moodley, *The Negotiated Revolution* (Johannesburg, 1993).

Alhadeff, Vic, *A Newspaper History of South Africa* (Cape Town, 1976).

Arnheim, M. T. W., *South Africa after Vorster* (Cape Town, 1979).

Attwell, Michael, *South Africa: Background to the Crisis* (London, 1986).

Baskin, Jeremy, *Striking Back: a History of Cosatu* (Cape Town, 1991).

Bickford-Smith, Vyvyan, *Cape Town on the Eve of the Mineral Revolution* (Cape Town, 1985).

Buthelezi, M. G., *White and Black Nationalism* (Johannesburg, 1974).

Davenport, Rodney, *South Africa: a Modern History* (London, 1987).

Desmond, Cosmas, *The Discarded People* (Harmondsworth, 1971).

Frederickse, Julie, *South Africa: a Different Kind of War* (Cape Town, 1986).

Friedman, Steven, ed., *The Long Journey: South Africa's Quest for a Negotiated Settlement* (Centre for Policy Studies, London, 1993).

Gerhart, Gail, *Black Power in South Africa* (Berkeley, 1978).

Hancock, Sir William, *Smuts*, 2 vols (Cambridge, 1962).

Hanlon, J., *Apartheid's Second Front* (Harmondsworth, 1986).

Harrison, David, *The White Tribe of Africa* (London, 1981).

Hepple, Alexander, *Verwoerd* (London, 1967).

Howe, Geoffrey, *Conflict of Loyalty* (London, 1994).

The Illustrated History of South Africa (Reader's Digest, Cape Town, 1994).

Johnson, R. W., *How Long Will South Africa Survive?* (London, 1977).

Kane-Berman, John, *Soweto: Black Revolt, White Reaction* (Cape Town, 1978).

Karis, Thomas and Gwendolyn Carter, *From Protest to Challenge*, vol. 3 (Hoover Institution, 1977).

Leach, Graham, *South Africa* (London, 1986).

Lodge, Tom, *Black Politics in South Africa since 1945* (Cape Town, 1983).

Luthuli, Albert, *Let My People Go* (London, 1962).

Mandela, Nelson, *Nelson Mandela Speaks* (New York, 1993).

Mandela, Nelson, *Long Walk to Freedom* (Boston, 1994).

Matanzima, Kaisar, *Independence My Way* (Pretoria, 1976).

Modisane, Bloke, *Blame Me on History* (Johannesburg, 1986).

Nasson, Bill, *All Here and Now: Black Politics in the 1980s* (Cape Town, 1991).

O'Meara, Dan, *Volkscapitalisme: Class, Capital and Ideology in the Development of Afrikaner Nationalism, 1934–48* (Cape Town, 1983).

Paton, Alan, *The Long View* (London, 1968).

Pollack, Luis, *The Inquest into the Death of Stephen Vantu Biko* (Lawyers' Committee for Civil Rights, Cape Town, Feb. 1978).

Rhoodie, Eschel, *The Real Information Scandal* (Cape Town, 1983).

Ross, Richard van der, *The Rise and Decline of Apartheid* (Cape Town, 1986).

Sampson, Anthony, *Black and Gold* (London, 1987).

Sampson, Anthony, *Nelson Mandela* (London, 1999).

Sandbrook, R. and R. Cohen, eds, *The Development of an African Working Class*

(London, 1975).

Schrire, Robert, *Adapt or Die* (Ford Foundation, USA, 1991).

Select Committee on Foreign Affairs, UK House of Commons, *South Africa Report and Minutes* (London, HMSO, 1986).

Silk, A., *A Shanty Town in South Africa: the Story of Motterdam* (Cape Town, 1981).

Slabbert, Frederik van Zyl, *The Last White Parliament* (Johannesburg, 1986).

Sparks, Allister, *Tomorrow is Another Country* (Cape Town, 1994).

Stultz, Newell, *Afrikaner Politics in South Africa, 1934–48* (Berkeley, 1974).

Thatcher, Margaret, *The Downing Street Years* (London, 1993).

Waldmeir, Patti, *Anatomy of a Miracle* (London, 1997).

Walshe, Peter, *The Rise of African Nationalism in South Africa* (London, 1970).

Wilkins, Ivor and Hans Strydom, *The Super Afrikaners* (Johannesburg, 1978).

Young, Michael, Unpublished minutes of the Mells Park talks.

Index